W9-AVR-967

The Best American Short Plays

2004–2005

The Best American Short Plays

2004–2005

edited with an introduction by
Barbara Parisi

APPLAUSE THEATRE & CINEMA BOOKS
An Imprint of Hal Leonard Corporation
New York

The Best American Short Plays 2004–2005
Edited with an intoduction by Barbara Parisi

Published in 2008 by Applause Theatre & Cinema Books
An imprint of Hal Leonard Corporation
7777 West Bluemound Road
Milwaukee, WI 53213

Trade Book Division Editorial Offices
19 West 21st Street, New York, NY 10010

Printed in the United States of America
Book interior by UB Communications

ISBN 978-1-55783-711-0 [cloth]
ISBN 978-1-55783-712-7 [paper]
ISSN 0067-6284

www.applausepub.com

To William and Gloria Parisi,
Rochelle Martinsen,
and my husband—
Michael Ronald Pasternack

contents

Introduction by Barbara Parisi   ix

Crazy Eights   1
David Lindsay-Abaire

Such a Beautiful Voice Is Sayeda's   27
and Karima's City
Yussef El Guindi

fin & euba   85
Audrey Cefaly

The Devil Is in the Details   107
Jill Elaine Hughes

Arkadelphia   125
Samuel Brett Williams

Charlie Blake's Boat   165
Graeme Gillis

Reading List   189
Susan Miller

The News   207
Billy Aronson

Heights   221
Amy Fox

He Came Home One Day   251
While I Was Washing Dishes
K. Biadaszkiewicz

Letty on a Bench   259
Jolene Goldenthal

Erros—Love Is Deaf   279
Cherie Vogelstein

I'll Do It Tomorrow . . .   317
Michael Roderick

Acknowledgments   333

introduction
by Barbara Parisi

As the new editor for The Best American Short Plays, I have had the opportunity to read many new one-act plays and choose the ones that are part of
this anthology. The journey through this selection process has been
extremely rewarding. It has really made me think about the complex artistic
and technical qualities needed to write a one-act play.

In the book *Contemporary One-Act Plays* by B. Roland Lewis, written in
1922, Lewis states:

> The one-act play is with us and is asking for consideration. It is challenging
> our attention whether we will or not. . . . The one-act play is claiming recogni-
> tion as a specific dramatic type. It may be said that, as an art form, it has
> achieved that distinction. . . . Artistically and technically considered, the one-
> act play is quite as much a distinctive dramatic problem as the longer play. . . . It
> is a truth that the one-act play is well made or it is nothing at all.

I am convinced the one-act play form is a unique and difficult genre to
write effectively. There can be many subgenres of the one-act play, such as
drama, comedy, tragic-comedy, black comedy, melodrama, mystery, and
science fiction. Time requirements make the play take place in a single act
or scene, and it is usually easier to produce since it has fewer technical
requirements and cast members. One-acts can be short in duration or half

an evening's entertainment, and sometimes they can last a whole evening. One-act plays do not have a break in the action. They reveal their theme and plot in depth through the challenge of character development and resolution of the conflict in a shorter amount of time than the full-length play. They must quickly develop engaging, believable characters and a meaningful theme depicted through solid action. The conflict faced by the main character will be revealed early in the piece, and the climax of the play will happen near the end, with the story revolving around one event.

One-act plays are usually produced in festivals and then published in a series of anthologies and collections. Secondary school and university drama students as well as small to large nonprofit theatres and dinner theatres produce this genre.

In analyzing the diverse plays that make up this anthology, many themes that reflect the current social issues of our twenty-first-century society are revealed. To write this introduction, I asked the playwrights to express their meaning and inspiration for creating their one-act plays.

David Lindsay-Abaire

In *Crazy Eights* by David Lindsay-Abaire, inspiration was the "24 Hour Plays" at the American Airlines Theatre in New York City. The "24 Hour Plays" is an annual benefit in which several one-acts are written, cast, directed, and performed on Broadway in less than a day. The *New York Times* says, "By creating their shows on the fly, the artists of the '24 Hour Plays,' which are dependably messy, spontaneous and occasionally in bad taste, prove to be even fringier than the Fringe."

In 2005, *Crazy Eights* was produced by the Ensemble Studio Theatre's festival of new one-act plays, directed by Brian Mertes and featuring Rosie Perez. The *New York Times* states:

> In an appetizing slice of life called *Crazy Eights*, David Lindsay-Abaire presents a budding, off-centered romance that quietly exudes the aching and amused compassion found in his *Fuddy Meers and Kimberly Akimbo*. He makes ingenious and surprising organic use of the blurring of personal and professional roles, in what may or may not be the beginning of a beautiful relationship.

This play, which tells the story of a parole officer who develops unusual feelings for his parolee, was produced at the Ottawa Fringe Festival in June '07. The story reveals Connie coming home late one night. She finds her parole officer waiting in her apartment with a list of questions. The interrogation/courting dance that follows is further complicated by the after-hours arrival of her charming card-playing buddy.

Yussef El Guindi

In *Such a Beautiful Voice Is Sayeda's* and *Karima's City* by Yussef El Guindi, both plays deal with the struggle of a woman trying to find her voice in a hostile environment. It is a hostility that is found in most places around the world, including the West and not just in the Middle East. A hostility borne of reacting to those who decide to go outside the norm, who won't conform to the prevailing sentiment. A hostility that becomes all the more crippling for being expressed in terms of wanting to protect the person, and thus supposedly to prevent these two women from doing harm to themselves. But both Sayeda and Karima have something inside them—a voice, a spirit—that demands to see the light of day.

The inspiration for these two plays occurred when a friend, Dina Amin, suggested the playwright adapt Salwa Bakr's story "Such a Beautiful Voice Is Sayeda's." He picked up the story not sure what to expect and ended up falling in love with the main character. After going through some of Salwa Bakr's other stories in order to write a companion play, he came across her story "Thirty-one Beautiful Green Trees" (retitled *Karima's City* for the play). He recognized in Karima a kindred spirit. Both Sayeda and Karima are trying to find and share their voice, their love of something. As a writer, there was of course instant identification.

The story of *Such a Beautiful Voice Is Sayeda's* finds Sayeda, late in life, discovering she possesses a beautiful singing voice and wanting to share it. But this news is met with hostility and ridicule, both by her family and from those she seeks help. It's not clear if this voice is real or—as those around her suspect—evidence of Sayeda's mental breakdown.

The story of *Karima's City* centers on an idealistic woman struggling against the corruption and destruction of the city she loves. The play opens in a hospital jail cell, where Karima begins to narrate the events through reenactments that led to her imprisonment. Her conflicts with her mother, her vocal reactions to the conformity she sees in her workplace, her attempts to stop the deterioration around her—especially the cutting down of trees and the blow-up that occurs when she goes to vote on Election Day—result in making her wonder whether or not she should cut her tongue out for getting her into so much trouble.

Audrey Cefaly

In *fin & euba* by Audrey Cefaly, an unexpected piece of mail breaches the status quo and forces its hand insistently. The resulting quagmire examines the gap between inertia and action as well as the definition of friendship. The setting is a front porch, autumn, late evening in the Florida panhandle. Fin and Euba are friends and co-workers at a paper mill in Cantonment, Florida. They also share space in a rooming house, which they are desperately trying to escape, due to the tyrannical landlady who has a penchant for strict rules and tacky yard art. Unbeknownst to Euba, Fin submits some of Euba's amateur photos to *Life* magazine. Euba receives a reply from *Life*, but is reluctant to open it for fear of rejection, or worse—acceptance. Fin and Euba sit on the porch, drinking, smoking, flicking ashes into a coffee can, and contemplating their lives and their plans for escape.

The inspiration for *fin & euba* was an exercise in the structure of action. The playwright wanted to see what would happen if she wrote a theatre piece backward. So she started with a dramatic ending and worked her way back from there, attempting to justify the moment that had come before. For her, it proved to be a highly effective way of writing and much easier than it sounds. The great thing about this technique is that once you know where you are in your piece, the place before it always seems to present itself quite naturally.

Jill Elaine Hughes

The Devil Is in the Details by Jill Elaine Hughes was written in 2004 specifically for a festival to be held at Chicago's Boxer Rebellion Theatre. Each playwright participating in the festival was assigned a group of three actors, who each did auditions for the playwrights so the writers would get an idea of what their types/ranges were. Then each playwright was shown the image of a painting to serve as inspiration for their pieces. Hughes was shown *The Descent Into Hell* by a little-known nineteenth-century French artist. So she took that idea and melded it with the three young actors she was assigned and came up with a "hip-hop *No Exit*"–type of play, since the two male actors she was assigned had a kind of gangster edge to them. The female actor she had been assigned was an artsy foil to the other two, so she used that in the play as well by making her character a sophisticated, wealthy sculptor who just happens to be dating a L.A. gang assassin.

The play opens with the gang assassin and his sculptor girlfriend guarding a body in an abandoned warehouse used by L.A. gangs to dump dead bodies after gang killings. As the play progresses, though, it becomes clear that the warehouse isn't really a warehouse anymore, and the dead body the two lead characters dragged in isn't really dead, either. *The Devil Is in the Details* works well because it is not only entertaining in a Hollywood-slash-*Pulp-Fiction* kind of way but because there is a very slick twist at the end that almost no one sees coming.

Samuel Brett Williams

Arkadelphia by Samuel Brett Williams reveals the concessions that modern Southern Baptist teenagers make to live normal lives. Bobby returns to his hometown of Arkadelphia, Arkansas, after a semester of college in Manhattan. Seeking refuge in two childhood friends, he ends up exposing a secret the small, religious town would rather keep buried. Williams's inspiration for writing this play came from being born and raised in Arkansas by strict Southern Baptist parents. He lived in Arkadelphia until he moved north in 2003. He wanted to write a play about the conflicted feelings he had about where he came from and all that entails. On the one hand, he sorely missed the South, but on the other hand, he was glad to be experiencing the North. To this day, he has the same feelings of stay/leave with Arkansas. He goes home probably one and a half to two months out of every year.

Graeme Gillis

Charlie Blake's Boat by Graeme Gillis takes place in a small maritime town. Charlie Blake plans to sail to Scotland in a boat he's built himself. As his going-away party rages, his lost love appears on the dock to stop him. The play explores life by the water, love out of failure, and finding something to live for. Gillis's inspiration for this play began when he was growing up. His next-door neighbor was a man named Charlie Blake who built a boat in his driveway. When he finished the boat, he set out to sea. This seemed to Gillis a good thing to do with your life.

Susan Miller

Reading List by Susan Miller encounters people who come to a library, and despite the social and political climate threatening their freedoms, they are moved and transformed by what they find there. Her inspiration for this play was her response to the wonder and transformative nature of freely exchanged ideas, and the nefarious efforts that threaten to suppress what we hold dear.

Billy Aronson

The News by Billy Aronson reminds us of the need to say and do things about which nothing can be said or done. In this story, Karen has some really strange news, and as people realize what it is, they start acting really weird. Aronson's inspiration for the play occurred when he wanted to take this event that happened to him and regurgitate it in the form of a play—so he could stop the event from regurgitating him.

Amy Fox

Heights by Amy Fox explores the isolation that is still possible within relationships and the ways in which any change in our identity can impact those we are intimate with. In this play, three young New Yorkers confront each other's secrets and entanglements when they are locked in an endless rooftop dinner party. The play actually came out of a writing exercise in which the playwright had to choose a setting before establishing characters.

The rooftop setting with the table set for dinner inspired the rest of the play. On a deeper level, Fox was exploring her own feelings of isolation in the city.

K. Biadaszkiewicz

He Came Home One Day While I Was Washing Dishes by K. Biadaszkiewicz looks at humanizing conflict and the futility of violence. In this story, a teenage boy comes home to tell his mother the news she has dreaded. The inspiration for this play came from seeing the inanity of current world events and the resulting unconscionable waste of human potential.

Jolene Goldenthal

The inspiration for *Letty on a Bench* by Jolene Goldenthal came one evening at about seven o'clock as the playwright and a group of her friends were going out to dinner. As they walked along, laughing and talking, the playwright saw a figure on the sidewalk stretched over a grate directly in front of them. Many months later, she began to write *Letty on a Bench*. The play takes place in the waiting room of a deserted train station, with the final line of the play stating, "We thought . . . we thought . . . it would be . . . for always." Need I say any more?

Cherie Vogelstein

Erros—Love Is Deaf by Cherie Vogelstein explores people's fantasies of love that preclude them from experiencing the reality of it. Or: Love is not only blind but deaf and masochistic as well. Through six interlocking scenes, three men and three women blindly pursue unrequited love while failing to see the love right before their eyes. Vogelstein's inspiration for writing this play began after her reading of *La Ronde* and observing the love lives of her nearest and dearest. She wanted to take a crack at writing about neurotic love using the A to B, B to C structure. Then she rewrote the play for Ensemble Studio Theatre's Octoberfest and changed the scenes around to see how it worked out of order. Like Mary-Kate and Ashley's clothing line, she thinks the right director can mix and match the scenes for a great ensemble piece.

Michael Roderick

I'll Do It Tomorrow . . . by Michael Roderick asks the question: What would happen when you're told you don't have all the time in the world? In his play, a man finds out that his procrastination has angered God and that he will age ten years for every day of the coming week. He then seeks out his friend, who is a waitress, to accompany him on a journey to make things right with the people he wronged as a result of his procrastination. Roderick's inspiration for this play began when he was out with a friend, who asked him to write a short play that involved the following: growing old before your time, candle wax, and seashells. This play was the result.

The Best American Short Plays

2004–2005

Crazy Eights

David Lindsay-Abaire

David Lindsay-Abaire

David Lindsay-Abaire is a Pulitzer Prize-winning American playwright, best known for *Fuddy Meers* (1999) and for the 2007 Pulitzer Prize in drama for *Rabbit Hole*, which premiered on Broadway in 2006 at MTC's Biltmore Theater. The play, which featured Cynthia Nixon, Tyne Daly, and John Slattery, received five Tony Award nominations, including Best Play, and the Spirit of America Award.

Mr. Lindsay-Abaire concentrated in theatre at Sarah Lawrence College, and was accepted into the Lila Acheson Wallace American Playwrights Program at the Juilliard School, where he wrote under the tutelage of Marsha Norman and Christopher Durang.

He has received commissions from South Coast Repertory, Dance Theater Workshop, and the Jerome Foundation, as well as awards from the Berilla Kerr Foundation, the Lincoln Center LeComte du Nuoy Fund, Mixed Blood Theater, Primary Stages, the Tennessee Williams/New Orleans Literary Festival, and the South Carolina Playwrights Festival.

Mr. Lindsay-Abaire returned to the Manhattan Theatre Club in 2000, with *Wonder of the World*, starring Sarah Jessica Parker, about a wife who suddenly leaves her husband and hops a bus to Niagara Falls in search of freedom, enlightenment, and the meaning of life. Other plays include *Kimberly Akimbo* (2000), *Dotting and Dashing* (1999), *Snow Angel* (1999), *The L'il Plays* (1997), and *A Devil Inside* (1997).

He also has writing credits on two screenplays, *Robots* (2005) from 20th Century Fox and *Inkheart* (2007) from New Line Cinema, and he is currently at work on screen adaptations of *Rabbit Hole* for 20th Century Fox, starring Nicole Kidman, and *Kimberly Akimbo* for DreamWorks. His most recent projects are the book for the musical *High Fidelity* and the book and lyrics for the Broadway-bound musical *Shrek*.

Mr. Lindsay-Abaire is a proud member of New Dramatists, the Dramatists Guild, and the WGA.

···production note···

Crazy Eights was originally presented as part of the "24 Hour Plays on Broadway," a one-night-only benefit for Working Playground, Inc., on September 15, 2003, at the Roundabout Theater in New York City. It was directed by Nick Philippou. The cast was as follows:

CONNIE   Rosie Perez
BENNY   Frank Whaley
CLIFF   Matt McGrath
VOICE OF MR. DUGAN   Ned Eisenberg

A revised version of *Crazy Eights* was produced by the Ensemble Studio Theatre (Curt Dempster, Artistic Director) in New York City, opening on May 31, 2005. It was directed by Brian Mertes; the production designer was Maruti Evans; the production stage manager was Elis C. Arroyo; the sound design was by Lindsay Jones; and the assistant director was Jordan Young. The cast was as follows:

CONNIE   Rosie Perez
BENNY   Keith Reddin
CLIFF   Tom Pelfrey
VOICE OF MR. DUGAN   Thomas Lyons

characters

CONNIE, mid- to late 30s
BENNY, mid- to late 30s
CLIFF, just a little younger and a little more attractive
VOICE OF MR. DUGAN, 60s

set

A humble apartment on the sixth floor of a crappy walk-up. There's at least one window and a fire escape outside that window.

···

[*A dark apartment.* BENNY *naps in a chair. He's fallen asleep waiting. After a couple beats, we hear a key turn in the lock, and the apartment door opens.* CONNIE *enters, tosses her purse onto a counter, and walks across the dark room, unaware that* BENNY *is there. Eventually she clicks on the light, revealing* BENNY. *She lets out a terrified scream.* BENNY *bolts up and looks around, not sure where he is at first.*]

CONNIE   [*Realizing who he is.*]
Jesus Christ, Benny. What are you tryin' to do to me?

BENNY   [*Still waking up.*]
Where you been?

CONNIE   I was out. Shit. You can't be waitin' up like that, sittin' in the dark. There's heart disease in my family.

BENNY   [*Tries to make out his watch.*]
You know what time it is?

CONNIE   I could've dropped dead. I get spooked real easy.

BENNY   It's ten past twelve.

CONNIE   And I got a clock, Benny. I don't need you tellin' me what time it is.

BENNY   You were supposed to be home at midnight.

CONNIE   My train got stuck. We had to wait for the signal to change.

BENNY   Ah, that ol' chestnut.

CONNIE   You think I'm lyin'?

BENNY   Wouldn't be the first time.

CONNIE   Ten minutes. Cut me some slack.

[*She takes off her jacket-catches her breath.*]

How'd you get in here anyway?

BENNY   You left the window unlocked.

CONNIE What window? I live on the sixth floor.

BENNY I came up the fire escape.

CONNIE What are you retarded? What if you fell?

BENNY Nah, baby, I'm like a cat.

CONNIE This ain't legit, Benny.

BENNY What ain't?

CONNIE The way you do things. All the time you doin' shit like this. It ain't on the level.

BENNY Sure it is.

CONNIE None of my other parole officers ever did this.

BENNY Did what?

CONNIE Break into my apartment!

BENNY Come on—

CONNIE It's creepy. You climbin' in my window. Waitin' in here with all the lights off. What if I didn't realize it was you? What if I freaked out and maced you or stuck a knife in your gut or something?

BENNY Well, for one thing, that'd probably qualify as a parole violation.

CONNIE You wanna check up on me, wait on my doorstep. I don't wanna come home and find you layin' all over my furniture. I don't even know you hardly.

[*Beat.*]

Besides, don't you need a warrant or something to come in here like that?   .

BENNY Whoa-whoa, let's not get all hung up on warrants and legalities, okay? We're talking about your curfew right now and your blatant disregard of it.

CONNIE   My train. Got. Stuck.

BENNY   You need to allow for setbacks then. 'Cause trains get stuck all the time. And if you're late, then I am obligated to report that to the parole board. Ya understand? I'm their conduit.

CONNIE   [*He's full of shit.*]
Uh-huh, right, conduit, that's terrific.

BENNY   I'm sorry, but late is late. Midnight is midnight. You gotta hop in your pumpkin and get your ass home, otherwise you're goin' back to jail, Connie. And I know you don't wanna go back to jail.

[CONNIE *finds a torte on the kitchen table.*]

CONNIE   What's that?

BENNY   Oh, that's a . . . It's a torte.

CONNIE   A what?

BENNY   A torte. A tomato-basil torte. It's a little like a quiche.

CONNIE   What's it doin' here?

BENNY   I made it. In case you were hungry when you got home.

CONNIE   You made a torte? In my kitchen?

BENNY   Yeah.

CONNIE   And you carried all the ingredients up the fire escape?

BENNY   That's right.

CONNIE   And nobody stopped you?

BENNY   No.

CONNIE   Fuckin' neighborhood. I'm tellin' ya.

[*Yells out the window.*]

Hey, assholes! If ya see a guy crawl in my window with bags of food, call the frickin' cops! What is wrong with you people?!

[*Slams the window closed.*]

BENNY What's the matter, you don't like torte?

CONNIE What I don't like, Benny, is you coming up into my house, and bustin' out my pots and pans like you own the place. You can't be bakin' shit in my kitchen. I know you're my parole officer, but you got no business in my oven.

BENNY You're right, I'm sorry.

CONNIE Alright then.

[*Beat, glances at the torte.*]

It does look good, though.

BENNY Right?

CONNIE I'm hungry too. I'ma get a fork.

[*She does.*]

BENNY There's some porcini mushrooms in there too. I don't know if you like porcini or not.

CONNIE I like portobello better, but that's okay.

[*Takes a bite.*]

BENNY I hope it's still warm.

CONNIE [*In heaven.*]
Mmmm.

BENNY It's good, right? I actually went to culinary school for a few months. That's what I wanted to do, but . . . that didn't work out. So . . .

CONNIE You should go back.

BENNY   Nah. I don't think they'd let me. There was an episode with a grease fire that got a little crazy, so . . . Besides, I'm not sure where that school is anymore. They had to relocate.

CONNIE   That's too bad. This is some tasty torte.

[BENNY *just watches her eat for a couple beats.*]

So you gonna report me? For bein' late?

BENNY   I don't know. Where were you?

CONNIE   My cousin's house. She lives in Flatbush, and you know that Q train's for shit.

BENNY   She was having a party or something?

CONNIE   No, no party. You tryin' to trick me, Benny?

BENNY   No, I'm not trying to trick you.

CONNIE   You know I don't go to parties no more. I was just watchin' videos with Tina and her kids. I lost track of time. You ever see *Spy Kids*? The original?

BENNY   No.

CONNIE   It's a good movie.

BENNY   Who else was there?

CONNIE   That's it. Just me and Tina and the kids.

BENNY   No guys in the house?

CONNIE   No, there were no guys. Her neighbor Raul popped in to borrow some tinfoil, but—

BENNY   What's he look like?

CONNIE   Who, Raul? I don't know what he—He looked like a guy, just a regular—You know, like a normal person. Why you asking me what he looked like?

BENNY   I need to have a sense of the type of people you're spending your time with.

CONNIE   I didn't spend no time with him. He borrowed some foil. He was there for a minute and went home. He's just some old guy from next door.

BENNY   Oh, okay then. He's an old man.

CONNIE   Yeah.

BENNY   Well, you didn't say that.

CONNIE   'Cause I didn't understand what you were asking me. What's he look like, you wanna know. What the hell's that? Maybe next time I'll take a picture for you.

BENNY   Hey, come on, don't get mouthy. You know I gotta ask this stuff.

CONNIE   No, I don't. I don't know that. None of my other parole officers ever asked me the goofy shit you ask me. I don't like it.

BENNY   How 'bout the torte?'

CONNIE   The torte I don't mind. Next time, though, do portobello.

[*She smiles in spite of herself.*]

BENNY   Connie, I got something to tell you.

CONNIE   Oh yeah? What is it?

CLIFF   [*From down on the street.*]
          CONNIE! HEY! CONNIE!

[*Silence.*]

          CONNIE! YOU UP THERE?!

BENNY   You expecting somebody?

CONNIE   What, I'm not allowed to have company now?

BENNY Well, that depends on who it is, doesn't it?

CONNIE He ain't a convicted felon if that's what you're askin'.

CLIFF CONNIE!

CONNIE You're done, right? Did your little surprise pop-in, gave me a good talkin' to?

BENNY You're not gonna gimme the bum's rush now, are ya?

CLIFF CONNIE! YOU AWAKE?!

VOICE OF MAN WE'RE ALL AWAKE, SHITHEAD! YOU KNOW HOW TO RING A BELL?

CLIFF HER BUZZER IS BUSTED! WHY DON'T YOU MIND YOUR BUSINESS?

VOICE OF MAN HOW 'BOUT I COME DOWN THERE INSTEAD AND CUT OFF YOUR HEAD, MOTHERFUCKER?!

CONNIE That's Mr. Dugan. He's always threatening to cut off somebody's head.

CLIFF CONNIE!

BENNY This guy your boyfriend?

CONNIE Come on, Benny, you gotta go.

BENNY But I wanna meet this gentleman caller of yours.

CONNIE You've got some real boundary problems, ya know it?

BENNY Yes, yes I do, and you're not the first person to say so.

[*Leans out the window.*]

HEY! HOW YA DOIN'?

CLIFF HOW AM I DOIN'? MY THROAT IS SORE, MAN. LET ME UP THERE.

BENNY LET YOU UP? I DON'T EVEN KNOW WHO YOU ARE.

CLIFF IT'S ME, MAN. CLIFF.

BENNY HOW CAN I HELP YA, CLIFF?

CLIFF IS CONNIE UP THERE?

BENNY YEAH, CLIFF, SHE'S HERE.

CLIFF WELL, THROW DOWN THE KEY, MAN.

BENNY THE THING IS, CLIFF, CONNIE HAS A CURFEW.

CLIFF YOU HER FATHER?

BENNY NO, I'M NOT HER FATHER, CLIFF.

CLIFF WHY YOU KEEP SAYIN' MY NAME, MAN?

BENNY YOU GOT SOME BUSINESS HERE WITH CONNIE?

CLIFF YEAH, I GOT SOME BUSINESS, NOW LEMME UP.

VOICE OF MAN YEAH, LET HIM UP! I GOTTA WORK AT SIX A.M.

CONNIE [*Rushes to the window.*]

WHY YOU LYIN', MR. DUGAN? YOU BEEN OUT ON DISABILITY FOR THREE MONTHS! YOU DON'T HAVE NO WORK TO GO TO!

[*To herself, or maybe* BENNY.]

I hate these stupid people.

CLIFF CONNIE! THAT YOU?!

CONNIE YEAH, IT'S ME.

CLIFF THROW DOWN THE KEY!

VOICE OF MAN I AM TRYING TO SLEEP!

CONNIE YOU AIN'T TRYIN' TO SLEEP EITHER! YOU OVER THERE WATCHIN' THE SPICE CHANNEL! I CAN SEE IT FROM HERE! WHY DON'T YOU BUY SOME SHADES, YOU DIRTY PIG?!

CLIFF CONNIE!

CONNIE WAIT A MINUTE!

[*To* BENNY.]

Hand me that sock.

[BENNY *hands her the sock. She puts the front-door key inside and tosses it out the window.*]

YOU GOT IT?

CLIFF NAH, MAN, IT GOT STUCK ON THE TELEPHONE WIRE. IT'S HANGIN' THERE.

CONNIE SHIT.

[*To* BENNY.]

Hand me your shoe.

BENNY For what?

CONNIE I gotta try to knock that sock off the wire.

BENNY [*Hands it over.*]

Why don't you use your own shoe?

CONNIE You crazy? I just bought these.

[*Leans out the window and drops shoe.*]

CLIFF [*After a beat.*]

OW, MAN!

CONNIE YOU GOT IT?

CLIFF NO!

CONNIE Gimme your other shoe.

[BENNY *hands over his other shoe.*]

OKAY, CLIFF, NOW LOOK OUT THIS TIME!

[*Throws shoe.*]

YOU GOT IT NOW?

CLIFF YEAH.

CONNIE ALRIGHT THEN. COME ON UP.

[*Closes window.*]

[BENNY *is seated comfortably with his feet up.*]

So what, you stayin' now?

BENNY I gotta get my shoes back, don't I?

CONNIE Well, don't go cross-examining my friend. Just get your shoes and go home.

BENNY Connie, you seem to forget that this is my job.

CONNIE Nah, this ain't your job. This is harassment. You think I'm not gonna report all this? Breakin' and enterin' and cookin' tortes? That ain't right. I been through the system, remember? And ain't none of this shit kosher.

BENNY Just tell me this guy's not your dealer.

CONNIE Now come on, why you gotta be like that?

BENNY You know I have to ask.

CONNIE Didn't I say I spent the night watching movies? Why you gotta bring up drugs? That's just tacky. You just sullied a nice night with my cousins.

BENNY I'm sorry.

CONNIE You should be. You need to get yourself a partner, 'cause you can't be playin' good-cop-bad-cop by yourself. You only confuse people.

BENNY I confuse you?

CONNIE Yeah, you confuse me.

BENNY Well, the feeling's mutual.

CONNIE [*Beat.*]
See, I don't even know what that's supposed to mean. You're cryptic. You know that word?

BENNY I'll look it up when I go home.

CONNIE Well, you should. You might find a little picture of yourself in there. It'll say, "Cryptic. See this guy."

[*There's a knock at the door.*]

BENNY Who is it?

CLIFF It's Cliff, man! Who do you think it is?

[CONNIE *opens the door.* CLIFF *enters with* BENNY's *shoes, the key, and sock. He's winded.*]

Damn, those stairs just about killed me.

CONNIE This is my parole officer.

CLIFF For real? You didn't commit any infractions, I hope.

BENNY What brings you out tonight, Cliff?

CONNIE You don't have to answer his questions. You ain't on parole.

[*Hands* BENNY *his shoes.*]

CLIFF Connie and I have a date.

BENNY Huh. A date. Interesting. Where you kids headed?

CLIFF We're not headed anyplace. It's more of an indoor date.

BENNY Ahh, an indoor date.

CONNIE [*To* CLIFF.]
> See that? He tried to trick you into saying we were going out.

CLIFF Crafty.

BENNY You're not a bad influence, are ya, Cliff?

CLIFF Nah, man. I'm wholesome.

BENNY Good. 'Cause, ya know, I gotta look out for this girl.

CONNIE You ain't gotta look out for me.

CLIFF You don't have to worry 'bout us. I treat Connie real nice, don't I, baby?

CONNIE [*To* BENNY.]
> You done now?

BENNY Almost. There's just one last thing. It's been a couple months, after all.

CONNIE A couple months since what?

[*He pulls a plastic cup and lid out of his pocket.*]
> You kiddin' me?

BENNY It's part of the program, you know that. Random tests.

CONNIE Right. Except this don't feel so random to me.

BENNY What's the big deal? You're clean, right?

CONNIE Yeah, I'm clean.

BENNY Alright then, no worries. Gimme a little pee and I'll get lost.

CONNIE Except I don't have to pee at the moment.

BENNY That's okay, I can wait.

CONNIE Gimme the fuckin' cup.

[*He hands her the cup. She storms off to the bathroom and slams the door.*]

CLIFF Damn . . .

BENNY I'm used to that. I get a lot of hostility on my job.

CLIFF Yeah, me too.

BENNY What do you do?

CLIFF I work at Au Bon Pain. Customers there are fuckin' animals, man.

[*Takes out a deck of cards and starts shuffling.*]

BENNY So how do you guys know each other?

CLIFF We met at church.

BENNY Huh. I didn't know Connie went to church.

CLIFF Not church-church. Just the basement. That's where the meetings are.

BENNY Oh, I see.

CLIFF N.A.

BENNY Right.

CLIFF I've been clean for eight months.

BENNY Congratulations.

[*Beat.*]

And how long you been with Connie?

CLIFF What?

BENNY   Connie. You just start dating her?

CLIFF   I ain't datin' her, man.

BENNY   Oh. I thought you said this was a date.

CLIFF   Yeah, a date like we set a date to hang out. We're platonic, man. I just come up here to play Crazy Eights.

BENNY   Oh.

CLIFF   I got a boyfriend. I can't be foolin' around with Connie. He'd kill me.

BENNY   I see.

CLIFF   Saturday nights me and Connie stay up late playin' cards together, that's all, so we don't go out and do what we used to do, you know? Get fucked up and in trouble and whatnot. It's like a buddy system.

BENNY   Right. That's good. That's a good system.

CLIFF   You thought I was screwin' her?

BENNY   I wasn't sure.

CLIFF   You were jealous of me?

BENNY   No.

CLIFF   Yeah, you was. You were jealous. That's some funny shit.

[*Chuckles for a couple beats, and then . . .*]

You know what?

BENNY   What?

CLIFF   You don't look how I pictured.

BENNY   What do you mean?

CLIFF   I mean the way she described you. You're not how I pictured.

BENNY   She described me?

CLIFF   Yeah, only not too good.

BENNY   Why, what'd she say?

CLIFF   She said attractive.

BENNY   Really?

CLIFF   I know, that's what I'm thinking. Really? I mean, no offense, but . . . Anyway, eye of the beholder, I guess.

BENNY   What else she say?

CLIFF   Nah, man, I ain't playin' that game. High school is over. You sort that shit out yourselves.

BENNY   [*Pause.*]
She seemed upset.

CLIFF   Yeah, she is.

BENNY   I gotta stop doing that.

CLIFF   Making people upset?

BENNY   Yeah.

CLIFF   Yeah, well, we all have our habits to break.

BENNY   [*Beat.*]
Yes. Yes, we do.

CLIFF   Maybe you should get in a program.

[*Off his blank look.*]

Something to make you stop . . . doin' whatever it is you keep doin'.

BENNY   What is it that I keep doin'?

CLIFF   How should I know? I just met you.

BENNY   Oh.

CLIFF   I'm just sayin', a program's good. Structure and whatnot.

BENNY   Yeah, well, I don't think they really have a program like that. For what it is I do.

CLIFF   You'd be surprised. My cousin couldn't stop getting' tattoos. He was like . . . addicted, for real, same as me, only it was body art. Crazy skulls and devils, evil pixie tattoos, whatever, all over his body. And he found a program, made him stop. So if they got something for him, I bet you can dig something up. You should Google that shit.

[*Toilet flushes.* CONNIE *reenters with a full cup. She places it on the table next to* BENNY, *icy.*]

CONNIE   Here. Now get out.

BENNY   Hey, come on now.

CONNIE   No, your duties are done. Now go home.

BENNY   Are you mad?

CONNIE   Nah, I ain't mad.

BENNY   Yes, you are. Why are you mad?

CONNIE   Your little power trip. Cliff comes up here, so you gotta start flappin' your dick around?

CLIFF   That was a misunderstanding. He thought I wanted to get with you.

CONNIE   I don't care what he thought. Don't be defendin' him.

CLIFF   I wasn't.

BENNY   Listen, I gotta tell you something.

CONNIE   Well, tell me some other time, 'cause I got company right now.

BENNY   It's why I came up here tonight. Why I made you that torte.

CLIFF   You made that? It looks good.

CONNIE   Go home, Benny.

BENNY   Hold on, Connie, let me just—

[*Look over to* CLIFF.]

CLIFF   It's okay, just pretend I ain't even here.

BENNY   [*Back to* CONNIE.]

   I'm not very good at this kind of stuff. And I should've just come out with it right off instead of—

CONNIE   I know you ain't asking me out. Please, God, don't let him ask me out.

BENNY   Look, I've been having feelings for you for a few weeks now. You could tell, right?

CLIFF   Yeah, she could tell.

BENNY   And that's a big no-no in the department, as you can imagine. A lot of conflict of interest. So I went in the front office today and came clean about it. I was real upfront with them. So naturally they took me off your case.

CONNIE   What do you mean?

BENNY   I mean, they're gonna assign you a new parole officer.

CONNIE   You're not my parole officer?

BENNY   No.

CONNIE   Since what time?

BENNY   Since, I don't know, noon, I guess. But the point is, now we're free to, you know, hang out or whatever. I don't even know if you're open to that at all, but—

CONNIE   So wait, you came up here, and broke into my apartment—

BENNY   I know.

CONNIE   And questioned me and threatened me, and you're not even assigned to my case no more?

BENNY   I didn't know how else to—

CONNIE   And right in front of my friend you make me piss in a cup?

BENNY   Clearly that was a misjudgment.

[*She throws the cup of piss in his face.*]

CONNIE   Clearly.

CLIFF   Oh shit.

CONNIE   Get the fuck out of here.

BENNY   Connie—

CONNIE   No Connie. I have been with some sick people in my day, but you beat 'em all.

[BENNY *puts his shoes on over the following lines.*]

You up here waitin' for me, intimidating me, sayin' I'm gonna go back to jail, holdin' me hostage in my own apartment so you can . . . what? Ask me out? Tell me you got a crush on me? That's smooth. You're a real Romeo, you know it?

BENNY   I'm sorry.

CONNIE   Yeah, you're sorry. You're sorry you got a face full of piss.

BENNY   Look, this was stupid, I know. I do stupid things sometimes. I just wanted to—I didn't know how else to talk to you.

CONNIE   You call me up, you say, hey how you doin'. Like a normal person. You don't know to be a normal person?

BENNY [*Pause.*]

I'm gonna go.

CONNIE You do that. And take your nasty torte with ya.

[*Throws it at him.*]

Tasted like dog shit anyways. I was just bein' polite.

[*He doesn't move.*]

Get out!

[BENNY *takes one last look at* CONNIE, *and exits.* CONNIE *joins* CLIFF *at the table. Silence . . .*]

You believe that shit?

[*Beat. She and* CLIFF *share a moment. Then* CLIFF *bends over and cleans the torte off the floor.*]

What are you doing?

CLIFF Doing what I always do. Cleaning up your mess.

CONNIE Well, you don't need to do that. Leave it for the maid.

CLIFF [*A little chuckle.*]

Maid.

[*But he keeps cleaning.*]

CONNIE I'm serious, leave it alone. I wanna play cards.

[CLIFF *stops the cleaning and heads over to the table. He takes the cards and begins shuffling. After a couple beats . . .*]

I cleaned up your messes plenty of times.

CLIFF I didn't say you didn't.

[*Pause as he shuffles some more.*]

He didn't look at all like you said he'd look.

CONNIE Deal the cards, please.

[*He deals eight cards to each of them in silence.*]

CLIFF You gonna call him?

CONNIE Cliff, please.

CLIFF You're gonna call, though, right? Maybe after a couple weeks or something?

[CONNIE *just arranges the cards in her hand.*]

It's not like you've never done anything stupid.

CONNIE Flip the card.

CLIFF [*Flips the card.*]

I think you oughta call him. You're gonna, right? Someday, maybe?

[CONNIE *plays a card.*]

I hope you do. 'Cause it's hard to find a man who can cook.

[CLIFF *plays a card. Then* CONNIE. *They play Crazy Eights as the lights fade.*]

• • •

Such a Beautiful Voice Is Sayeda's and Karima's City

Yussef El Guindi

Adapted from the

short stories by

Salwa Bakr

Such a Beautiful Voice Is Sayeda's and *Karima's City*
by Yussef El Guindi
adapted from the short stories by Salwa Bakr

For my father

Acknowledgments:

My deep thanks to Salwa Bakr for writing such wonderful stories; to Dina Amin for introducing me to Bakr's work; to Golden Thread Productions for first staging them; to the Lark Play Development Center for first pairing them up at a staged reading, and to The Fountain Theatre for giving the two pieces a full production.

Yussef El Guindi

Yussef El Guindi's most recent production was *Back of the Throat*, winner of the 2004 Northwest Playwright's Competition held by Theater Schmeater. It won *LA Weekly*'s Excellence in Playwriting Award for 2006. It was also nominated for the 2006 American Theater Critics Association's Steinberg/New Play Award and was voted Best New Play of 2005 by the *Seattle Times*. It was first staged by San Francisco's Thick Description and Golden Thread Productions, then later presented in various theatres around the country, including The Flea Theater in New York. Another play of his, *Ten Acrobats in an Amazing Leap of Faith*, staged by Silk Road Theatre Project, won the After Dark Award for Best New Play in Chicago in 2006. *Acts of Desire*, consisting of two related one-acts, was staged by the Fountain Theatre in Los Angeles. *Back of the Throat* and those two related one-acts, now titled *Such a Beautiful Voice Is Sayeda's* and *Karima's City*, have been published by Dramatists Play Service. Yussef holds an MFA from Carnegie-Mellon University and was playwright-in-residence at Duke University.

···author's note···

The plays were written a couple of years apart and were first presented individually by Golden Thread Productions. Ideally they should be presented together, as they were done at The Fountain Theatre; and before that, as staged readings at the Lark Play Development Center—with an intermission between the two pieces. It is up to the director to decide which play should go first.

They can also be done individually, of course, as originally presented.

Both plays are best staged if kept fluid, moving, with lighting changes where necessary, but with no prolonged blackouts.

Also, with *Such a Beautiful Voice Is Sayeda's* in particular, there may be a temptation to characterize the men as heavy-handed or unlikable. It is much more effective if the men come across as human and familiar. The forces arrayed against Sayeda and Karima are much more insidious and widespread than a prevailing patriarchy. One of the reasons I wanted to adapt these two short stories was because I felt these two women could be living, and struggling, anywhere, including the United States. Fighting to have one's voice heard is always an uphill struggle, regardless of location or culture.

···production note···

Such a Beautiful Voice Is Sayeda's was produced by Golden Thread Productions (Torange Yeghiazarian, Artistic Director) in San Francisco, California, opening on August 8, 2002. It was directed by Hal Gelb; the set design was by Jay Lasnik; the costume design was by Svetlana; the lighting design was by Robert Ted Anderson; and the sound design was by Michael Santo. The cast was as follows:

SAYEDA Bella Warda
SAYEDA 2, SISTER Claudia Rosa
SAYEDA 3, MOTHER Pamela Marsh
ABDEL HAMID Ric Prindle
AM ISSA, DOCTOR Ali Dadgar
VIOLIN Morgan Fichte
SINGING VOICE Barbara Jaspersen

Such a Beautiful Voice Is Sayeda's was produced by The Fountain Theatre (Deborah Lawlor and Stephen Sachs, Artistic Directors; Simon Levy and Stephen Sachs, Producers) in Los Angeles, California, opening on October 28, 2005. It was directed by Deborah Lawlor; the set design was by Scott Siedman; the costume design was by Naila Aladdin-Sanders; the lighting design was by Kathi O'Donohue; and the sound design was by David B. Marling. The cast was as follows:

SAYEDA   Sarah Ripard
SAYEDA 2   Naila Azad
SAYEDA 3, SISTER   Grace Nassar
ABDEL HAMID   Navid Negahban
AM ISSA, DOCTOR   Marc Casabani
MOTHER   Marisa Vural

characters

SAYEDA	**DOCTOR**
ABDEL HAMID	**SAYEDA 2**
MOTHER	**SAYEDA 3 / STAGEHAND**
SISTER	**A WOMAN'S VOICE**
AM ISSA	

Note: Sayeda 2 and 3 play the Mother and Sister.
Am Issa plays the Doctor.

• • •

[*Sheets and clothes hang on an upstage clothesline. If possible, a soft wind blows these items so that they billow slightly. There is a table and chairs on one side of the stage. A bathtub is positioned in another area. Inside it, a woman, her back to the audience. The lighting is muted, perhaps tinged with blue, or some other color to impart an otherworldly tone. SAYEDA stands some yards from the bathtub. She is transfixed by the sight of the woman in the tub. Sayeda is dressed in drab house clothes. Music is heard. An ethereal sound? Over that, an Arabic song, perhaps. A woman singing. A beautiful voice. And overlaying that (an actor talking over the speakers) a WOMAN'S VOICE is heard.*]

WOMAN'S VOICE   Sayeda . . . Don't be afraid. [SAYEDA *approaches the woman in the bathtub.*] There's nothing to be afraid of anymore . . . Sayeda.

ABDEL HAMID   [*Offstage.*] Sayeda. [*Beat. The woman in the bathtub looks at* SAYEDA.] Sayeda! [*Blackout.* ABDEL HAMID*'s voice continues:*] What's keeping you in there? Come out here. [*Beat.*] Sayeda! [*The sound of tea glasses, spoons are heard clattering to the ground. Lights up. The woman in the bathtub is gone. The billowing of the laundry has stopped.* SAYEDA *is kneeling on the floor next to the fallen tea glasses, sugar cubes, and spoons. She holds a tray.* ABDEL HAMID *stands nearby. Perhaps he holds a newspaper, or is smoking a cigarette.*] What's the matter with you? It's like you're a million miles away. You've been dropping things all afternoon. [*She places the fallen items on the tray and wipes the floor with a cloth from her apron. Does he bend down to help her?*] What's going on?

SAYEDA   Nothing.

ABDEL HAMID   Every time you tell me it's nothing, I hold my breath. Your nothings have a way of ruining my day. What is it? What has happened? [SAYEDA *starts to exit.*] Sayeda. Don't walk away from me when I'm talking to you.

SAYEDA   I'm going to get you some more tea.—I'll get us some more, then I'll . . . Yes . . . There is—. . . I would like to have a word with you about something.

ABDEL HAMID   Uh-huh. [*She exits.*] I knew it. It's about money, isn't it. What else could it be. The only time you're afraid to ask for something is when you want to bleed me of more money. What emergency is it this time? It's funny how all your emergencies turn out to be luxuries in the end. Well, for your information, I don't have a piaster more to give. [*Opens newspaper.*] It's enough what I pay you for household expenses each month. The pennies I give myself to have coffee with my friends is the last pleasure I have left. You want to rob me of that too? I get it from my boss at work, then I come home and I get it from you? [SAYEDA *enters with tray.*]

SAYEDA   It's not about money.

ABDEL HAMID   [*Beat.*] What are you keeping from me? . . . Is it the children?

SAYEDA   No.

ABDEL HAMID   Is someone talking about us?

SAYEDA   No.

ABDEL HAMID   Then spit it out! Before I think the worse has happened.

SAYEDA   [*Beat.*] Well, I . . . the fact is . . . I don't know how to tell you . . . [*Her hand goes to her throat.*] I've discovered that I'm . . .

ABDEL HAMID   God help us. Again? Sayeda. How is it possible? I'm up to here with children. My pockets are empty. Which means you can neither have the baby nor do I have the money for an abortion. So you figure it out yourself, because we're not having another child.

SAYEDA   It's not—no. I'm not pregnant.

ABDEL HAMID   [*Throws down his newspaper.*] What? What is it? Tell me.

SAYEDA   The fact is, I've . . . Something has happened to my—voice.— When I sing. I've discovered that my voice has become—very beautiful. [ABDEL HAMID *stares at his wife for a few seconds. He bursts out laughing.*] Don't laugh.

ABDEL HAMID   How can I not laugh. My wife is a comedienne.

SAYEDA   Don't laugh, please.

ABDEL HAMID   And I was sure it was something serious.

SAYEDA   It is. I just don't know how to explain it.

ABDEL HAMID   But that's why I married you. Every time I'm about ready to throw you out the window, you make me laugh. [*He moves to hug her; she tries to push him away.*]

SAYEDA   Wait.

ABDEL HAMID   Come here.

SAYEDA   Listen to me! [*She pushes him away.*] Something happened this morning and I need to tell you. Because I don't know where it came from or how to explain it. [*A final laugh—beat—then a shrug from* ABDEL HAMID.]

ABDEL HAMID   Sure—sure. Go ahead. I like a good joke.

SAYEDA   It's not a joke. It happened after you left for work this morning. It's . . . I don't know where to begin . . . [*As* SAYEDA *narrates what happened,* ABDEL HAMID *will sit down to drink his tea, plopping in three or four sugar cubes.*] As soon as you left and I—I sent the children off to school . . . I went about my usual routine: I prepared dinner, cleaned the house and all those other household chores that never seem to end. And then when I heard the noon call to prayer, I thought, why not take a bath. I deserved a break. So I did. [*Lights up on the bathtub. "*SAYEDA*"—or* SAYEDA 2*—is in the tub.*] I got a bucket of water.—I washed my hair, and I, as I sometimes do, I began to sing, to amuse myself. You know how I do sometimes. But as I was singing and scrubbing myself, I experienced the strangest thing. [SAYEDA *looks at* SAYEDA 2.] You see—the voice that was singing . . . it wasn't my own.—At least it wasn't my normal voice and nothing I recognized. It was like someone else had stepped into the room and was singing instead. [SAYEDA *approaches the bathtub.—We hear this other voice singing faintly over the speakers.*] And it was so beautiful. This voice. That felt like it might be coming out of my mouth but that wasn't mine. Well, beautiful or not, you can imagine how I reacted. I thought someone had come into the room. But when I washed the soap from my eyes and looked around—there was no one there. Everything was as it should be.—I was so scared.—I muttered a prayer to God to protect me . . . and went back to cleaning myself . . . And I started to sing again. [*The beautiful voice is heard again. At some point, also, the light breeze causes the sheets to stir.*] And again this voice rang out more powerful—and serene and intense, rising and falling like perfect dunes—and bubbling up like water in a spring. Well, I was ready to run. You know I don't believe in ifrits, or jinns. But right then I called on God to protect me from the devil and any and everything He doesn't sanction. Abdel Hamid, my heart was pounding so strong it felt like each heartbeat was a punch in my chest. I was scared to open my mouth. . . . But . . . but again I calmed down and I . . . this time I called out my name.

WOMAN'S VOICE and **SAYEDA 2**   [*Together.*] Sayeda.

SAYEDA   And then again.

WOMAN'S VOICE and **SAYEDA 2**   [*Together.*] Sayeda. [*Beat; joyous now, as if sung.*] Sayeda! [SAYEDA 2 *clamps her hand over her mouth.*]

SAYEDA   Then I thought, what if the neighbors heard me? Or you came back and heard me call my name? You'd think I'd gone crazy. Who in their right mind calls out their name with such amazement and wonder? And it was wonderful. Not because of my name but because of this voice that was pronouncing it. [SAYEDA 2 *hurriedly puts on her galabeya, looking around as if still not convinced she's alone.*] I know this all sounds like craziness and I thought so too. Worse, I thought there might be some truth to those stories of spirits that haunt us and make us their playthings, and I uttered the prayer—

SAYEDA and **SAYEDA 2**   [*Together.*] "Say: I seek refuge / With the Lord of the Dawn, / From Mischief. I seek refuge / With the Lord of Dawn, / From Mischief."

[SAYEDA 2 *and* SAYEDA *come downstage and look out as if through a window.*]

SAYEDA   Once I looked out the window and saw people going about their business I relaxed. . . . I breathed again. I finished drying. . . . And I started to comb my hair. [*The two* SAYEDAS *turn to each other.*] And in front of the mirror . . . [*The beautiful voice is heard singing.*] Can you believe it, my love . . . my voice was even more beautiful than before. I felt no fear now. And without that fear, my voice rose higher than ever before and played in the air like a bird enchanted with its own wings and flight and knowing it was free to fly wherever it willed. And I knew then for sure this was no genie. It couldn't be. This was a human voice. This was my voice. And I was singing. It was me. . . . It was me. . . . Listen. Listen, Abdel Hamid, I'll show you.

[SAYEDA *opens her mouth, ready to sing.* ABDEL HAMID *slams his tea down. The lights in the bathtub area go down and* SAYEDA 2 *exits.*]

ABDEL HAMID   Who have you told about this?

SAYEDA   No one. It just happened this morning. I haven't spoken to anyone.

ABDEL HAMID   This is to stay between ourselves. You are not to tell anyone, especially the children.

SAYEDA   You don't believe me.—I'll prove it to you.

ABDEL HAMID   Sayeda.

SAYEDA   I'll sing you something.

ABDEL HAMID   No. Come here.

SAYEDA   Have I ever lied to you?

ABDEL HAMID   Just come here. It has nothing to do with believing you or not.

SAYEDA   I'm not going soft in the head either. And I know it's not the work of ifrits. We've been in this house twenty years and I haven't laid eyes on one of them once.

ABDEL HAMID   Sit here. [*Pats his knee.*] Keep me company for a second.

SAYEDA   I can sing that song you like, "What a Sweet, Sweet World." [*She sits on his lap.*]

ABDEL HAMID   I'm sure you could sing it wonderfully. I know I've been ignoring you. I know I have, and I'm sorry. I just can't seem to get ahead of my work.

SAYEDA   I swear before God that all I've told you is the truth.

ABDEL HAMID   I am not doubting you. But imagine how this would sound. I mean really imagine how your story would sound to someone who doesn't know you. They would think you were light in the head.

SAYEDA   But it was the most amazing thing.

ABDEL HAMID   I know you've been exhausted recently. What with this horrible heat we're having—

SAYEDA   That's not it. It has nothing to do with that.

ABDEL HAMID   [*Overlapping.*] And the children, misbehaving, giving you a hard time. I will give them a good talking to, I promise you. [*If she hasn't got off his lap before, she gets off now.*]

SAYEDA   There's only one way to show you. Listen. [*She opens her mouth to sing.*]

ABDEL HAMID   [*Hits the table.*] Sayeda . . . What's gotten into you? . . . Have you no shame? . . . This nonsense does you no credit, and will make you the laughingstock of your children. So what if what you say is true? What do you want to do about it? Sing? Become a singer? At your age? You are over forty; a mother of four and you're acting like a child.—Stop it. [*Behind the sheet, we now see the shadow of* SAYEDA 2. SAYEDA *also notices her. Beat.*] Look. [*He goes up to her, holds her.*] Let's forget all this . . . forget my job . . . and we go lie down together. Take this time before the children come back; relax a little. Mm? What do you say . . . I missed you . . . Sayeda?

WOMAN'S VOICE   [*Over the speakers.*] Sayeda.

[*Blackout apart from the light throwing* SAYEDA 2*'s shadow onto the sheets. Then that goes out and we go to a blue-tinged work light, or some transitional lighting as the following scene change takes place. Also, music or sounds accompany the transition. Perhaps either a metronome-like sound or something repetitive, mechanical.* SAYEDA 2 *and the stagehand—a third woman—are dressed in the same outfit as* SAYEDA. *They represent* SAYEDA *as she goes about her household chores. First they bring on a small bed, or mattress.* ABDEL HAMID *will go over to it, undress, and get in.* SAYEDA *will move downstage.* SAYEDA 2 *takes down the laundry.* SAYEDA 3 *takes out the tea tray.*]

WOMAN'S VOICE   Sayeda . . . What are you doing? . . . The laundry can wait.

SAYEDA   It has to be done.

WOMAN'S VOICE   The cleaning up can wait.

SAYEDA   That has to be done too.

WOMAN'S VOICE   The dishes can wait.

SAYEDA   They have to be washed.

WOMAN'S VOICE   The floor can wait.

SAYEDA   That has to be cleaned too. [SAYEDA 3 *will cross the stage pushing a mop across the floor before her.*]

WOMAN'S VOICE   Your soap opera can wait.

SAYEDA   It's only half an hour.

WOMAN'S VOICE   Their dinner can wait.

SAYEDA   Who will feed them?

WOMAN'S VOICE   Your husband's needs can wait.

SAYEDA   He'll get angry, I can't.

WOMAN'S VOICE   The children can wait.

SAYEDA   How can you say that?

WOMAN'S VOICE   Sayeda. You can't wait. . . . Not anymore.

[*The metronome/mechanical sound stops. Lights up on the bathtub area and* SAYEDA 2 *combing her hair.*]

SAYEDA 2   A beautiful voice was meant for singing.

SAYEDA   You have to be realistic, Sayeda.

SAYEDA 2   If a relative left a house for you in her inheritance, would it be realistic to walk away from it? What's yours is yours, use it.

SAYEDA   Just like that? I wish it was that simple.

SAYEDA 2   Why can't it be? It costs nothing. And why shouldn't others hear you?

SAYEDA   You're being so arrogant. If you want to sing, sing in the bathroom. You don't have to make a spectacle of yourself.

SAYEDA 2   You, who's always worried about doing the right thing: not to let others hear you would be selfish. If it's pleasing, if it brings joy to others, then that gift is meant to be shared. That's what you're supposed to do with a gift like that. And it doesn't matter how old you are.

SAYEDA   He needn't have said that.

SAYEDA 2   Age has nothing to do with it.

SAYEDA   People can enjoy the voice of a human being regardless of age.

SAYEDA 2   So sing.

SAYEDA   I want to.

SAYEDA 2   Sing.

SAYEDA   All right. Yes . . . I will.

SAYEDA 2   Take a deep breath, and the right song will come and fill you.

[*They both take a deep breath. Music begins. They open their mouths to sing.*]

ABDEL HAMID   What's the matter? . . . Sayeda?

SAYEDA   I'm going to get a glass of water. . . . Can I get you anything?

ABDEL HAMID   Hurry up and come back to bed.

SAYEDA   I will. I'll just be a second.

[*Blackout apart from spotlights on the two* SAYEDAS *as the music swells, and the beautiful voice is heard singing again.* ABDEL HAMID *exits.* SAYEDA 3 *crosses the stage with a mop before her, cleaning as she goes along.* SAYEDA *sees this and takes the mop from her and continues the cleaning.* SAYEDA 2 *quickly steps in front of* SAYEDA, *stopping her. Lights up.* SAYEDA 2 *grabs hold of the mop.*]

SAYEDA 2   That's enough.

[SAYEDA *tries to resume cleaning but* SAYEDA 2 *throws the mop to the floor. The music stops.*]

SAYEDA   What?

SAYEDA 2   Look at you.

SAYEDA   How do you mean?

SAYEDA 2   Well, look at you. Walking around in a worn housedress, and covering your hair in that ugly handkerchief. You look like a walking poster for refugees.

SAYEDA   Is it that bad?

SAYEDA 2   Can't you tell anymore?

SAYEDA   What do I need to dress up for?

SAYEDA 2   Must you have a reason to look nice? Others make an effort, but not you?

SAYEDA   I'm cleaning. Why would I—? My God: Am I that terrible to look at?

SAYEDA 2   Just the opposite. [SAYEDA 2 *has taken* SAYEDA *to stand before a mirror—which can be an imaginary one downstage. Upstage,* SAYEDA 3 *hangs a beautiful dress and a neck scarf on the laundry line.*] You've forgotten how attractive you are.

SAYEDA   Don't say that. I'm not.

SAYEDA 2   You are. . . . Or will be when we remove that little mustache. [SAYEDA, *horrified, covers it up with her hand.* SAYEDA 2 *takes out a blush and lipstick from her pocket and hands it to* SAYEDA.] Use this for now. We'll wax it off later. And those eyebrows could use plucking.

[*As* SAYEDA *powders her face,* SAYEDA 2 *gets the dress and scarf and brings them back to* SAYEDA.]

SAYEDA   No wonder he's been ignoring me.

SAYEDA 2   Forget him. It has nothing to do with him.

SAYEDA   How could I have let myself go like this?

SAYEDA 2   Put on the lipstick.

SAYEDA   He doesn't like lipstick.

SAYEDA 2   He doesn't have to wear it then. Put it on. . . . Put it on. [SAYEDA *hesitates . . . then applies the lipstick.*] And wear this.

SAYEDA   There's no reason in the world for me to wear that. [*Beat.*] I haven't worn that since I was engaged.

SAYEDA 2   All the more reason to wear it then.

[*Beat. She pulls off her housedress and proceeds to put on the dress and scarf. SAYEDA laughs.*]

SAYEDA   This will get the neighbors talking.

SAYEDA 2   Let them.

SAYEDA   They'll think I'm having an affair.

SAYEDA 2   You are. How can you possess the voice you do and not look like you're in love. To be able to sing . . .

SAYEDA   I should feel beautiful. [SAYEDA 2 *picks up the housedress and exits.*] Now what? . . . Sayeda? . . . Can you assure me that you're not going crazy? [*Beat, as she seriously considers the question.*] Yes. . . . A voice this lovely can't be a sign of craziness.—God wouldn't be so cruel to torment you with something so wonderful. You can sing.—I've always felt I could, now I know for sure. Why it took me forever to appreciate what was right in front of me I don't know, but now that I do, I'm not going to bottle it up again. I'm going to sing. I am.—I'll sing. In front of people. I'll tell Abdel Hamid tonight.—Or tomorrow . . . How am I ever going to tell him? . . . If only I had someone who could advise me.—Om Hassan—We're not that intimate. When did I stop knowing people I can share secrets with? . . . I can't tell my mother and sister.—Or should I? [*Lights up on the MOTHER and SISTER.*]

MOTHER   It's menopause. What else could it be.

SISTER   I don't know why he hasn't divorced her.

MOTHER   She wants to embarrass her family.

SISTER   Who does she think she is, Om Kulthoum?

MOTHER   Wait until your auntie Hoda hears about this, she'll have a fit.

SISTER   You're the one who spoilt her.

MOTHER   It could be worse, I suppose.

SISTER   How?

MOTHER   She could want to be a dancer. [*The* SISTER *and* MOTHER *laugh.*]

SAYEDA   I'll tell them last. Definitely tell them last.

MOTHER   And now with this singing, I hear she has no time to feed her children.

SISTER   [*Scandalized.*] No. [*Lights out on* MOTHER *and* SISTER.]

SAYEDA   Oh my God, dinner. I've forgotten to buy dinner.

[*Lights change as* SAYEDA *steps into a different space, representing the grocery store. The grocer—*AM ISSA*—enters holding a plastic grocery bag.*]

AM ISSA   Here we are: ten eggs, ten slices of "gibna rumi," macaroni, bread, and five of the sweetest mangoes you'll ever find.
[SAYEDA *doesn't take the bag at first but stares distractedly in front of her.*] If you can't pay me now, pay later. [*Then remembering where she is,* SAYEDA *takes out the money, gives it to him, and takes the bag.*] What is it, Sitta Sayeda? This is the first time I've seen you this upset. . . . You are too young to be talking to yourself. You have to wait until you get to my age before you start muttering under your breath in the middle of a street and not give a damn.—Has something happened? [SAYEDA *looks at him, on the verge of crying.*] Come with me. Rest a while. [*He leads her to a chair. He sits her down, then draws up a chair to sit beside her.*] Knowing you, you've

been on your feet since dawn and not stopped once. What is the matter? I've known your family long enough to want to know you're okay; and where I can be of help, I'll do what I can. Has something come between you and Abdel Hamid? . . . Have you had a quarrel?

[SAYEDA *looks like she might say something but instead tries to hold back tears.*]

Shh, it's all right. Whatever has happened, I'm sure it's not that bad. Abdel Hamid is a good man. You're both good people, and where that is the case, a solution is always possible. If he's quarreled with you, he's just under a lot of stress, I'm sure. How can he not be. With the cost of everything, and living in this city. The price of essentials is devouring us all. Just putting food on the table is an achievement. It's like you've gone through the Olympics just to get through the day, and by the end of it, you have no time for your family. If his temper is short now and again, you must be patient with him.

SAYEDA It's—it's not that.

AM ISSA Then what? Don't be shy with me. If there is a problem, we'll put our heads together and find an answer.

SAYEDA Am Issa: If I tell you . . . promise me you'll never let on that I spoke to you.

AM ISSA Of course; if you want.

SAYEDA I'm serious. He has taken an oath to divorce me if I ever discuss this matter with anyone. But I have to tell someone. I have to. And I can't tell my mother and sister, they'd laugh at me and—well—you've always been so kind. . . Maybe . . . maybe you'll understand.

AM ISSA Whatever you say stays between us, I promise; have no fear about that. Now tell me, what is the matter?

SAYEDA [*Beat.*] It's the strangest thing. . . . Yesterday morning . . . While I was having a bath . . . [SAYEDA *freezes. Perhaps there is also a light change.*]

AM ISSA Poor Abdel Hamid . . . As if his burdens aren't enough, now he has to deal with this.—And to come out dressed this way; and for what, to buy bread, and draw attention to herself? A singer?—What next? The embarrassment she will cause her family all because of some silly notion she's gotten into her head. Truly the private lives of my customers are better than anything I watch on TV. And who would have thought: She always seemed so normal.

[SAYEDA *unfreezes.*]

SAYEDA And I swear that is what happened. However strange it might sound. In fact—there's only one way to prove it: With your permission, I'll sing you something.

AM ISSA Sitta Sayeda.

SAYEDA Any song you like. I know most of them.

AM ISSA Calm yourself. I'll get you a glass of tea.

SAYEDA But I want to sing. I know you don't believe me.

AM ISSA Of course I do; but this is a grocery store, not the opera house; anyone might come in.

[ABDEL HAMID *enters. He and* SAYEDA *look at each other, as if back in their house. Beat.*]

ABDEL HAMID I passed by Issa's grocery on the way home. . . . I've made an appointment with a doctor and you're coming with me. [*Perhaps* ABDEL HAMID *and* AM ISSA *exchange looks briefly, before* AM ISSA *exits.* SAYEDA 2 *enters and moves the two chairs to another part of the stage. She lines them up next to each other.* ABDEL HAMID *and* SAYEDA *sit in them. They are in a psychiatrist's office.* SAYEDA 2 *hovers not far from* SAYEDA. *Beat.*] You understand why I'm doing this. . . . I care for you, Sayeda. . . . I love you. . . . I want no harm to come to you. We don't know what's going on. It could be a— anything, a simple matter—and the sooner we deal with it the better. And there's nothing to be ashamed of in coming to see a psychiatrist. Who are we to understand these things? It is said and I believe it that a fathomless sea exists inside every person and no one can unravel that mystery except God. And when you think about it—how are we supposed to understand ourselves when something breaks down? We cannot be rational when we are ill. Doctors are to be consulted in these matters. And who knows, this story of your voice could simply be from exhaustion. It's certainly not genies or demons. Even though I have a modest education, I do have faith in God; and the Holy Quran says that God has erected a solid barrier between man and genies. So . . . if it's not that . . . why not give this a try. . . . If it brings about a remedy and everything goes back to normal—then . . . the expenses for this will be worth it. . . . Am I wrong? [*Beat.*] And please don't forget you actually told the grocer.—What about tomorrow, or the day after. You might blurt it out to someone else, or worse, do something that would make us look ridiculous. And to come out in this dress; I want him to see this. I have worked too hard to have us become a cheap story people laugh about. I don't know what's gotten into you. . . . If it was just you and me, I might have closed my eyes, kept my mouth shut, but you are the mother of my children and I will not put their welfare in jeopardy. [*The doctor enters.*]

DOCTOR Sorry to keep you waiting.

[ABDEL HAMID *stands to greet him.* SAYEDA *remains seated.*]

ABDEL HAMID Thank you for seeing us, Doctor.

DOCTOR Not a problem. How can I help you?

[ABDEL HAMID *starts to speak but both he and the* DOCTOR *freeze.* SAYEDA *turns to* SAYEDA 2.]

SAYEDA What if he's right? What if it's an affliction? And my children are put in danger by it.

[SAYEDA 2 *sits next to* SAYEDA.]

SAYEDA 2 All you have to know is that you've discovered something that is only beautiful. And it belongs to you. . . . A beautiful voice was meant for singing. How dangerous can that be?

[ABDEL HAMID *and the* DOCTOR *unfreeze.*]

DOCTOR Thank you, but I would prefer it if she would tell me the story, if you don't mind. [*Turns to* SAYEDA.] In her own words. If that's okay with you, Sayeda. [SAYEDA 2 *gets up as the doctor comes around and sits next to* SAYEDA.] Take your time. . . . There are no pressures here. I want you to be at ease. . . . and tell me what has happened? . . . What is troubling you?

SAYEDA [*Beat.*] Nothing . . . I don't think.

[*The* DOCTOR *takes out a small notepad and a ballpoint pen which he clicks open. Beat.*]

DOCTOR Tell me about this incident.

[*Beat.*]

SAYEDA Well . . . [*Beat.*] I was having a bath . . . I began to sing—as I sometimes do. . . . And—discovered—I was singing better than I had before. . . . I was singing in a way . . . in a voice more beautiful than I've ever heard. [*Beat.*] That's all. [*Beat.*] Except I was shocked by it. . . . I didn't know I had it in me. . . . It was like I was filled with a feeling that I was another person completely. . . . Almost— separate from the Sayeda I know. The Sayeda who goes about her day . . . Who binds her head with a handkerchief because she doesn't have the time to pull a comb through her hair. [*Beat.*] It filled me with a—a calm. . . . A sense of peace, and strength. It was like I'd stepped into a palace. . . . But that palace was— . . . It was the palace of my—voice. [*The* DOCTOR *continues to look at her.*] If you'd like: I could sing a little song for you.

DOCTOR   [*Smiling.*] I'm sure you have a charming voice but that won't be necessary. [*Writes in his notepad.*] Here's what I suggest. I can appreciate how unsettling this must be. There's a new medication out on the market that's proven very effective for this sort of occurrence. And please don't be alarmed that you hear voices. It is commoner than you think. Three pills daily should do it. [*Tears out paper and gives it to* ABDEL HAMID.] And, Sayeda: [*He turns to her.*] For the time being, you must avoid situations that create stress. I know day-to-day problems can be challenging, but you must rest for a while. I would also prefer it if you didn't stay alone. Invite a neighbor over or your family. And switch on the radio when you take a bath. Another thing: You may want to think about losing a little weight, because clearly that is affecting the way you see yourself. And if you get very depressed, hurry back to the clinic. All right? [*He pats her hand and gets up.*]

ABDEL HAMID   Thank you, Doctor.

DOCTOR   You're quite welcome.

[*As he exits, the stagehand comes on with a glass of water and a bottle of pills. She hands them to* ABDEL HAMID, *then takes the two chairs back to the table before exiting.* SAYEDA *stands looking at* SAYEDA 2. ABDEL HAMID *holds out the glass and pills.*]

ABDEL HAMID   Sayeda . . . Sayeda. [SAYEDA *walks over to her husband. She takes the glass as he opens the bottle and gives her one pill. She takes it, looks at it, then swallows the pill and drinks. She looks over at* SAYEDA 2, *who starts backing up, receding . . . and then exits.* ABDEL HAMID *takes the glass from her and places it, along with the pill bottle, on the table. He returns to* SAYEDA *and holds her, or takes her face in his hands.*] Everything's going to be all right. . . . I know it will. . . . Inshallah. [*He kisses her.*] I love you.

[*He exits.* SAYEDA 3 *comes on with the laundry basket and starts hanging sheets on the laundry line.* SAYEDA *lethargically takes off her dress and puts on the housedress that is also placed on the laundry line, along with the handkerchief. She ties on the handkerchief around her hair as she comes downstage to stand before the mirror-the imaginary one downstage. SAYEDA 3 exits once she's finished. SAYEDA looks at herself . . . then opens her mouth and sings. For the first time we actually hear SAYEDA's singing voice. It is cracked, hoarse, and devoid of any harmony. She tries snatches of different songs before giving up. For a moment she stands there looking apathetic, resigned. . . . She turns to look at the bottle of pills. She walks over to the table. She opens the bottle and pours out all the pills. She brings the pills to her mouth . . . then stops . . . and instead flings them all away, scattering them across the stage.]*

WOMAN'S VOICE   Sayeda. [SAYEDA *lights up at the sound of the voice.*] Sayeda.

[*Perhaps the shadow of* SAYEDA 2 *is thrown on the sheets.*]

SAYEDA   I'm here . . . I'm here.

[*Blackout.*]

• • •

• • • property list • • •

Tray of tea glasses, spoons, sugar	Plastic grocery bag with food
Newspaper	Money
Cloth	Chairs
Bed	Notepad, pen
Mop	Glass of water
Comb	Bottle of pills
Blush, lipstick	Laundry basket

• • • sound effects • • •

Ethereal music
Metronome

• • • production note • • •

Karima's City was produced by Golden Thread Productions (Torange Yeghiazarian, Artistic Director) in San Francisco, California, opening on October 30, 2003. It was directed by Arlene Hood; the costume design was by Keri Fitch; the lighting design was by Paul Measom; and the sound design was by Steven Klems. The cast was as follows:

KARIMA and ENSEMBLE   Bernadette Quattrone
MOTHER and ENSEMBLE   Lynne Soffer
MR. AZIZ and ENSEMBLE   Ali Dadgar
NADIA and ENSEMBLE   Denmo Ibrahim
NURSE and ENSEMBLE   Deborah Ben-Elizier

Karima's City was produced by The Fountain Theatre (Deborah Lawlor and Stephen Sachs, Artistic Directors; Simon Levy and Stephen Sachs, Producers) in Los Angeles, California. It was directed by Deborah Lawlor. The cast was as follows:

KARIMA   Naila Azad
MOTHER, MATRON, OFFICE WORKER, CANDIDATE 3, OLD WOMAN   Marisa Vural
SUITOR, NUT VENDOR, DOCTOR 1, OFFICE MANAGER, CANDIDATE 1, VOTING OFFICIAL   Marc Casabani
BUTCHER, DOCTOR 2, MR. AZIZ, TREE, CANDIDATE 2   Navid Negahban
FRUIT SELLER, NADIA, WEASEL, CANDIDATE 4   Grace Nassar

characters

Six to seven actors can play the 26 roles:

KARIMA	TREE
HOSPITAL MATRON	WEASEL
MOTHER	OLD WOMAN
S/A 1	S/A 2
SUITOR	S/A 3

VENDOR	**MANAGER**
FRUIT SELLER	**DESK MOVER 1**
BUTCHER	**DESK MOVER 2**
DOCTOR 1	**CANDIDATE 1**
DOCTOR 2	**CANDIDATE 2**
MR. AZIZ NADIA	**CANDIDATE 3**
OFFICE WORKER 1	**VOTING OFFICIAL**
OFFICE WORKER 2	

• • •

[*A prison cell. If possible, there are moveable flats representing the walls of the cell. Though a spotlight/lights could also be used to isolate and define spaces. Also, if possible, behind the walls, lining the sides of the stage, are trees, or something symbolic of trees. These trees are not yet visible. (One could also just project shadows of branches/trees; or, use the other actors to stand in for the trees.) In the cell,* KARIMA *looks out to the audience. She clutches a manuscript of loose paper to her chest.*]

KARIMA   I am going to presume you're out there. . . . It would be nice if you are. Listening . . . Keeping me company . . . There's only so much a mind can do looking at four walls every day. After I don't know how long, I think I should be allowed to change things around. Do some interior decorating. Have these sentries called walls be you. And you.—And you over there. Because I'm not going anywhere, so why not imagine you're here. You'll eventually exist even if you're not here now. You'll be reading what I'm going to tell you. I've written it all down. Just the way it happened. Every detail about how I ended up in this charming hell-hole from which I know I'll never get out. I mean they'll never let me out, I know that; so I said, write it down, Karima, put it on paper for that future audience you'll surely have—if everything you've gone through is ever to make sense. Someone will read it—and see how you were wrongly, unjustly confined all because you wanted to remain silent. Eternally silent, that day you decided to shut up that tongue of yours, that trouble-making tongue that got you into so many arguments by picking up a pair of scissors and cutting it out once and for all.

HOSPITAL MATRON   Karima. [*The* HOSPITAL MATRON *enters. She holds several sheets of paper.* KARIMA, *perhaps, attempts to hide the manuscript under her shirt, or in the folds of her dress.*] The doctors have looked over your complaints . . . . And—after careful study . . . they wish to assure you that you have nothing to fear from these walls. It's official now. You don't have to take my word for it. Screaming will not push them back any further. If you continue to scream at night, then we might have to consider other measures. These walls are not moving in on you; they have not moved, and will not in the future move. They're walls. Walls don't threaten and close in on people. They don't have anything against you. Secondly, the . . . [*She reads from the sheet of paper.*] "fat woman with the double chin . . ." I presume you're talking about me-is required to give you an injection. I will continue to do so until the doctors order otherwise. I'd appreciate it if you didn't laugh in my face while I carry out my duties. I too have feelings. [*Half to herself.*] And I hardly think I have a double chin. Thirdly . . . [*The* HOSPITAL MATRON *places several sheets of paper on the table.*] We're not trying to poison you. We want you to get well. You have to eat more; we insist on it. Otherwise . . . well . . . I'm sure it won't come to that. . . . I left you more paper in case you have any more requests. [*The* HOSPITAL MATRON *moves to the exit.*] And I'll see if I can't get you a potted plant. . . . There's no reason why we can't make this a cheerier place. [*With one last look at* KARIMA, *the* HOSPITAL MATRON *exits.*]

KARIMA   Bitch . . . I'm sorry but she is. I hate it when everything done is for my good. All your goods sicken me! And these walls are moving in on me. Live here all these years and see if they don't.

[*Collects herself.*] But . . . I won't talk of that—or anything else that happens in this bloody-minded model of good health and sanity. It would just get me too mad to speak. No: What's important, what you should know is everything that happened before I got here. When I started seeing the world around me changing horribly.

[*Perhaps* KARIMA *starts laying out sheets from her manuscript on the floor.*]

It's so depressing when nobody else is seeing what you see. And you end up being the only one warning of the disasters to come. Which always begin slowly, with a few words, a few rules and regulations and buildings that rise up and block out everything beautiful before it all floods your whole life and you find yourself drowning in it. [*Perhaps she stops what she's doing to look at the audience.*] If I seem tense during any of this, I'm sorry. I never want you to think you can't rely on me to tell this story. Because I can. Please allow me to show you what happened. [*The walls move in on* KARIMA.] No!

[*The walls stop, then break open and are moved away. Hopefully they're light enough that stagehands/actors from behind can lift them. If the back of these walls are painted with some of the elements she talks about below—storefronts, human figures—then perhaps these murals can be incorporated into the scene.* KARIMA's *mother enters.*]

MOTHER   Karima.

KARIMA   Oh no.

MOTHER   What are you yelling about?

KARIMA   I'm sorry, sorry.

MOTHER   Your brother's trying to sleep. He's home for a couple of days. The least you can do is think about someone else for once.

KARIMA   Mummy . . . one of the benefits of being shut up in this place is that I don't have to worry about you or my brother anymore.

MOTHER   What's the matter with you?

KARIMA   Can he still hear me all the way from my cell?

MOTHER   What cell? What are you talking about? Are you so wrapped up in your fantasies that you imagine you're some heroine locked up in a dungeon?

KARIMA   I would like to tell my story if that's all right with you.

MOTHER   God help us. Why you want to embarrass the people who love you the most, I don't know.

KARIMA   [*Holds out a sheet to her.*] Do you want to help me?—You can if you want.

[MOTHER *ignores the sheet of paper and walks out. A stagehand/actor* [S/A 1] *takes the sheet of paper from* KARIMA *and reads from it.*]

S/A 1   "This is the catastrophe. This is the deluge. This is the deluge that came and washed away everything beautiful in my amazing city." [*A second stagehand/actor* [S/A 2] *has picked up a sheet of paper from the floor. While* S/A 2 *reads, another stagehand/actor* [S/A 3] *helps* KARIMA *change out of her hospital gown into a dress.* KARIMA *listens as* S/A 2 *reads.*]

S/A 2   "Since the day I graduated and was given a job at the water company, a few drops of this deluge hovered on the horizon, touching people, plants, and animals. Most of us brushed it off as something that didn't concern us; or saw it as a sign of progress or some other excuse that allowed us to ignore it and get on with our lives. I did that too, in the beginning. What did I know but what was in front of my nose."

[S/A 3 *has left her to finish dressing and has picked up a sheet of paper.*]

KARIMA   [*Scrambling to get dressed.*] Wait, wait, I'm not ready.

S/A 3   "I noticed the first signs of this calamity on the very street I lived on."

KARIMA [*Still buttoning her dress.*] That's right, I did.

S/A 3 "Which ran a straight line to the water company, which I walked to every day."

KARIMA Others noticed it too, but we shrugged it away.

S/A 2 "Little things at first, then not so little; then things that made my heart sink."

KARIMA Could someone help me do this up, please?

[S/A 3 *returns to help her finish dressing.*]

S/A 1 "It was uprooted; completely torn out. It looked like the carcass of an innocent bird slaughtered."

KARIMA [*Overlapping.*] You've got the pages out of order, let me do it.

S/A 2 "He scolded me: 'How dare you do that in a public place.'"

KARIMA Wait.

S/A 1 "And this animal with its smooth body crept closer—"

KARIMA All right, everyone shut up. We can't have everyone talking at once or they'll think we're demented. The point is to show how the city and its dwellers went off the deep end, not us.—At least not me especially.

S/A 3 "Radiant with joy."

KARIMA Yes. [*Remembering what she wrote.*] "Up to this moment as I sit down to write, I feel radiant with joy." . . . Thank you, I'll take it from here. [*The stagehand/actors exit.*] I loved my street.—It made me proud to live in this city.—This mess of a wonderful city with its bright colors and little shops nestled next to each other like a bunch of women at a loud party; sharing gossip and compliments, and this one shop that had this shiny blue and orange awning that looked like it might have been the parachute of a spaceman, but really quite charming all the same. And this other one that shaded the Star of Liberty store, which sold chickpeas, and seeds and all sorts of nuts. And the vendor who would say every day—

[S/A 1 *as vendor.*]

VENDOR [*Handing her a bag of nuts.*] The morning doesn't start without you.

KARIMA [*Handing him money.*] And I believed he meant it. Even if it was a lie, why shouldn't I believe him? We're all too quick to accept the bad things said about us, why not believe the lies that mean well?

VENDOR It's not a lie, my dear.

KARIMA I believe you.

[S/A 2 *as fruit seller.*]

FRUIT SELLER Freshly picked with the morning dew still on them. Try my pears. Eat the fruit that's good for you.

KARIMA [*Showing him her hands are full.*] Maybe on my way back.

FRUIT SELLER I'll be waiting for you.

KARIMA Even the butcher with his terrible carcasses was real in a way that nothing else is now.

[SA 3 *as butcher.*]

BUTCHER Don't think about how it looks hanging in my store; but how it'll taste all cooked with roast potatoes and vegetables. Meat is the good life too.

KARIMA After a while even his greetings disappeared.—As the changes began, this street that was so dear to me started to lose its spirit.—I don't know what happened. . . . It was like a funeral pall had descended and we were all mute before the death of something we couldn't name. . . . And beyond my street, over the awnings, huge structures started appearing. Buildings rising like scarecrows to scare away everything beautiful. And on top of them the size of houses were these neon signs—that spelt nonsensical words telling you to buy things you didn't need; and somehow if you didn't have these things you didn't want you wouldn't be a complete human being. A complete moron more likely. But—I don't want to talk about that just now either. I still haven't told you about the best thing on my street. [*Lights up on the trees.*] The thirty-one beautiful trees. Lining the street from my house to my work. And they too greeted me each day. I'm not saying they talked to me, okay. I'm saying they were so alive with their own beauty, they spoke to me that way. They sang. Through their leaves. In the clear sounds of something that has no doubt about what it is. That simply delights in what it is. All of them: the camphor trees. The Indian ficus. And this really special one. Right next to the water company. I never knew its name, but when it blossomed, my God, it was as if the entire street was at a festival. Large, violet flowers up and down its long limbs. Looking like a choir of petals singing their colors and making the whole street pay attention. And we did. And then one day walking to work, I found the tree lying on the street. [*Suggestion: This "special tree" could be one she sees out in the direction of the audience, and might be suggested by a change in lighting.*] At first I didn't know what it was doing there; and felt it somehow unseemly, as if I'd caught it doing something it shouldn't. Then I saw it had been uprooted. Completely torn out. It looked like the carcass of an innocent bird, slaughtered. And no act of nature had done this but a human act. . . . In the next weeks, other trees followed. One by one.— That's when I began to feel the changes in me. . . . Little headaches at first. Then big ones. Then cramps that wouldn't go away. Then a sensation under my skin that felt like spiders crawling around my nerve ends. After a month these pains became excruciating, and when breathing began to feel like something I had to attend to or it would stop, I went to a doctor.

[*Suggestion: During the above speech, it might be effective to have a disconcerting, piercing sound of some sort build behind her speech. It might end when the doctor enters.* DOCTOR 1 *enters.*]

DOCTOR 1   Now what seems to be troubling you?

KARIMA   Several of them.

[DOCTOR 2 *enters.*]

DOCTOR 2   Where are you experiencing these pains?

KARIMA   I tried to tell them.

DOCTOR 1   Uh-huh.

[DOCTORS 1 *and 2 proceed to write prescriptions.*]

KARIMA   But I didn't know how to explain what was going on.

DOCTOR 1   [*Hands her a prescription.*] Good, good. Why don't we start you off on this.

DOCTOR 2   [*Hands her a prescription.*] Try these. They're very effective.

KARIMA   What could I say, I'm upset because my street is vanishing and they're ruining my city?

DOCTOR 2   That's hardly a thing to collapse about. Upset, yes, but migraines and cramps?

KARIMA   And finally I was diagnosed with—

DOCTOR 1   Chronic colitis with neurotic tension.

DOCTOR 2   I'd go along with that.

KARIMA   The medications were useless.

DOCTOR 1   [*Under his breath as he exits.*] Neurotic tension, without a doubt.

DOCTOR 2   [*Approaches KARIMA.*] If you'll allow me to make a suggestion. As a doctor, but also as an older person. A young woman, such as yourself, all alone—it is bound to put stress on you. And why? It is unnecessary, and the solution is easy.

KARIMA   What are you doing? I didn't write that.

DOCTOR 2   Nothing is written, my dear. Stop thinking you have control over things you don't. Concentrate on what you can change. You have duties. Look to what you can do. You can marry. You can bring life into the world. This will give a center to your life and go a long way to calming you.

[*The* DOCTOR *smiles and exits.*]

KARIMA   I wrote no such thing. What are you doing?

[*The* MOTHER *enters carrying groceries.*]

MOTHER   Have you nothing better to do than stand in front of the mirror talking to yourself? What you do all day when you're not working, I don't know. Help me with the groceries.

KARIMA   I'm worried, Mother. Why aren't we doing anything to stop them ruining our street? They're hacking down the trees. There're only three left. What's got into everyone?

MOTHER   People want to build. There's a housing shortage.

KARIMA   They're killing our neighborhood.

MOTHER   Forget the street, worry about yourself. Make use of the mirror and change what looks back at you.

KARIMA   [*To audience.*] Not that this has any relevance but during this period I also put on a bit of weight. [*To* MOTHER.] Why, what's the matter?

MOTHER   You're fat.

[MOTHER *deposits her bags offstage.*]

KARIMA   [*To audience.*] I also lost my sense of humor. And I used to have a very good one.

MOTHER   How are you going to find someone to marry you? [*Takes the other bag from* KARIMA.] Let me take that. I'm going to make a feast for your brother. Try and be pleasant when he's around.

KARIMA   It's always nice talking to you, Mother.

MOTHER   [*As she exits.*] No wonder nobody invites you out anymore. How is anyone going to want you looking like that?

[*The* MOTHER *exits.*]

KARIMA   [*To* MOTHER.] I don't want to go out; it's my choice, and I don't want to get married. [*To audience.*] And for the record, I'd like to say I was never considered unattractive. You might think differently. You might consider me a real hag, and if you do, the exit's that way. Really. I don't want anyone here who has a low opinion of my looks, or anything else about me. If I'm ugly, it's for me to say and not anyone else. I hate it how we bury ourselves under other people's ugly thoughts about us. I won't have it! [*Calms herself.*] And anyway. I had no intention of getting married and bringing children into this city. How could I? It would be selfishness on my part to want comfort at the expense of a child's happiness. And how could they be happy when they looked around them and saw a large forest of nothing but cement? And what of my grandchildren, and their children? Would they know what a flower is outside of a book? You think I exaggerate: When you leave tonight, look around you. I mean it, take a look. . . . And besides—I never liked any of the men I met. Who brought these men up, I want to know. How did they end up so brain-dead with only the stupidest thoughts surviving? I know there are wonderful men out there, I've just never met them. My luck. But I really would like someone to investigate the disappearance of all the decent men. . . . Except . . . there was this one man. [*The* SUITOR *appears.*] This one particular man . . . I'd always hoped to find a man who cared about the same things I did. Who loved this city with the same passion. Who wouldn't think it stupid to remark on something lovely we might come across . . . as we walked along . . . on hot summer evenings; hand in hand . . . with the moon shining brightly on us . . . I would close my eyes and dream of this.

SUITOR   Karima.

KARIMA   Then one day he appeared. In the person of a colleague of mine from the water company.

SUITOR   Karima . . . I wonder if you would like to, er . . . Would like to . . .

KARIMA   [*Beat.*] Yes?

SUITOR   Would like to . . .

KARIMA   Would like to what?

SUITOR   You know—whether or not . . . Perhaps . . .

KARIMA   Yes?

SUITOR   On the way home . . . after work . . .

KARIMA   Yes?

SUITOR   You know . . .

KARIMA   [*To audience.*]
He was very shy.

SUITOR   Never mind.

[SUITOR *starts to walk away.*]

KARIMA   Yes, I would. Thank you.

[*The* SUITOR *turns around.*]

SUITOR   You would what?

KARIMA I'd love to.

SUITOR Love to what?

KARIMA What you came to ask me.

SUITOR What did I come in to ask?

KARIMA Mahmoud!

SUITOR Yes?

KARIMA I said yes.

SUITOR You would?

KARIMA Why not?

SUITOR Perhaps we could go to a coffee shop and have a Coke.

KARIMA All right.—Except I don't like Coke. Why don't we walk along the river instead?

SUITOR Okay. That would be nice too. I'd like that.

KARIMA Great . . . God, that was exhausting. [*Change in lighting to suggest a beautiful sunset. It will change to moonlight gradually. They slowly amble along. At some point during the exchange below, they might find a place to sit.*] But once he relaxed I discovered what I'd always guessed about him. That he was kind; and curious; and was interested in what I cared about and didn't think my concerns silly. On top of that, he was handsome.—At least I thought so. And with the sun setting and the moon rising, the moment was better than any scene I could have imagined. And he was even moved to talk of the moon. As if it was the most natural thing in the world.

SUITOR Did you know that the moon is four hundred and six thousand, nine hundred and ninety-seven kilometers from the earth?

KARIMA I didn't know that.

SUITOR Yes. There're many interesting theories regarding its origins.

KARIMA I love mysteries. Think how boring life would be if God gave us all the answers.

SUITOR People think its orbit is circular. But it's not. It's actually elliptical.

KARIMA I started to feel like the moon he was talking about; revolving around him. And the more he talked, the less elliptical I felt. Watching him talk . . . the way his-lips moved . . . the way the sunset brightened his eyes.

SUITOR Plus it's not that big. Its mass is approximately one-eightieth that of the earth.

[KARIMA *leans over and kisses him on the lips. The* SUITOR *jumps to his feet-or, if they're standing, he steps away.*]

KARIMA What's the matter?

SUITOR What—why did you do that?

KARIMA [*Worried.*] I—I wanted to.—Didn't you like it?

SUITOR Are you—[*Looks around him.*]—crazy?

KARIMA What did I do? I'm sorry.

SUITOR In public?

KARIMA It's okay, there's no one around.

SUITOR That's—not the point.

KARIMA Didn't you want me to?

SUITOR Yes. No. You can't do that.

KARIMA I wasn't thinking. I just did it.

SUITOR In public? What are you—? How dare you do that in public?

KARIMA There's no public around to worry about. [*The* SUITOR *looks at her, then walks away.*] Where are you going? . . . I'm sorry. I won't do it again.

[*The* SUITOR *stops.*]

SUITOR   This isn't going to work out.

KARIMA   Why not? It was just a kiss.

SUITOR   Karima . . . have you no shame?

KARIMA   Yes, I have shame. I have all the shame in the world! [*The* SUITOR *shakes his head and starts to exit.*] Don't walk away from me. [*The* SUITOR *exits.*] To hell with you! [KARIMA *sits down. She cries . . . The crying subsides and she makes the effort to collect herself again.*] And so what? [*Beat.*] So what? . . . In the end . . . so what? [*Beat.*] The incident that directed their attention to me had nothing to do with that. . . . I never saw him again. . . . What led me here and confirmed that I belonged to a different world began on the day I overslept. [*Lights up. Also lights up on trees.*] That night I had dreamt all the trees on my street had returned—in full color—with every branch heavy with fruit. And at the bottom of my favorite tree was a basket full of pears. I don't think I'd tasted a more delicious fruit. . . . I woke up with that wonderful taste in my mouth.

MOTHER   [*Offstage.*] Karima! You're going to be late. Aren't you supposed to be at work?

[KARIMA *snaps out of her reverie and looks at her watch. Panic.*]

KARIMA   Why didn't anyone wake me up? [*She rushes to one side of the stage, then realizes she needs to be on the other side. She is trying to take off her dress.*] Where are my clothes? [*Perhaps a dress is thrown out onto the stage, or an arm emerges from the wings, dress in hand.*] I've worn that for a month, I can't. [*Another dress is thrown on or handed to her. It looks exactly the same as the other one.*] Thank God I don't have any fashion sense. Think of all the choices I'd have to make if I did. [*A pair of shoes are thrown out onto the stage or are handed to her by a stagehand/actor.*] Thank you. [*She slips into the new dress while also getting into her shoes. The mother comes on beating eggs in a bowl.*]

MOTHER   You're going to be fired.

KARIMA   Don't say that.

MOTHER   They already think you're careless at work.

KARIMA   That was then. I know what I'm doing now.

MOTHER   Plus they think you're strange, no?

KARIMA   Who told you that?

MOTHER   You did. Why expose yourself to so much unpleasantness?

KARIMA   They don't know me yet. I'm going to succeed in this job, Mother. I'm going to surprise them all and break every record in their book. People will be able to say the word "efficiency" in my office without laughing. And don't be surprised if within five years I end up running the water company myself. Goodbye, Mother.

[*She strides off confidently.*]

MOTHER   Haven't you forgotten something?

[KARIMA *stops and clutches her chest. The* MOTHER *exits.* KARIMA *looks down at her chest. She looks tentatively around. She is apprehensive, embarrassed.*]

KARIMA   How could I forget? [*She starts off in one direction then stops.*] You can't go back, you'll be late. They'll demote you if you show up late again. [*She looks down at her breasts.*] It's okay. It's not bad. I have to go back for it. [*She starts off but stops again.*] Karima, stop. You can't be this spineless. You've forgotten your bra, not your mind. They require your mind, and your mind on time, not a bra. Your breasts in a bra is optional. They don't hang down, or make a spectacle of themselves. They're fine. No one will notice. [*Starts walking again.*] It's all in your head. [*Walks in the opposite direction.*] Don't kid yourself. This isn't a thought you can hide, these are breasts. [*Ticked off.*] Oh for godsake! [*She stops again.*] Who

invented these stupid bras in the first place! How absolutely
ridiculous. [*Perhaps three mannequins are brought on by the stagehands.
Each mannequin sports a bra. Note: This could also be done with one
mannequin or with the stagehand/actors wearing the bras themselves.*] I
mean, look at them. What kind of monstrous mind came up with
that? [*She goes up to the bras on the mannequins.*] They look like
shackles. Handcuffs for the breasts. Breastcuffs. For the crime of
puberty I sentence your breasts to a lifetime of confinement in
these—these—I mean look at them. And what is so embarrassing
about breasts? Really. I mean let's look at what we're talking about
here. [*She looks at her breasts.*] Are they that dangerous? Of grave
national concern? And if they're supposedly that erotic to some, is
that my fault? I should be punished for other people not having
control? Everyone needs to grow up and let go of this nonsense.
[*Stagehands bring on a desk. Either she picks up papers from them, or
papers are handed to her.*] Sometimes I think we all agree on
something and then forget how silly that agreement was in the
first place. We just keep on with a practice that should have been
dropped ages ago. And to think this is a modern invention. This
was a sign of progress. Imagine. [MR. AZIZ *enters. She moves towards
him as if entering his office.*] Besides—it's conceited on my part to
think anyone's going to notice. People are too busy and a lot
more mature. Mr. Aziz? Are you ready to sign the papers? [*She
extends her arm.* MR. AZIZ *moves to take them, then freezes, his gaze on
her breasts.*] Oh no. [MR. AZIZ *remains frozen.*] Oh no.—Mr.
Aziz? . . . Are you all right? . . . Can I get you a glass of water?—Or
something?

[MR. AZIZ *snatches the papers from her.*]

MR. AZIZ   [*Curt.*] That will be all. [*He starts signing the papers.*]

KARIMA   Is there anything else I can get you?

MR. AZIZ   No.

KARIMA Would you like me to bring in—

MR. AZIZ [*Interrupting.*] No. Thank you. You can leave now.

KARIMA [*Exiting, under her breath.*] Okay.

MR. AZIZ Nadia!

KARIMA Wait until I head this department. I'll never be that rude to people. [NADIA *comes on.* MR. AZIZ *talks to her. As if to* MR. AZIZ:] Civility is also like a bra, you know. It holds a company together. Why aren't you wearing that? Huh?—Scratch that analogy.— Here she comes. Stay calm. Don't say anything stupid.

NADIA Karima.

KARIMA Good morning.

NADIA Please follow me to the ladies' room.

KARIMA Okay. You don't want to try the men's room. It's usually less busy. [*Tries to laugh at her joke.* NADIA'*s not amused.*] I'm—. Sure.

[*They both take a few steps into the "ladies' room." NADIA faces her.*]

NADIA Didn't your mother and father bring you up properly?

KARIMA Whatever you have to say to me, please leave my parents out of this.

NADIA Mr. Aziz is very upset.

KARIMA Really, why?

NADIA You know very well the reason.

KARIMA No, I don't, tell me.

NADIA This company will not tolerate your kind of impudence.

KARIMA What impudence? I'm one of the hardest workers here.

NADIA How dare you come to work without a bra?

KARIMA Oh no, not that. We can't be that dull.

NADIA Who do you think you are?

KARIMA It's more who I was hoping everyone else here was.

NADIA Mr. Aziz regards this as a dangerous precedent for the company, one that he cannot overlook.

KARIMA I'm sorry he doesn't have enough on his mind that he has to worry about bras.

NADIA It's not just him.

KARIMA Really.

NADIA You've upset others.

KARIMA That's their problem. Tell them to grow up.

NADIA You are going to be penalized for this indecency.

KARIMA Is that so? Where do you get off talking to me about decency with all those layers of makeup? Have you looked at yourself recently? You'd need an archaeologist to find your face.

NADIA If you thought coming to work in this provocative manner would sway Mr. Aziz with your charms, you calculated wrong. You'll actually have to work hard here to earn a promotion.

[KARIMA *is stunned by the accusation.*]

KARIMA [*To herself/audience.*] I swear to God, I was this close to slapping the makeup off of that bitch. Instead: [*She storms into* MR. AZIZ'*s office.*] May I talk to you for a second, Mr. Aziz. [MR. AZIZ *starts to talk but* KARIMA *cuts him off.*] For your information the reason why I am not wearing a bra is because I was worried I'd be late. I actually thought it more important to get to work on time than to strap on a meaningless piece of cloth which nobody can see anyway. Obviously I got my priorities wrong. How stupid of me. That I should think efficiency and productivity to be of greater value than whether or not my breasts hang down. [MR. AZIZ *opens his mouth but is again cut off. Other office workers approach to listen.*] Furthermore, from now on, I will categorically and unequivocally never ever for as long as I live come to work with anything even resembling a bra. They are antiquated modern inventions that criminalize parts of my body that will not be made to feel ashamed! What's more, your belly hangs out, Mr. Aziz. Have you ever heard me say that you should strap something on that? Well, you should. It's obscene. And I have to see it every goddamn day!

[*Beat.*]

OFFICE WORKER 1   She's mad.

OFFICE WORKER 2   Completely.

[*Blackout. In the dim light, we see* KARIMA *take one of the bras from the mannequins. She undresses and puts it on. If it's a complete blackout, then lights slowly come up as we see her finishing strapping on the bra. The mannequins are removed.*]

KARIMA   [*Beat.*] There was another incident at the company . . . that happened two weeks before. . . . Which further endeared me to my co-workers. . . . Which should have endeared me to my coworkers but once again I presumed too much. But—you know what . . . you don't need to hear about it. Why drag you through another incident where things didn't quite live up to expectations. And to think this is a life.—And to live it under the glare of our worst moments. Brought on by people who have no business in your life, but there they are, whether you want them or not. All right, I'll tell you, one day, I'd decided I'd had enough of the grey, unrelenting horrible grey colors of our office. [*A bright red desk is brought on.*] And bought this. [MANAGER *enters and stops the desk from being moved further.*] Lovely, right?

MANAGER   [*To desk movers.*] What is this?

DESK MOVER   A desk for Ms. Karima.

MANAGER   For who? [*One of the* DESK MOVERS *hands him the sales slip.* KARIMA *goes over to them.*]

KARIMA   [*To* DESK MOVERS.] Thank you: You can put it over there.

[*The* DESK MOVERS *start to move the desk but the manager blocks them.*]

MANAGER   This is yours?

KARIMA   Isn't it wonderful? [*To* DESK MOVERS.] Right over there.

MANAGER   [*Blocking them.*] You can't bring this in here.

KARIMA   Excuse me?

MANAGER   [*To* DESK MOVERS.] Take it back. [*The* DESK MOVERS *start carrying the desk away.*]

KARIMA   [*Stopping them.*] Stop. Put it down, please. There must be a misunderstanding. I bought this with my own money.

MANAGER   I don't care if you bought it with your life savings. It's not coming in here.

KARIMA   May I ask why?

MANAGER   I think the reason is obvious.

KARIMA   No, it's not. Please explain. As our office manager, I have learnt so much from you already, I feel anything you have to say on whatever subject will surely be illuminating.

MANAGER   The desk is red.

[*They all look at the red desk.*]

KARIMA   That is the color I asked for, yes. Pomegranate red. Don't you like this particular shade?

MANAGER   Do you see any red desks in here?

KARIMA   That's exactly the point. I don't see anything in here. Everything has disappeared into everything else. It's all a sea of grey. And with those horrible lights it all makes us look like corpses.

MANAGER   And your solution is what? To turn our office into a circus?

KARIMA   My solution is to bring a little life into this mortuary so we don't feel like we're suffocating. In addition, it's been proven scientifically that creativity increases many times over when you're working in a cheerful environment.

MANAGER   Ms. Karima: We are paying you to do a job, not to be creative. This sort of idiocy will run us into the ground and make us the laughingstock of every other department. Now you two will pick up this desk and go back the way you came.

[*The* DESK MOVERS *start moving.*]

KARIMA   [*Stopping them.*] You will do no such thing.

MANAGER   Are you disobeying me, Ms. Karima?

KARIMA   I am appealing to your better nature. You haven't even noticed how clean the office is today. I came in early and swept it. And where do you think all those flowers on the desks came from? And the windows. We actually have sunlight streaming in; I cleaned them.

MANAGER   [*To* DESK MOVERS.] Take the desk back.

[*The* DESK MOVERS *start moving it again.* KARIMA *leaps on top of the desk and stands.*]

KARIMA   This desk is not budging! What's more you should know that when I have saved enough money, I plan on buying more desks: yellow desks, green ones, orange and blue desks. Somebody in this company has to stand up to the flood of mediocrity. And if you can't see it in your heart to do it, then you leave me no choice but to take a stand and do it myself! [*Back to talking to the audience.*] My stand was brief. I have in the past unfortunately suffered from vertigo. Quickly followed by a fainting spell. A fact I forgot when I leapt up on the desk. Today was no exception. . . . Damn it. [KARIMA *faints. The* OFFICE MANAGER *catches her. The* DESK MOVERS *take the desk off. Lights change. Perhaps the reddish-tinted colors of a sunset. The* OFFICE MANAGER *walks with* KARIMA *in his arms. A stagehand comes on.* KARIMA *is handed over to him. Perhaps this passing of* KARIMA *is done with a third stagehand. The stagehand stops.* KARIMA *wakes up.*] Where am I?

STAGEHAND/TREE   You're safe. You're up in the tree. You climbed up and fell asleep.

KARIMA   Oh . . . [*Beat, hugging him.*] I always feel safe with you.

TREE   I like having you too.

KARIMA   [*Beat.*] I'm not too heavy?

TREE   I've got pretty strong branches.

KARIMA   Are you sure? [*She bounces slightly as if testing their strength.*]

TREE   [*Strain showing.*] Don't push it.

KARIMA   Sorry.

TREE   I'm okay. Scoot a little closer to my trunk, will you?

KARIMA   [*Does so.*] Better?

TREE   Thank you.

KARIMA   [*Beat.*] I wish the men I meet were like you.

TREE   That would be very boring. I'm a tree. We don't do much.

KARIMA   You do. I'm surprised you don't know how much you do, do.

TREE   That's sweet of you to say.

KARIMA   It's strange how none of us seem to know how much we do for each other. . . . Funny that.

TREE Well . . . I'm happy when you're here.

KARIMA You are?

TREE Yes.

KARIMA Do you feel me when I'm around?

TREE Yes I do. Very much so.

KARIMA You're not just talking about my weight.

TREE [*Laughs.*] No. [*Beat, feeling the weight.*] Scoot a little closer, will you.

KARIMA Sorry. [*Beat.*] Do you know what I secretly dream of doing? [*Beat.*]

TREE What?

KARIMA Promise you won't be shocked.

TREE Outside of a lightning bolt, it's hard to shock me.

KARIMA On summer nights—when it's very humid . . . I dream of coming here . . . taking all my clothes off . . . climbing up—and lying naked on your branches.

TREE Karima!

KARIMA You promised you wouldn't be shocked.

TREE I'm not, I'm . . . shocked.

KARIMA It's just a dream. Am I forbidden even to imagine it?

TREE No, but . . . You do?

KARIMA Yes.

TREE [*Beat, intrigued.*] And what happens?

KARIMA Nothing. . . . It's more how I feel. Looking over the city. Feeling the breeze on my skin . . . Not hiding . . . And yet being hidden among all these leaves.

TREE [*Beat.*] It's a pity you'll never be able to do it.

KARIMA [*Beat.*] And if I did, would you mind?

TREE No . . . I like holding you in my arms. . . . Still . . . you wouldn't want to start a trend or anything. . . . We wouldn't want people strolling along the street and say, "Oh, Mummy, look, there's another naked person on the branch." "Yes, honey, they must be in season."

KARIMA [*A laugh.*] Naked fruit.

TREE When ripe, they're picked.

KARIMA Or they fall. [*Beat, sleepy.*] They're going to cut you down, you know.

TREE [*Beat.*] I know. [*A stagehand enters wearing an animal mask, preferably a weasel's—though it could also be the mask of any sinister-looking animal. He slowly approaches* KARIMA.] Shouldn't you be going somewhere?

KARIMA Where?

TREE I don't know. But I know today's a special day.

KARIMA I want to stay here.

TREE [*Seeing the weasel.*] Wake up.

KARIMA Just a few more minutes.

TREE Karima, wake up.—Wake up.

KARIMA Why? [*Sees the weasel, scared.*] Oh.

TREE Don't panic. Stay calm.

KARIMA Oh God.

TREE It's okay. Listen carefully.

KARIMA Shake him off.

TREE Climb down. Move to my lower branches.

KARIMA Shake him off!

TREE I can't. You'll have to climb down.

KARIMA It's too far. There isn't enough time. [*She starts moving around in his arms.*]

TREE Stop squirming.

KARIMA Help me.

TREE You'll lose your balance. Karima, stop it!

KARIMA Do something! [*She falls out of his arms onto the floor.*]

TREE Karima!

[*The weasel and the tree look at* KARIMA *for a beat. Then exit. Lights change: It's day. An* OLD WOMAN *walks over to* KARIMA. KARIMA *stirs and sits up.*]

OLD WOMAN My dear, my poor dear. Are you all right? What happened? Are you all right? [KARIMA *tries to get her bearings.*] Did you hurt anything? . . . Let me see.

KARIMA I'm fine.

OLD WOMAN One minute you're walking; the next . . . let me take a look.

KARIMA Really, I'm fine . . . I just . . .

OLD WOMAN What is it?

KARIMA Didn't you see it? The weasel? It ran right in front of me— into the school.

OLD WOMAN No.

KARIMA In broad daylight. It had a terrible face.—Like it was sneering at me.

OLD WOMAN   It wouldn't surprise me. With all this garbage around. Come on, let's get you up. [*She helps* KARIMA *stand.*] Are you going into the school to vote? Let's go in and vote together. Maybe there'll be a candidate who can do something about this garbage. We're turning the city over to the rats. Is it any wonder if a weasel feels comfortable enough to walk right up and shake your hand. Are you okay?

KARIMA   I'll follow you in a second.

OLD WOMAN   As long as you're okay, my dear. I'll see you inside.

[KARIMA *smiles. The* OLD WOMAN *exits into "the school" where the voting takes place.*]

KARIMA   This is the day. . . . This is the day that led to my imprisonment. . . . The events of today will lead to my being called a mad woman. . . . Election day. [*Another possible light change as cast members enter dressed as* CANDIDATES *wearing large buttons on their lapels with recognizable visuals: e.g., a palm tree/a watch/a pineapple/a camel. The* CANDIDATES *move amongst the audience handing out fliers, saying, "Vote for us," "Vote where you see the sign of the palm tree," "Cast your future with our party; you'll see the difference," etc. Also, if a fourth* CANDIDATE *is desired to swell the sense of busyness, then a few of the lines spoken by the other* CANDIDATES *can be given to him. Overlapping:*] When it came to picking candidates . . . my interests never helped me in finding someone worthy of my vote.—But I voted anyway. Even if I felt it didn't make the slightest difference.—That's a mad thought all by itself, come to think of it. . . . What happened next I'm not sure anymore.

CANDIDATE 1   [*Handing her a flier.*] Read this. Our record speaks for itself.

CANDIDATE 2   [*Handing her a flier.*] His record may speak for itself, our party speaks for you.

CANDIDATE 3   [*Hands her another flier.*] These parties only want your vote. We care about you long after that.

KARIMA   I'm sorry, I . . .

CANDIDATE 3   Vote for us and you'll see the changes.

KARIMA   [*Dazed.*] What changes?

CANDIDATE 1   If you care for your country, your conscience and your vote must go to us.

KARIMA   What do you care about again?

CANDIDATE 2   His record is empty rhetoric and wishful thinking; our actions speaker longer, louder and will provide three nutritious meals a day.

KARIMA   What? Wait. I'm not remembering this right.

[KARIMA *starts to leave the stage.*]

CANDIDATE 3   Where are you going? You can't leave. This is your day.

CANDIDATE 1   As a good citizen, you must vote.

CANDIDATE 2   It's your constitutional right and you must exercise it.

KARIMA   [*Facing them.*] What are you talking about? None of what you're saying makes sense.

CANDIDATE 1   [*Holding up his flier.*] Our record, read it. Have you even bothered to do that?

KARIMA   I don't need to. I see it every day when I step out of my house. That's my proof of what none of you are doing.

CANDIDATE 2   Our hard work on your behalf is not always apparent.

KARIMA   Then what good does it do us?

CANDIDATE 3   There's a great deal to government that requires a level of expertise which only we can provide.

KARIMA   To do what?

CANDIDATE 2   To keep the government functioning.

KARIMA   To what end?

CANDIDATE 3   To serve you.

KARIMA   I'm not feeling served!

CANDIDATE 1   Our good deeds would be noticed if you voters bothered to look.

KARIMA   I'm looking! I've looked! Every day. With my own eyes. I see how you've allowed the trees to be hacked down and left in the street to rot—and replaced with cement monstrosities that rise up and kill the joy in our hearts. I'm looking! I see the light in people's eyes die out as they lose hope of anything ever changing. What are you doing about that? What exactly are you doing to make our hearts sing, or is that not important? Sing with the joy of being proud to live in this city and be alive and be human, just to be human. Do you have a policy on any of that?

[*Beat. The* CANDIDATES *turn back to working the audience. Their lines overlap.*]

CANDIDATE 3   Vote for us. We're the party you want.

CANDIDATE 1   Don't waste your votes. Cast where you see the sign of the watch.

CANDIDATE 2   You can't go wrong with our party.

CANDIDATE 3   You'll be doing yourselves a favor, vote right here.

[*The* CANDIDATES *continue to work the audience, handing them fliers, speaking to them—variations on the above lines—while ignoring* KARIMA *as she addresses them.*]

KARIMA   [*Overlapping.*] And why aren't there more women running? We're half the population! And what are you doing about the weasels, and the garbage and the flies they breed? And excuse me but what is it with you all being overweight? Is that a requirement to run? To have fat necks on bloated bodies and waddle around like you've just swallowed a cow? [*A* VOTING OFFICIAL *enters and approaches* KARIMA.] Is that any example to set for our youth? Is it any wonder you can't do anything useful?

VOTING OFFICIAL   Miss.

KARIMA   Think diet. Stop eating. Skip dessert.

VOTING OFFICIAL   Miss.

KARIMA   Do something for yourselves if you can't do anything for us.

VOTING OFFICIAL   Miss!

KARIMA   What?

VOTING OFFICIAL   Come with me.

KARIMA   Why? [*At some point the* CANDIDATES *will perhaps stop working the audience.*]

VOTING OFFICIAL   Just come with me.

KARIMA   Why?

VOTING OFFICIAL   You're causing a disturbance.

KARIMA   I'm voicing my opinion.

VOTING OFFICIAL   You're disrupting people's business.

KARIMA   It's election day: There's supposed to be a disturbance; that's what voting is supposed to do, change things.

VOTING OFFICIAL   Just come with me.

KARIMA   I thought we were pretending to be a democracy, or have we stopped pretending?

VOTING OFFICIAL   Show me your identity card.

KARIMA   No.

VOTING OFFICIAL   [*Menacing.*] I said—hand it over.

[KARIMA *hesitates, then hands it to him. The* VOTING OFFICIAL *studies the card. He takes out a pencil and pad.*]

KARIMA   All right, you've seen it. Give it back. [VOTING OFFICIAL *ignores her and starts to write down her name and address.*] What are you doing? Why are you writing my name down? I haven't done anything. Give it back. Who are you to take my name down? You have no right. Give me my card back. [*Tries to snatch the card back, he avoids her.*] Give it—[*Lunges for card, he avoids her.*] Give it— [*Lunges for card, he avoids her.*] Give it back to me! [*He avoids her again; with her next line she—*] I want my card back! [*—jumps on his back.*] You have no right! [*The candidates rush to pry* KARIMA *off the* VOTING OFFICIAL.] It's my identity card! [*There are cries of "Miss," "Get her off," "She's crazy," "Call the police," etc.*] It's mine! GIVE IT BACK TO ME! IT BELONGS TO ME!

[*Either they pry her off, or are in the process of doing so, but at this point everyone freezes. Lights change. Two people remain by* KARIMA*'s side as the others exit and the* MOTHER *enters. When she does, the remaining two men also exit.... Beat.*]

MOTHER   Has it come to this? [*Beat.*] This shame. [*Beat.*] This terrible insult . . . to our family . . . To everything your brother has worked for? [*Beat.*] To the sacrifices I've made to make sure not one word of reproach would ever fall on our name. [*Beat.*] And you throw it away with your . . . [*Beat.*] Does your selfishness know no end? [*Beat.*] You are a dark cloud in our lives. . . . Whenever things are going well . . . along you come . . . and ruin it for us. [*Beat.*] Because of you your brother's career as an officer is now in jeopardy. . . . He may have to resign.

[*Beat.*]

KARIMA   I was trying to get my card back.

MOTHER   I don't want to hear it. . . . I don't want to hear anything from you. [*Beat.*] You deserve to have your tongue cut out.

[*The* MOTHER *exits. Silence.* KARIMA *stands transfixed where she is.*]

KARIMA   Yes. [*Beat.*] Yes . . . You're right. [*Beat.*] You should have cut it
out as you wanted to, Mummy. . . . All those years ago . . . Do you
remember? . . . When I told on my brother . . . For breaking the
vase . . . And you came at me with scissors. Ordering me to stick
out my tongue so you could slice it off. So I would never let out
another secret. [*Beat.*] My poor tongue. You don't know how to
behave. . . . You live in such a big mouth, no wonder you're lost.
[*Beat.*] What have I accomplished by speaking out? . . . [*Beat.*]
Nothing. [*Beat.*] Who have I helped by speaking up? . . . [*Beat.*] No
one. [*Beat.*] What good have my opinions done me? [*Beat.*] You
don't have the courage to end it. But a tongue . . . Cutting it out
will not make you die. . . . I would not be committing a sin. . . . I
may prevent future sins by doing so—I would stop hurting people.
Myself.—The cause of my miseries would end.—One snip. [*A hand
slides a pair of scissors from the wings towards Karima. Or it can also be
handed to her by a stagehand. She sees it. Beat.*] It doesn't even feel like
it belongs to me half the time. [*Beat.*] Come. [*Picks up scissors.*] The
pain will only last a little while. A little blood and it's done. This is
not a punishment. It's that piece of flesh that punishes you. Miseries
greater than any knife could inflict. This is no different than your
circumcision and you survived that. This one will do you more
good. [*She sticks out her tongue. . . . She opens the scissors. . . . She positions
her tongue between the blades. She stands there, tongue between scissor
blades. . . . She lowers the scissors from her mouth.*] Karima, please. . . .
For once in your life listen to me. I'm trying to save you. You
won't lose anything. . . . We'll still be able to talk. . . . We'll just
make sure no one will hear us. [*Beat. Once again she places her tongue
between the blades. . . . She wills herself to complete the act. A strangled,
tongueless sound is heard: a scream building up. Then a garbled:*] DO IT!
[*Her* MOTHER *enters—sees her daughter about to cut out her tongue, and
screams.* KARIMA *at this point, perhaps, turns her back to the audience,
tongue still between the blades, as: The stagehands move the flats back in to*

reconstruct the cell. Any other objects seen earlier in the cell are brought back on. The mother takes the scissors from KARIMA *and exits. A stagehand will hand her her manuscript.*] My mother's screams gathered the neighbors and I was brought here. To this cell . . . This—place. Where I have stayed ever since. . . . I have lost count how many years. [*At some point,* KARIMA *turns to face the audience.*] My mother visited me regularly. Then stopped. My brother came once and said nothing.—I have told my story to the doctors and nurses but they don't listen. I explained why I tried to do what I did.—That it was with the best interests of everyone in mind. But when you're considered a little cracked, it's hard to convince anyone of anything. [*Beat.*] My mother should have let me finish the job. [*Beat.*] But since she didn't—here I am. . . . My big mouth still open and my tongue still flapping. [*Beat.*] Don't you wish now she hadn't interrupted me. . . . And I'm also writing. In the hope some of this will make sense to me one day. And, because—I'd like to get out. If just for an hour . . . I have noticed the white in my hair. . . . And my city is moving on too. I would like to see it again. . . . Walk down the street I loved . . . See the vendors. Smell the scents of what they're selling . . . Wave to people. [*Beat.*] How I wish I could see those thirty-one beautiful green trees again. [*Fade to blackout.*]

• • •

··· property list ···

Papers	Desk with papers
Bag of nuts	Red desk
Money	Animal mask
Prescription pads, pens	Buttons, fliers
Bags of groceries	ID card
Whisk, bowl	Pencil and pad
Mannequins with bras	Scissors

fin & euba

Audrey Cefaly

Audrey Cefaly

Audrey Cefaly, an Alabama native, now resides near Annapolis, Maryland. Her one-act *fin & euba* was developed at Silver Spring Stage and received its premiere at the Pittsburgh New Works Festival, where it was a finalist. It went on to win many festivals, including the Strawberry One-Act Festival and UMBC's In 10, a yearly festival which fosters plays with clearly defined roles for young women. *fin & euba* has become a popular performance piece among college and high school students across the U.S. and Canada. Cefaly is a writer in residence at Quotidian Theatre Company, which recently produced her commissioned play *Mill Town Girls* (a full-length prequel to *fin & euba*). Other one-act plays include *Piano Man*, *Pierced*, and *Cottonwood*.

running time

23–25 minutes

setting

The setting is the yard of an old boarding house, autumn, late evening in the Florida panhandle. There is an abundance of tacky yard art, gnomes, and all things ridiculous. The house overlooks both a lonely highway and in the distance...a paper mill. A porch light is visible near an area that represents the house.

characters

    EUBA, quiet; a follower; any age, any ethnicity

    FIN, self-assured; dry and gritty, any age, any ethnicity

note to actors

Fin and Euba are poor and scrappy. They say and do things that may seem surreal or comical, but in all things there is a truth to their ways...they are not caricatures. That is to say...they are very real people with real problems. Every effort should be made to make them as human and as genuine as possible, to identify their core beliefs and to portray them honestly.

• • •

[EUBA *comes out and sits on the front porch bench. The yard is filled with gnomes, flamingos, whirly gigs, and tacky yard art.* EUBA *stares out at the highway. We can hear the sound of spring peepers and crickets. The air is thick and the silence surrounds this place, except for the occasional car that speeds by on the highway. She begins to light a cigarette but notices that the gnome sitting next to her on the bench appears to be staring at her. She turns it the other way before lighting her cigarette.* FIN *comes out. They smoke cigarettes and flick ashes into an old coffee can.*]

FIN   Hey.

EUBA   Hey.

FIN Can I bum one?

[EUBA *passes her the pack.*]

        Where is she?

[FIN *looks back at the house.*]

EUBA Same as always. Back in the back watching Home Shoppin'.

FIN God. Ain't she got enough of them creepy critters?

EUBA They keep disappearing. She keeps buyin' more.

[FIN *points to a gnome and looks to* EUBA *for explanation.* EUBA *reads the notation on the bottom of the gnome.*]

        It's new. [*Reading.*] Buddy.

FIN Buddy? They have names?

[EUBA *nods yes.*]

FIN Eww.

EUBA Yeah.

[*They stare out at the highway. An occasional car speeds by.*]

FIN It's gettin' cold.

EUBA Yeah.

FIN Don't you think it's gettin' cold?

EUBA Yeah, it's gettin' cold.

[*Silence.*]

FIN Bernice told me you got a letter in mail-call today.

EUBA [*Somewhat annoyed.*] Yeah.

FIN From *Life* magazine?

EUBA Bernice talks too much.

FIN Well, ain't you gonna tell me what it says? You been waitin' for that letter since June.

EUBA No.

FIN No?

EUBA I ain't read it.

FIN Why not?

EUBA Personal reasons.

FIN What?

EUBA Private reasons.

FIN Oooh. Oh, I see. OK Alright. That's fine . . . you don't want to tell me.

EUBA Good.

FIN Your best friend.

EUBA Yup.

FIN The only person you could trust in the whole wide world.

EUBA Yup.

FIN But if you don't want to tell me—

EUBA Nope

[*Silence.*]

FIN [*Annoyed.*] I shoulda' worn my jacket.

EUBA Mnnn hmn.

FIN Two weeks til' Thanksgiving . . . can you believe that?

EUBA Double shifts again all next week.

FIN You're kiddin'?!

EUBA   Fat Charlie told Thelma—'n' Thelma told me.

FIN   Good! I need the money.

EUBA   I need sleep more than I need the money.

FIN   That's the truth. [*Pause.*] I heard something, but you ain't gon' like it.

EUBA   What?

FIN   Miss Vera's fixin' to raise the rent next month.

EUBA   Where'd you hear that?!

FIN   Bernice. Said she overheard her *talkin'* about it on the phone to Brother Herbert.

EUBA   Shit.

FIN   Yup.

EUBA   How much?

FIN   [*Through an exhale of cigarette smoke.*] I don't know.

[*Pause.*]

EUBA   [*Bravely.*] You know I'd move in a heartbeat.

FIN   Me too.

EUBA   Too many rules.

FIN   I know it!

EUBA   You better not let her see you smokin' out here. She'll kick us out for sure.

[FIN *blows a defiant puff of smoke toward the house.* FIN *takes a moment to ponder the logistics.*]

FIN   Let's do it.

EUBA   What?

FIN Move.

EUBA You're crazy.

FIN I'm serious!

EUBA It's too far, Fin. The next rooming house is two miles down . . . that's way too far to walk to work.

FIN Lou Anne lives down there at Scooter's. We could ride in with her. And he don't have no rules, neither, except cash only.

EUBA Cash only?

FIN Cash only. And no pets.

EUBA No pets?

FIN No pets.

EUBA What about a fish? [*Pause.*] Could I have fish?

FIN I bet you could have a fish.

EUBA Maybe I'd like fish.

FIN What . . . like a goldfish?

EUBA No . . . one of them pretty ones . . . with the pretty colors.

FIN Oh yeah! I like them. Fish are good. [*Pause.*] What do you think?

EUBA I don't know.

FIN I'll call Scooter tomorrow.

EUBA [*Annoyed at FIN's persistence.*] I don't know.

FIN We could think on it.

EUBA Yeah.

FIN Let's just think on it.

EUBA OK

FIN We'll just think on it. That's what we'll do.

EUBA [*Trying to close the subject.*] OK Let's *think* on it.

FIN [*Overlapping.*] OK [*Pause.*] I'm thinkin'.

[*They both sit quietly for a moment trying to work through the details.*]

EUBA We got any beer?

FIN [*Mischievously.*] Hangin' off the dock out back!

[FIN *exits.*]

EUBA [*Calling.*] You better hope she don't find it.

FIN I hope she does!

[EUBA *pulls out the unopened letter and holds and walks around the yard a bit, contemplating.*]

EUBA [*To herself.*] Stupid.

[EUBA *looks at Buddy, who is staring back at her.*]

[*To Buddy.*] Oh shut up.

[EUBA *hides the note as* FIN *returns with several dripping wet beers.*]

FIN Shiiiiittt, these are cold!

EUBA Well, what do you expect? The pond's about froze over.

[FIN *hands* EUBA *a beer.*]

Damn!!

FIN I told you.

[EUBA *and* FIN *open their beers and try to bundle in their clothes and hold their beers with their shirt sleeves. They both drink in their beers and savor the flavor heartily.*]

[*Enthralled.*] Man . . . there's nothin' better!!

EUBA Nope.

FIN   I love a good cold beer.

EUBA   [*A whisper.*] Really cold . . .

FIN   You alright?

EUBA   Yup.

FIN   Ice headache?

EUBA   Yup.

FIN   Well, drink some more, you'll be alright.

EUBA   [EUBA *nods yes as she drinks.*]

[*A factory whistle is heard in the distance. They look out at the factory, which can be seen from the yard.*]

BOTH   10 o'clock.

FIN   They got a new foreman comin' in next week.

EUBA   Where's Lila?

FIN   Fat Charlie sent her home. She couldn't keep up.

EUBA   [*Amused.*] When's the baby due?

FIN   Any day.

EUBA   How's she look?

FIN   She looks good. She looks real good. Big.

EUBA   I miss havin' her on my shift.

FIN   I know it. She's so funny. You remember back last fall when we had that real bad storm and everybody was down at Winn Dixie fightin' over toilet paper? Well, I saw Lila, Terrell, and I don't know who all else . . . a big ole crowd of folks standin' around Bobby Johnson's butcher counter . . . cuz one of the stock boys had gotten all pissed off at Bobby one night and had went and built . . . a Kotex Maxi-pad display inside the meat case.

EUBA   I forgot all about that.

FIN   So Lila says . . . *That's a mighty fine display, Bobby. Are you havin' a special?* I'm gon' miss her.

EUBA   She'll be back.

FIN   Nuh uh! She's movin'.

EUBA   What?

FIN   Well, you remember how her husband went through basic training last summer?

EUBA   Yeah.

FIN   They just assigned him to a unit at Ft. Bragg and they're movin' soon as the baby's born.

EUBA   What?

FIN   She's mad as a hornet too. She just got the baby's room all fixed up and everything.

[The front porch light flashes.]

BOTH   *[Ad lib.]* Oh . . . Oh man . . . Shit

[They hide their beers for a moment.]

FIN   *[To Euba.]* 15 minutes. *[Calling.]* Yes, *ma'am!*

EUBA   God, I can't stand that woman!

FIN   *[Overlapping.]* She gives me the creeps! Her and them *13 cats.*

EUBA   *Seventeen.* Ginger had her litter this mornin'.

FIN   *[A warning.]* That's it! We're movin' to Scooters. *[Pause.]* I mean it, Euba! I'm callin' Scooter tomorrow. My hands are frozen.

EUBA   I'll get a blanket.

[EUBA *goes into the house to get a blanket.* FIN *sips her beer quietly looking around the yard. She goes over to* BUDDY, *the gnome, and quietly picks him up. She takes him offstage and throws him into the pond. We hear a splash. She re-enters cavellierly rolling up her shirt sleeves.*]

FIN   Oops.

[FIN *notices that* EUBA *has left her letter behind. She casually picks it up and tries to decode it from the outside. She is nearly caught as* EUBA *returns.*]

EUBA   [*Calling back.*] Yes, ma'am! [*Mimicking.*] *Aren't you girls comin' in? I flashed that light a hundred times.* Here, I stole you a cookie.

[EUBA *hands* FIN *the blanket . . . then looks at the letter and then looks at* FIN, *who is casually looking away.*]

FIN   Yumm. What'd you tell her?

EUBA   Nothing. I just looked at her. She was still yacking away when I left.

FIN   Yack. Yack. That woman could talk the chicken off a bone. [*Pause.*] I wonder how somebody could do that much talkin' and still not *say* anything. [*Pause.*] Euba?

EUBA   Yeah?

FIN   When you gon' open that letter?

EUBA   [*Grimacing.*] *Life* magazine does not care about any of the stupid pictures I took in high school, Fin. Get real.

FIN   I didn't send 'em those, Miss *smartie pants*. I sent 'em the ones you took at the plant during the strike last year.

EUBA   [EUBA *has a moment of hope, but quickly dismisses it.*] Whatever.

FIN   What if it's a job offer?

EUBA   Oh, get serious, Fin. You think you can just send my pictures to some big shot at *Life* magazine and expect a job offer?

FIN [*Overlapping.*] Oh, give me a little more credit, will ya? I did not just send them to any old *big shot*. [*Proudly.*] I sent them to the *Executive Editor*, if you must know. I took his name right off the inside cover.

EUBA [*Sarcastically.*] Now, that makes all the difference, don't it?

FIN [*Staring at* EUBA *blankly.*] You are so negative. *Negative. Negative. Negative.*

EUBA [*Overlapping.*] *Realistic.*

FIN Yes. That too! And negative. [*Pause.*] I bet it's a job offer! What do ya think?

EUBA I don't know and I don't care.

FIN Don't lie.

EUBA I ain't lyin.' I don't want to know.

FIN Why?

EUBA It's better not knowing.

FIN Better?

EUBA I didn't send the pictures, Fin! You did!

FIN It's what you wanted.

EUBA No, Fin. It's what *you* wanted.

FIN You said. You *dreamed* about it.

EUBA No I didn't.

FIN Don't lie! Euba. You have been dreamin' about taking pictures for *Life* magazine ever since high school.

EUBA OK, yeah, alright. Yeah, I dreamed about it, but that don't mean I *want* it.

[*Pause.*]

FIN   [*Annoyed.*] That don't make no sense, Euba. Dreamin'... wantin'... same thing.

EUBA   No, it ain't. Dreamin' is dreamin,' that's all it is. Wantin' means you're willin' to work for it and I ain't and that's *all*.

FIN   What are you *talking* about?

EUBA   Do I dream about it? Yes! Of course, I do. When I'm out there on that line all day and my feet are so swole up I can't think straight? I dream about it. Or when Bugger James comes into *my* room stead of his own at 4 a.m. cuz he's so *blind* from drunk. I dream about it. Or how bout, every mornin' scrambling for a warm shower 'stead of ice cold, cuz I slept in two minutes late. Fin, I dream about getting out every minute of every day of my life.

FIN   Well, what are you waitin' for? [*Holding up the letter.*] This is your *chance*, Euba.

EUBA   [*Taking the letter.*] Because. If I open this letter. And it says what I know it's gonna say...

FIN   What?

EUBA   ... then I have nothin'.

FIN   But what if they *want you*!?

EUBA   What if they don't?

FIN   What if they do?

EUBA   What if they don't?! What if I open that letter, and it tells me I'm no better than anybody else in this—

FIN   Oh, come on!!! If I had *half* your talent, I'd march right down to that office and I'd tell that *fat-bastard* Charlie to kiss my ass. I'd *quit*. With no notice! And I'd start walking til' I hit Atlanta. And you wanna know what else?!?! I WOULDN'T LOOK BACK!!!

I'D NEVER LOOK BACK! Not even for you, baby. Not even for you.

EUBA Well, thanks a lot.

FIN It's nothing personal.

EUBA I know it.

FIN Open the damn letter!

EUBA Stop it!

FIN Euba!

EUBA Leave it alone, Fin.

FIN It's a *sin* what you're doin.' Throwin' away your God-given talent.

EUBA How come you can't just drop it?!

FIN You oughta' be ashamed.

EUBA Stop!!

FIN No, I won't. And you wanna know why?

EUBA 'Cause you ain't got any dreams of your own, that's why!

[*Pause.*]

FIN [*Stung.*] *Nice.* Turn it back on me why don't you?

EUBA [*Overlapping.*] I didn't mean it, I'm sorry.

FIN [*Overlapping.*] Oh, save it, Euba! I know what I want. And you can call it dreamin', wantin' WHATEVER. Kids? Yep. On the list. One girl. One boy. And a husband some day, if I can find one who'll have me. Somebody to *love.* Somebody who will love me back. A white house, with a little wrap around porch . . . on a little quiet street—

EUBA [*Overlapping.*] Don't forget the white picket fence.

FIN   [*Continuing defiantly.*] . . . in a little quiet city—that don't smell like . . . something . . . *dead*. And just maybe, when I'm old and ugly, I want a bloodhound named Jake . . . who knows his name, who will come when I call him and who will love me, no matter what, cuz that's what dogs do.

EUBA   [*Softening up now.*] Sounds like you got it all planned out.

FIN   [*Sincerely.*] Yeah, well, I ain't special like you, Euba.

EUBA   Oh, come on—

FIN   No, no, it don't bother me. You bother me. You say you want a fish, but you don't even know what kind!

EUBA   Fish? Fish? We're talking about fish now? I know what kind of *fish*, Fin, I just can't think of the *name*, that's all.

FIN   My point exactly.

EUBA   I know what I want.

FIN   No, you don't.

EUBA   Yes, I—

FIN   No! No you don't, Euba. You sit here and bitch and you moan about this place . . . about *gettin' out*. But it's all just words, idn't it? You never do anything. You never do anything about it.

EUBA   I'm happy right where I am, thank you very much.

FIN   [*Aghast.*] Don't say that! Don't you ever say that!

EUBA   Leave it alone, Fin.

FIN   You know—[*Calculating.*] OK Fine. Have it your way.

EUBA   I think I will. Thank you.

FIN   *As long as you can live with it.* [*Pause.*] Come Sunday morning and you're sittin' there, *7th row center* at Southside Baptist. Trying to explain to the Good Lord why you took the gifts—*the gifts*—he gave you and THREW THEM ALL AWAY! You hear me?!?! Just threw 'em away. Now what do you think he would have to say about that?

EUBA I can't speak for Jesus, Fin.

FIN Well, I can. [*Pause.*] And I'll tell you what he'd say. Shame. On. You! Shaammme on you, Yolanda Eubanks!

[EUBA *quickly pulls out the letter and starts ripping it up.*]

Stop it! What are you doing?!?! Are you insane?!?! Euba!!

[EUBA *holds a lighter up to the letter in warning. A cold menacing demeanor washes over her.*]

EUBA Get back, Fin. I'm warning ya. I got a Dale Earnhart Intimidator and I ain't afraid to use it.

FIN You wouldn't!

[EUBA *flicks the lighter "on."*]

EUBA You wanna take that chance?

FIN Don't do it. You'll never live it down, Euba.

EUBA [*Overlapping.*] You better *get back*, Fin! Now, I need you to leave me be on this, you hear me?!?!

FIN Euba, please!

EUBA BACK AWAY!

FIN Euba—

EUBA I'll torch it!

FIN I believe you would. I do. I'm backing away . . . see me . . . I'm back. Now put the lighter down.

EUBA [*Pointedly.*] Now, this is *my life*. My life. And it's mine for me to decide if I want to throw it away, you got it?

FIN Yes!

EUBA No more TALK! No more fish! No more nothin'!!

FIN [*Overlapping.*] OK Yes. Yes. OK I'm sorry. Please . . .
just . . . just . . . just . . . put the lighter down.

[*Overlapping.* EUBA *accidentally burns herself on the lighter. She drops the lighter and the papers on the ground.*]

EUBA Ow! Shit!!

[*Silence.*]

[*A realization.*] I'm crazy.

FIN No.

EUBA I am. I'm crazy. That's the only explanation.

FIN No. No.

EUBA I mean it, Fin. Whatever this is . . . It ain't normal. It ain't—
something's wrong with me.

FIN Euba?

EUBA [*Overlapping.*] I'm scared, Fin. You hear me? I'm scared!

FIN Of what? A letter?

EUBA No! Of . . . of everything. Afraid to go. Afraid to stay. Livin'.
Dyin'. We're screwed, you know that? We're screwed! Stuck in
this house with that crazy witch. No car. No phone.
[*Triumphantly.*] BETA FISH!

FIN Beta Fish! Yes!

EUBA With no nothin', Fin, when you think about it. We work in a mill
that spits poison twenty-four seven. . . . And the smell, God, that
smell . . . it turns my stomach, Fin. I can't get away from it. It's in
my clothes, it's in my hair, it's in my sheets! FIN! It's in my sheets!

FIN I know.

EUBA I've probably got some sort of deadly disease . . . eatin' away at me on the inside. . . . For Christ's sake, Fin, we have to wait for a northern wind to barbecue! God, I hate it here! I hate this fucking place.

FIN Then leave!

EUBA [*Quietly.*] What if the next place is no better? Ya ever thinka that?

FIN Wha—

EUBA What if the next place . . . is *worse* . . . than this?

FIN [FIN *takes in her surroundings.*] That's a scary thought, Euba.

EUBA You make it all sound so easy. Just pick up. . . . Go somewhere . . . do something . . . I know there's better places, Fin. Don't think I don't know that. But, Fin . . . I can't. I can't . . . *move*. I can't— I'm—I'm stuck.

FIN You are NOT stuck. You listen to me. You are NOT stuck. Ain't none of us stuck.

EUBA Yeah, I am.

[*The porch light flashes another warning.*]

    OH, SHUT UP!!!

[EUBA *hurls the empty beer can towards the porch.*]

    Oh, God, I can't breathe!

FIN Shh shh . . . OK, OK, caaallmmm down. Calm down.

EUBA I'M CALM!!

FIN OK, well, calm down a little bit more for me then.

EUBA OK.

FIN   Take a deep breath.

EUBA   OK.

FIN   Take another one. Sit down here for a second and catch your breath. Where's that beer? Whooo whooaa OK, now keeeep breathing. . . . Don't forget to breathe. Everything's gon' be back to normal here . . . now just keep breathing.

EUBA   OK.

FIN   Here, have a drink.

[EUBA *drinks.*]

Alright?

[EUBA *nods her head yes.*]

Have another one. Alright. You OK?

[EUBA *nods yes. They sit in silence for a minute.* FIN *pats* EUBA's *back and pushes the hair back from her eyes.*]

It's tough. I know. But . . . it might help if you remember . . . God never gives us more than we can handle.

[EUBA *slowly turns and stares blankly at* FIN.]

[*Backpedaling.*] Well, sometimes. Sometimes he does. Sometimes, it is just a *little* bit more than we can handle. [*Pause.*] But that's why we have each other.

[EUBA *takes a deep swig of beer. She gathers the pieces of the letter and stands for a moment looking down at the them. She is resolved now. She lights the papers. As they burn . . . she takes a cigarette out of the pack and lights it from the flame. She throws the burning pieces into the can.* EUBA *sits and stares out at the lonely highway.*]

EUBA   [*Vacantly.*] Fin?

FIN   [*Stoic.*] Yep?

EUBA   What happened to Buddy?

FIN He went for a swim.

EUBA Oh?

FIN Yeah.

[FIN *puts the blanket around her and grabs her beer and sits. The lull of the crickets and heaviness of the air envelope them both. They resume once again to staring out at the lonely highway.*]

It's getting' cold out here.

EUBA Yeah.

FIN Don't you think it's gettin' cold?

EUBA Yeah. [*Pause.*] Yeah, it's gettin' cold.

[*Lights fade.*]

• • •

The Devil Is in
the Details

Jill Elaine Hughes

Jill Elaine Hughes

Jill Elaine Hughes's plays have received productions and staged readings at thirty-plus small- and medium-size theatre companies in ten United States, Canada, and the United Kingdom. In 1999, she founded the nationally renowned Stockyards Theatre Project, Chicago's only theatre company dedicated exclusively to women's theatre and performance art, and served as its artistic director/producer for five years. She served for three years as president of Chicago Women's Theatre Alliance (2000–2003) and formerly served as treasurer on the executive board of the International Centre for Women Playwrights (ICWP).

Ms. Hughes's plays have been produced or have received staged readings in Chicagoland at Theatre of Western Springs, Stockyards, Boxer Rebellion Ensemble, Chicago Writers' Bloc, Chicago Dramatists, Bailiwick Arts Center, Stage Left, Speaking Ring Theatre Company, Wood Street Theatre, Women's Theatre Alliance, Around the Coyote, Theatre Entropy, and WNEP Theatre, among others. Her works have also been seen around the U.S. and in Canada at such companies as Whole World Theatre (Atlanta, GA), East Village Experimental Theatre Co. (Philadelphia, PA), NewGate Theatre (Providence, RI), A Working Theatre Co. (Portsmouth, OH), Brooklyn College, Belleville Theatre Guild (Belleville, Ontario), Insurrection Theatre Co. (Phoenix/Scottsdale, AZ), Mae West Fest (Seattle, WA), Rockland Productions (Los Angeles, CA), and the University of Massachusetts-Dartmouth. Her plays and monologues have been excerpted and anthologized by Smith & Kraus, Applause Books, and Meriwether Publishing, and she has written plays for the high school drama market, which are published and licensed by Brooklyn Play Publishers. In addition to her theatrical endeavors, Jill Elaine is a fiction writer, essayist, and humorist, and has contributed to many newspapers and national magazines, including the *Chicago Tribune*, *Chicago Reader*, *Missouri Review*, *New Art Examiner*, *Dialogue*, *Cat Fancy*, *Black Gate*, and many others. She also has completed five novels of contemporary women's fiction.

Jill Elaine was a Chicago Dramatists Network playwright from 2000 to 2007 and is also a member of the Dramatists Guild, the Playwrights' Center (Minneapolis, MN), the International Centre for Women Playwrights, the Romance Writers of America, and the National Writers' Union (AFL-CIO). An Ohio native, she received her BA from the University of Cincinnati and her MA from the University of Chicago. Ms. Hughes resides in Arlington Heights, Illinois, with her husband and son.

••• **production note** •••

Decalogue Commandment: "Thou Shalt Not Kill"
World premiere at Boxer Rebellion Ensemble Theatre, Chicago, IL, October 2004
Produced July–August 2005 at Whole World Theatre, Atlanta, GA
Produced March 8–11, 2006, at A Working Theatre Co., Portsmouth, OH

characters

> **LARRY**, very attractive man, late 20s, expensively dressed
>
> **SHEILA**, quirky young woman, early 20s, dressed like a well-to-do student
>
> **STEVE**, a wisecracking, sinister-looking corpse, early 20s, wearing rumpled and dirty street clothes

setting

The dank and dirty basement of a Los Angeles drug cartel's warehouse headquarters.

•••

[LARRY *is a mid-level L.A. gang executive.* SHEILA, *an artist, is his girlfriend and sometime business partner. They are in a cramped basement room having an argument. There are no furnishings except some old wooden crates and a battered chair; there is some random trash scattered about.* STEVE *is lying still as death on the floor, as* SHEILA *nervously watches* LARRY, *who paces back and forth while talking on his cell phone.*]

LARRY   [*On phone.*]

You didn't tell me there was gonna be other people there, man! I don't know. Twelve, maybe. Well, yeah, they all breathed it in too. How was I supposed to know Steve was having a party? I showed up at the appointed time. Huh? Jay—don't do this to me, Jay. Don't fucking do this to me, man. I know. Yeah, I know what happened over there! Well, Jesus H. Christ, Jay! I don't know what you're gonna do with twelve dead bodies, okay? That's not my fucking problem. You told me to take care of Steve and I took care of Steve. I did it quietly just like you said. I expect my payment. In full and on time. Yeah. Yeah, I have him. Aw, fuck you, man—

SHEILA   Larry, just hang up.

LARRY   [*On phone, covers mouthpiece.*] Sheila, no.

SHEILA   Larry—

LARRY   [*On phone.*] Sheila, shut up. Yeah, Jay, I'm here. Yeah. [*Pause.*] You can have him when you pay me.

SHEILA   Remember to tell him cash.

LARRY   Fifty thousand, cash. Non-negotiable. [*Pause.*] Well, if he starts to stink, I'll just cover up my fucking nose. You're not getting proof of kill until you pay up. That's how business is done, my friend. Well, I don't care how much it's gonna cost you to get rid of all those other bodies, Jay. Like I said, not my problem. You still owe me fifty thousand, cash. Yeah, well, you can fucking chalk it up to collateral damage, man. You pay me the fucking fifty thousand in full! Okay! Yeah, fuck you too. We're at the warehouse, basement room number three. Bye.

SHEILA   Is he gonna pay?

LARRY   No.

SHEILA   Are you sure?

LARRY   Yeah. Motherfucker's stiffing us right now.

SHEILA   Then what are we supposed to do?

LARRY   Wait.

SHEILA   For how long?

LARRY   Long as it takes. We'll stake him out with the body till he pays.

SHEILA   But you just said he's not gonna pay.

LARRY   He will. Eventually. He'll wanna see that body at some point.

SHEILA   When?

LARRY   I don't know.

SHEILA   You're really not making any sense right now, Larry.

LARRY   I told you, Sheila, he'll want to see the body at some point.

SHEILA   At what point, exactly?

LARRY   Eventually.

SHEILA   When is "eventually"? When his skin rots and his guts burst out? When the maggots have eaten out his eyes? When? When, Larry?

LARRY   I don't know. But he will. Jay always comes around on these types of things.

SHEILA   Are you sure?

LARRY   I'm sure, Sheila. Me and Jay go way back. He's a little mad now about the collateral damage—but he'll get over it. He always does.

SHEILA   Well, he better, because if we don't get paid, I am gonna be seriously pissed at you, Larry.

LARRY   If you want to get paid, we're gonna have to sit here and wait for Jay.

SHEILA   For how long?

LARRY   I don't know. Couple—three days. Maybe a week. There's a bathroom down the hall where we can shower, we can order in some food—no problem.

SHEILA   If you think I am going to stay here in this filthy fucking hellhole and babysit a dead body for a week, you have got another thing coming.

LARRY   Well, we've both got another thing coming, babe. It's called fifty grand in cash. Do you want your cut or not?

SHEILA   I can't wait here all week, Larry. I have a gallery opening in two days, remember? I need to get ready. The *Los Angeles Times* and *Art in America* are both coming to review the show. This is my big break, Larry. My art is finally getting noticed. I really don't need this level of stress right now.

LARRY   Then why the hell did you agree to help me? Huh? You didn't have to do it. Nobody held a gun to your head and forced you to help me work a contract out on a guy.

SHEILA   I need the money. You know that. I need the money for my sculpture.

LARRY   What, are you like, making a sculpture outa dollar bills now or something?

SHEILA   No, Larry. I need to buy supplies. Steel and blowtorches are expensive. And it's not like you could have mixed up those chemicals yourself. You needed my expertise.

LARRY   I'm sure I coulda done it. I woulda figured it out.

SHEILA   Yeah, and you would have blown yourself sky high. You're pretty good with a gun, Larry, but you've got a lot to learn about lethal gases. I swear, the things I do for the sake of our relationship—

LARRY   Well, like it or not, babe, you're in this as deep as I am. You know what's gonna have to happen now.

SHEILA   What?

LARRY We're gonna hafta split. We're gonna hafta go underground.

SHEILA Why? You kill people for a living and you never went underground before.

LARRY Babe, I'm a hit man for the fuckin Gangsta Kings. I kill people who are *expecting* to get killed. I ain't never accidentally killed twelve *other* people that I wasn't supposed to on a hit. Okay? There's gonna be some serious cop-sniffing around Steve's place, and we can't be around for it.

SHEILA Well, I'm not going underground, Larry. I have a gallery opening in two days and I fully intend to be there. Now if you'll excuse me, it's late and I am going to try and get some sleep here.

LARRY So I guess that means you're gonna stay here with me and Steve?

SHEILA I'll stay until tomorrow night. Morning after tomorrow at the absolute latest. But that's my final offer. And even if you have to stay here with that—*thing* all week by yourself, you still better pay me, Larry. I did more than my share mixing up all those chemicals for you. Those are dangerous, you know—

LARRY Sheila—

SHEILA Just shut up, okay? We'll talk more in the morning. Why don't you go to sleep too? You've had a big day.

LARRY Yeah, you're right. You can have the chair. I'll take the floor. Good night, babe.

SHEILA Good night, honey. Love you.

LARRY Yeah.

[LARRY *and* SHEILA *settle down to sleep. Lights shift to indicate a passage of time.* STEVE *sits up.*]

STEVE   You know the really cool thing about all this is, they think I'm dead. And I am, sort of. But not really. Have you ever heard of something called suspended animation, altered physical states? You know, the thing those guys in those old *Alien* movies did to make themselves sleep without aging for years while their ships traveled across the galaxy for decades? Well, that's the closest thing I can think of to explain it. I don't age, you see. Haven't in centuries. They of course think I'm dead, and who could blame them for thinking so? I'm not moving. I have no discernible breath pattern. Not to mention a *very* low body temperature. But I'm not dead. I'm not even unconscious.

I feel bad for poor Larry and Sheila here. You have to give them credit for trying. I mean, you at least have to give Sheila here credit for mixing and distributing all those lethal gases from stuff she just had sitting around her art studio when Larry found out the Gangsta Kings wanted poor old Steve bumped off all nice and quiet-like, with no gunshots or yucky blood. Actually, quite beautiful work, if I must say so myself. The perfect crime, you might say.

But not *quite* perfect. There was a little something they overlooked on their way down here.

[STEVE *returns to his corpse pose. Lights shift to indicate a passage of time. The next morning,* LARRY *and* SHEILA *wake up, stiff and rumpled from sleeping in their clothes.*]

SHEILA   What time is it?

LARRY   Mmmrggh?

SHEILA   What time is it, Larry?

LARRY   [*Looks for watch.*] Uhhhhh-nine-thirty.

SHEILA   How much longer do we have to wait?

LARRY   I told you, we have to wait until Jay calls.

SHEILA Well, what if he called you during the night? He could have left you a voicemail.

LARRY Huh? Sheila—

SHEILA Check your voicemail, Larry. I'm gonna go pee.

LARRY You can't go pee.

SHEILA What?

LARRY You can't go pee right now.

SHEILA Excuse me?

LARRY I have to escort you to the bathroom. No women walking the halls without a Gangsta King. That's the rule here.

SHEILA Screw that. I'm going to pee right now—

LARRY No. Sheila, seriously. This is a gangster building. I have to escort you to the bathroom. That's the rule.

SHEILA Well, *escort* me then. Escort me before I pee all over the place. Jesus—I don't think I've ever had to pee so much in my life.

LARRY Give me a minute, okay? I just woke up. Jesus. What day is it today, Tuesday?

SHEILA Yeah, Tuesday. Larry, *I* just woke up too, and *I* know what day it is. And furthermore, I have to PEE. NOW.

LARRY Okay, okay. Come on.

[LARRY *and* SHEILA *exit*; LARRY *is dialing his phone to check voicemail.* STEVE *sits up.*]

STEVE Like I said, there was a little something they overlooked. Well, more like there was a big something they overlooked. You see, today's not Tuesday.

LARRY [*Offstage.*] WHAT THE FUCK??

STEVE Ah, it begins.

[STEVE *reassumes his death pose just before* LARRY *and* SHEILA *enter.* SHEILA *is dancing up and down, trying not to pee.*]

SHEILA You *said* there was a bathroom! Where's the bathroom? Oh my God, Larry, I can't hold it much longer—

LARRY I swear, there's always been a bathroom right down the hall—it was there last night! I don't know—what the fuck can somebody do with a whole fucking bathroom in the middle of the night? And my goddamn phone has no signal—what the hell, man?

SHEILA That's it. I'm peeing in the hallway. I'm just going to pee in the fucking hallway.

[SHEILA *exits.*]

LARRY You can't do that! Sheila—

SHEILA [*Offstage.*] Yes I can. I'm doing it right now.

LARRY Agghhh—Sheila!!

SHEILA [*Offstage.*] You pee in alleys after rock concerts all the time, so I don't want to hear it.

LARRY You're gonna get us both in big trouble.

[SHEILA *enters.*]

SHEILA I think we're already in trouble.

LARRY Yeah, I'm starting to think you're right.

SHEILA Is your phone working yet?

LARRY Nope. Still no signal.

SHEILA Are you *sure* there was a bathroom here, Larry?

LARRY I'm sure.

SHEILA Are you *positive*?

LARRY I'm *positive*, Sheila! I've peed and showered in it a hundred times while I've waited here watchin' bodies after jobs. I've been working kills for the Kings for almost five years! I oughta know by now.

SHEILA Are you sure this is the same building you always hide out in?

LARRY I *passed* the bathroom on my way in yesterday. I'm telling you, it used to be there, but now it's just not.

SHEILA Well, an entire bathroom just does not get up and walk away in the middle of the night, Larry.

LARRY Well, I don't know what happened, but it used to be there and it's not there anymore. We'll just have to pee in a bucket or something until Jay shows up. No more pissing in the hallway.

SHEILA Well, I'm sorry, Larry, but I can't wait here when I can't even go to the bathroom. I'm leaving. I have to get ready for my opening anyway.

LARRY We agreed last night that you'd wait here for Jay for a while so you could get your cut. Do you want your cut or not?

SHEILA All I know right now is I need to go somewhere with a bathroom.

[SHEILA *exits.*]

LARRY [*Madly dialing and re-dialing his phone.*]
Jesus fucking H. Christ. Come on. Come on, goddamn it! Where's my goddamn signal? There is no signal. There is no fucking signal!!

[SHEILA *enters, distraught.*]

SHEILA How the hell do you get out of this place?

LARRY You walk down to the end of the hall and you go upstairs.

SHEILA Well, I couldn't find the stairs. I walked down the hall, all the way, and somehow I ended up just going in some kind of circle or something because I never found any stairs. I just ended up back here.

LARRY That's not possible.

SHEILA Yes it is.

LARRY There's no circle down here, Sheila. There's one hall, it goes in a straight line. Okay? There are four rooms and a bathroom. Well, there *used* to be a bathroom, but whatever. We're in room 3. The stairs are two doors down from room 3.

SHEILA Nope.

LARRY What do you mean, "nope"?

SHEILA I mean there are no stairs.

LARRY There are stairs, Sheila. There are definitely some fuckin stairs, because how else did we get down here last night? Huh? We dragged Steve's body down the fuckin stairs together, do you not remember that?

SHEILA I remember, Larry, but now there are no stairs.

LARRY Okay, Sheila, let's just drop the joke bullshit. I'm sorry that the bathroom got boarded up or concreted over or whatever the hell happened, but now you're just shitting me or something—

SHEILA I am not shitting you, Larry. There are no stairs. There is no way out of here. We're trapped.

LARRY You are completely full of shit, Sheila. We are not trapped down here. You just got lost. Come on, I'll take you to the fuckin stairs myself.

SHEILA Well, okay, but I am telling you, *they're not there.*

[SHEILA *and* LARRY *exit.* STEVE *sits up.*]

STEVE   You know, this is the part that I love. No matter how many times I see it happen, I just love the hell out of it. The new inmates, they always just refuse to accept the truth. It's right there in front of them, they can see it, but they don't believe it. Probably because whenever folks end up in my neck of the woods, it always looks very familiar to them. Usually looks like the last place they were before—you know, before they got *here.* But there's just the *slightest* differences, you see. The slightest differences between the old familiar place and the new familiar place, but it's the *slightest* differences that make *all* the difference. You see, the devil is in the details, my friends.

LARRY   [*Offstage.*]
        WHAT THE—WHAT THE FUCK????!!!!!!!

[STEVE *returns to his corpse pose just before* LARRY *and* SHEILA *enter. They are both in shock.*]

LARRY   There's no stairs.

SHEILA   I told you. You didn't believe me.

LARRY   There's no stairs.

SHEILA   Larry, I know.

LARRY   There are no stairs, Sheila!

SHEILA   Larry—

LARRY   We're trapped down here, Sheila! We're fuckin—we're fuckin trapped down here!

SHEILA   Maybe—maybe not. Maybe there's another way out—

LARRY   [*Near tears.*]   What the hell is goin' on, Sheila? Was there an earthquake last night or something? Did we sleep through a goddamn earthquake and now we're fuckin buried alive or what?

SHEILA   Larry. Larry, sweetheart, let's just calm down, okay? You've been through plenty of tough situations before. I'm sure we're gonna find another way out of here and Jay will show up with the money and everything will be just fine—

LARRY   Man—oh, Jesus H. Christ, man! I can't deal with this. Fuck—

SHEILA   Larry, you've killed over a hundred and fifty people in your life. You're a professional assassin for God's sake. I would think you'd be a little calmer in a crisis.

LARRY   Well, I'm sorry, Sheila. This is just a little out of my territory, okay? Just give me a second to think.

[*Silence for a few beats.* SHEILA *begins to pace. Lights slowly shift to a dark red.* LARRY *stands up and sniffs the air.*]

LARRY   What's that smell?

SHEILA   What smell?

LARRY   *That* smell. Do you smell that?

SHEILA   It just smells like a basement.

LARRY   Not that smell. The *other* smell. There's another smell. Do you smell it?

SHEILA   [*Sniffing.*]   I smell burning leaves.

LARRY   I think it smells more like a cookout. Barbecue.

SHEILA   It's getting stronger—oh my God, is the building on fire?

LARRY   Oh fuck. Oh fuckfuckfuck.

SHEILA   If there's a fire and we can't get out—Larry?

LARRY   What?

SHEILA   Larry, I think we're gonna die. I seriously think we're gonna die.

LARRY   I smell fire but I don't smell any smoke. If there's no smoke, then we should be okay. Hey—hey, I saw in a movie once, they used a dead body to keep smoke from coming in a room during a fire. Maybe we could do that. We have a dead body.

SHEILA   But we don't know where the fire is. And there's no smoke.

[*Lights shift to a deeper red.* STEVE *stands up, slowly.*]

STEVE   You can have fire without smoke, you know. Some people call it brimstone.

[LARRY *and* SHEILA *are stunned, then terrified.*]

LARRY   S-S-Steve? Ahhgggg—b-b-but I—but I killed you! We killed you!

SHEILA   Th—the gas. You know, the gas stuff—party—dead—oh my God—

LARRY   You're not dead.

STEVE   Hello, Larry. I've been waiting for you for a long time. A long time, indeed. How nice of you to drop in.

LARRY   B-but—but *we* brought you here—we killed you and then we brought you down here.

SHEILA   You're not dead. You're not even hurt. Who—who were all those other people who were with you when we—you know—

STEVE   Oh, just some friends. Some close friends and associates of mine. And yours, too.

LARRY   What—b-buh—

STEVE   You see, Larry and Sheila, when the Gangsta Kings sent you over to Steve's apartment to kill him quietly with that lovely ammonia and chlorine gas our lovely friend Sheila concocted, it wasn't Steve who was the real target. It was you.

LARRY Ugghhhhh—wha—

SHEILA But—but that's not possible! I distinctly remember spreading the gas, then getting Steve, then coming here—and Larry talked to Jay on the phone—I mean, we were alive for all of that—

STEVE Were you?

SHEILA I—

STEVE My friends, there are many theories in *your* world about what *my* world is really like. Some say it's a pit of fire and flame. Some say it's the place where you relive the worst parts of your life over and over again for all eternity. Some say it's an empty room with no exit. They're all right, in their own way. You see, it's different for everyone. But here it is, for you.

SHEILA What is this place?

LARRY Where the hell are we, really?

STEVE Why, the same place you were when you died, Larry and Sheila. The place you were when the noxious gas containers blew up and you breathed the same poison everyone else did. *My* place. This is my home. Welcome, my friends. Welcome to hell.

[*Curtain.*]

• • •

Arkadelphia

Samuel Brett Williams

Samuel Brett Williams

Samuel Brett Williams hails from Hot Springs, Arkansas, where he was raised by strict Southern Baptist parents. He received his BA in English from Ouachita Baptist University and his MFA in playwriting from Mason Gross School of the Arts, where he studied under Lee Blessing. Brett's plays have been produced at Stageworks/Hudson, Mile Square Theatre, New Orleans Theatre Experiment, and Readers' Theatre Repertory. His plays have been selected for the Eugene O'Neill National Playwrights' Conference, the Philadelphia New Play Festival, the Hatchery Festival, the ID America Festival, and the New Plays from the New South Festival. Brett is currently the playwright in residence at Playwrights' Theatre of New Jersey. He teaches screenwriting and expository writing at Rutgers University. He is twenty-six years old.

Brett would like to thank his family, Lia Romeo, Michole Biancosino, Lee Blessing, Sandra Nordgren, Jonathan Lomma, and Playwrights' Theatre of New Jersey.

characters

BOBBY, male, early twenties
TYLER, male, early twenties
JEREMY, male, early twenties

time

Present.

place

Arkadelphia, Arkansas. TYLER and JEREMY's living room.

• • •

••• scene one •••

[*Lights rise on the living room. BOBBY is on the outside of a large window, looking into the house. He touches the glass softly. A few prolonged seconds pass, and then he enters through the front door, nervously.*]

BOBBY   Hello? Anyone here?

[*After looking around for a few diffident seconds, he goes to the couch, sits down, and picks up a large hunting knife. Intrigued, he runs his finger up and down it—then, he notices a framed picture. He lays the knife down, and examines the picture. At this moment, TYLER and JEREMY burst into the room in mid-conversation.*]

TYLER   [*Mid-sentence.*]

... Even if you had mother F-ing Randy Moss, you still couldn't—

[BOBBY *rises quickly.* TYLER *and* JEREMY *stare at* BOBBY. *Silence. Awkward.*]

JEREMY   [*Finally.*]

It's the Bopper.

BOBBY   Hey, guys. What's up?

TYLER   Well, F me up the F-ing A, mother F-er—what the F are you doing in my house?

BOBBY   The door was open.

TYLER   It's Arkadelphia—everyone leaves the door open.

JEREMY   [*To* BOBBY.] It's okay.

[*To* TYLER.]

   Isn't it, Tyler? Tell him it's okay.

TYLER   I don't like coming home to intruders.

BOBBY   Intruders?

TYLER   [*Beat.*]

[*Laughing.*]

   I'm just S-ing you guys.

JEREMY   [*Relieved.*]
   Good one.

TYLER   I thought you were too F-ing cool to come back to Arkadelphia.

BOBBY   Come here.

[*They hug. JEREMY's embrace is more delicate while TYLER's is the personification of manliness.*]

BOBBY   I'm exhausted. I had a layover in Chicago.

[*To* JEREMY/*joking.*]

   If I had stayed overnight, I would have looked up your sister.

JEREMY   She hasn't talked to my family since she moved. We can't even send her a birthday present because we don't know her address.

BOBBY   Oh. Sorry.

JEREMY   Keep her in your prayers.

[BOBBY *says nothing. Nods.*]

TYLER   Why are you home now? I figured you would wait until this summer. If at all.

BOBBY   You guys didn't think I'd visit? Just because I'm in school doesn't mean I'm dead.

JEREMY   Well, it seemed that way—since you never call.

TYLER   Or return calls.

BOBBY   Guys, you have no idea how busy I am up there.

TYLER   We're busy too ya' know.

[BOBBY *says nothing. Awkward.*]

JEREMY   [*Finally.*] Well, I'm glad you came.

BOBBY   Thanks.

[*Trying to jumpstart conversation.*]

So . . . where are you guys coming from?

JEREMY   Well, it's Saturday night at ten. Where the heck do you think we're coming from?

TYLER   Soul saving, mother F-er.

BOBBY   I thought you guys went out witnessing to people on Wednesday nights.

TYLER   It's always been Saturdays.

[*Silence. Disappointment that* BOBBY *has already forgotten the soul-saving schedule. Awkward.*]

JEREMY   [*Finally.*]

Well . . . did you watch it?

BOBBY   [*Smiling.*] What?

TYLER   Of course he didn't—he's a city boy now.

JEREMY   Come on—I know you saw it.

BOBBY   The season finale of *Lost*?

TYLER   You're trying to P me off, aren't you?

BOBBY   I don't know what you guys are talking about.

TYLER   Fine. Whatever.

BOBBY   How did Toni Stewart not win that race? It was ridiculous.

JEREMY   [*Relieved.*] I knew you watched.

TYLER   Best Daytona 500 ever.

BOBBY   You're just saying that because Jeff Gordon won.

JEREMY   Dale Jr. was leading on lap four hundred and ninety-eight.

TYLER   Who won?

[*Beat.*]

>   I said—who won?

BOBBY   Gordon is more comfortable at that track—it's like a home field advantage. Now, Toni—

TYLER   We all know that Jeff Gordon is the best NASCAR driver ever.

JEREMY   BS. Dale Jr.—

BOBBY   Toni Stewart has the most talent.

TYLER   Why didn't he win then?

BOBBY   He was leading for, like, four hundred and ninety laps.

TYLER   I still don't see how you can like Toni Stewart. He has no friends—he doesn't use teammates—he just goes out there and tries to win every race by himself.

BOBBY   Well, look at Gordon—he uses people—he wouldn't have won the race if Kurt Busch hadn't bumped him up past Dale Jr.

TYLER   Stewart would have won if he wasn't a—

BOBBY   Lone wolf?

TYLER   Son of a bitty.

JEREMY   Everyone loves Dale Jr. because he runs a clean race, and he works hard.

TYLER   But, he's not a winner. He doesn't have his dad's balls.

BOBBY   Tyler's right. There are people who want things and there are people who take things.

TYLER   I'm surprised they even televised the race in Manhattan—I figured they would be too busy killing babies and marrying homosexuals.

BOBBY   Yeah—somehow they found time.

JEREMY   [Beat.] Well . . . speaking of . . . what's it like?

BOBBY   Intimidating. I go from a town with one street and two thousand people to a city that has buildings as big as our mountains and more people than our entire state. Everything is just . . . different up there.

JEREMY   Must be a whole lot of Wal-Marts.

BOBBY   You have no idea.

TYLER   [Intrigued now.] Really?

BOBBY   There's a Wal-Mart on every corner, and some are three stories high—you walk in and the floors are the whitest white you've ever seen—the aisles are ten feet tall and thirty feet long—you can buy anything from a can of soup to a mobile home—they have batting cages, basketball courts, and swimming pools for kids—the check-out lines are run by robots who sack your groceries, carry them out, and then wave good-bye as you drive away—and, they even sell . . .

JEREMY   Yeah?

BOBBY   Beer.

TYLER   You're F-ing lying.

BOBBY   Yeah, you're right.

TYLER   I knew they didn't sell beer.

BOBBY   Wal-Mart isn't the same up there—it's kind of ghetto.

JEREMY   [*Defending Wal-Mart.*] You're kind of ghetto.

BOBBY   [*Confused.*] What?

TYLER   So, you're too good for Wal-Mart now?

BOBBY   I miss the Super Wal-Marts more than I miss you guys.

TYLER   I should have turned the lights off, stabbed you in the face with that hunting knife, and said I thought you were a burglar.

[*Silence. Awkward.*]

BOBBY   [*Finally.*] Do you hear that?

JEREMY   [*Excited.*] Is it—

TYLER   [*Rolling his eyes.*] You know it is.

BOBBY   [*Becoming more and more excited.*] There's something outside, something that wants to get in. An animal, a beast—a beast that comes out only at night—a beast that wants to tear out our livers and eat them—a beast that wants to prematurely age our faces and give us the craps tomorrow—a beast that—

TYLER   Oh, for the love of our Heavenly Father.

BOBBY   Do you hear it?

[JEREMY *nods, excitedly.* TYLER *does not.*]

BOBBY Well?

TYLER The beast isn't as easy to catch now that Uncle Ned passed away.

JEREMY We have to drive two hours to Pine Bluff, and even then we're scared someone from the congregation will see, so we have to . . .

BOBBY What?

JEREMY [*Embarrassed.*] Wear fake mustaches.

[*BOBBY laughs, heartily. No one else does. Seeing this,* BOBBY *quickly regains his composure.*]

BOBBY Well, um, that's understandable.

TYLER Get the beer, Jeremy.

[*On command,* JEREMY *gets up and exits the room.* TYLER *looks at* BOBBY *and immediately begins playing a videogame, alone.*]

[*Watching the screen.*]

How's school?

BOBBY Good times. You know, a little Dylan Thomas, Lord Byron, e.—

TYLER I'm the assistant manager now. They finally moved me out of the nigger section.

BOBBY [*Beat.*] I really don't have time to get a job at school, because—

TYLER Since I'm manager—Wal-Mart lets me buy DVDs the day before they're actually released.

BOBBY Seen any good ones?

TYLER Monday. Double disc special edition with cast and crew commentaries. The Passion. My house.

BOBBY I'll try.

TYLER   I see a classic Bopper-back-out coming.

BOBBY   Whatever.

[*Challenging.*]

> Did you see *Closer*?

TYLER   No way—it had eighty-three F words in it.

BOBBY   How do you know?

TYLER   Looked it up on CineChristian.com.

BOBBY   You know my girl Nat's in it. Stripping. Great times.

TYLER   We're Christians, Bobby. We're not going to watch something like that at the movie theater.

JEREMY   [*Entering with beer.*]
> Yeah, we have to wait until it comes out on video.

BOBBY   Jeremy, where the hell were you?

[*Both* TYLER *and* JEREMY *are taken aback by the word "hell."*]

TYLER   [*Finally.*] We keep our beer in a lock box in the storm cellar, because my mom comes by and cleans the house every week.

[TYLER *gets up, closes the curtains, and locks the front door.*]

JEREMY   [*Opening the ice chest.*] Stand back—I'm opening the cage.

TYLER   Release the beast.

BOBBY   [*Grabbing a beer quickly.*] I never thought I would crave Milwaukee's Best.

[TYLER *nods to* JEREMY—*they both bow their heads.* BOBBY *does not.*]

JEREMY   [*Praying/sincere.*]
> Dear God, please, bless this beer and the hands that brewed it. Please, help it to be a nourishment to our bodies, and, please, help us to always be drunk in Christ. Also, please, help Bobby to

stop cussing and watching pornography at the movie theater, and,
God, Father, please, help Ray Allen to get a lot of steals this week
and, please, keep Lamar Odom on the injured reserved list,
so I can win my fantasy basketball weekly match-up with
SoulPatrol2000A.D.@yahoo.com, who has just gotten lucky
this season because—

[TYLER *elbows* JEREMY, *hard.*]

JEREMY   Ouch. Sorry. Amen.

[TYLER *and* JEREMY *raise their heads.*]

TYLER   Amen. Good pray.

BOBBY   [*Chugging his beer.*] Yeah, Amen. Good pray, good pray.

[TYLER *and* JEREMY *notice how quickly* BOBBY *downs his drink, and then takes another.*]

BOBBY   My dad told me the Badgers made it to state.

JEREMY   I think we could have won if we had a bigger crowd, but a lot
of people didn't have cars to get there.

BOBBY   Entire families can grow up in this town without ever going . . .
anywhere.

JEREMY   Why leave? We have the land, our families, and our football
team.

BOBBY   There's one street aptly named Central Street, one Super
Wal-Mart, one Sonic, one Exon, one school for kindergarten
through twelfth grade, and about two thousand people.

TYLER   What the F? You're a citified BIT-TAY![1]

BOBBY   Give me a break. I love Arkansas. I defend it to everyone.

JEREMY   [*Somewhat worried, insecure.*] What do people think of us?

---

[1] This is said in the same tone as "BEEATCH," or rather "bitch."

BOBBY   I'd rather not say.

JEREMY   Go 'head.

TYLER   Wait.

[*Beat.*]

You guys wanna get high?

BOBBY   You got some?

TYLER   It's a special occasion.

JEREMY   Sweet.

[TYLER *nods to* JEREMY. JEREMY *exits the room.*]

BOBBY   A lot of people up there have this stereotype of the Southern male. During my first month, anytime anyone wanted to make small talk with the hick, they would ask me about hunting, fireworks, *The Dukes of Hazzard*, and trucks. They were always asking about trucks.

TYLER   That's absurd.

BOBBY   Definitely.

JEREMY   [*Reentering the room.*] They really said that?

BOBBY   [*Surprised.*] That was a lot faster than the beer.

JEREMY   Well, I had it with me. We bought it tonight when we were soul saving.

TYLER   I was this close to saving T-Bone's soul.

BOBBY   Really?

TYLER   Well, after we got our dime bag, I told him about how much Jesus loves.

BOBBY   And?

TYLER   Well, he was kind of high—so he thought Jeremy was Jesus.

JEREMY   He tried to hug me.

TYLER   And then I told him that Jesus shook hands—in a really manly way—because he was, like, a carpenter, you know.

BOBBY   [*Noticing adhesive tape on the bag of marijuana.*] Jeremy, why is there tape on the weed?

[BOBBY *picks the bag up and inspects it.*]

JEREMY   Well, I couldn't keep it in my pocket—I'm not stupid. What if I had dropped it in front of Brother Eric or something?

BOBBY   [*Smelling the bag.*] So, where was it?

JEREMY   Taped to my balls.

BOBBY   [*Throwing the bag on the table.*] Oh, dear God.

JEREMY   [*Offended.*] Easy.

TYLER   [*To BOBBY.*] Cut the blasphemy, A-hole.

[BOBBY *says nothing. Silence.* JEREMY *goes about rolling a joint to ease the tension.*]

JEREMY   [*Quickly/holding up the joint.*] All right, let's hit it.

[JEREMY *takes a drag and then passes. After a few seconds the weed begins to set in, and he becomes more relaxed.*]

JEREMY   You know, trucks are sweet.

TYLER   [*After taking a drag.*]
            Yeah.

BOBBY   [*After taking a drag.*] They're great.

JEREMY   Harold Swan, down the block, just got a new Ram.

[*They continue hitting and passing.*]

BOBBY   I'm still a Tacoma fan.

TYLER   [*Laughing.*] Cousin Molly is going to get a Nissan.

BOBBY   Bless her heart, she tries.

TYLER   Holy F-ing S! We forgot to bless the weed. Here, put it down. I'll pray.

JEREMY   [*Putting the joint down.*] Sweet.

TYLER   Stop saying that.

JEREMY   Okay.

[TYLER *and* JEREMY *bow their heads.* BOBBY *does not.*]

TYLER   [*Praying/sincere.*] Dear God, thank you so much for this glorious day that you have given each one of us. Please, be with Bobby, Jeremy, and myself, and, please, help us to walk in your celestial footsteps, and, please, help Bobby to stop backsliding in his speech and help him to find a church when he goes back to Sodom and Gomorrah, and, please, don't let Bobby think that he is better than Arkadelphia just because Manhattan has better Wal-Marts, and, please, help me to lead T-Bone to Christ, and, please, bless this weed and the Colombian hands that prepared it. Hallelujah. Amen.

JEREMY   Good pray.

TYLER   [*To* BOBBY.] We're rooting for you, man.

JEREMY   [*To* BOBBY.] We miss you, dude. Seriously. It's not the same.

BOBBY   [*Changing the subject/laughing/to* JEREMY.] Remember the time Tyler and I held your shoes out the window and had you lay outside in the flower bed? I really thought Mrs. Clean was having a heart attack.

JEREMY   We got detention for a month.

TYLER   [*To* BOBBY.] You only got two weeks, though, because you ratted us out.

BOBBY   Great, though, wasn't it?

JEREMY   Best time of my life.

TYLER   Mine too.

[*They look at* BOBBY, *wanting him to agree. Instead, he picks up another beer and chugs it.*]

BOBBY   Stacey told me I was going to hell for that.

JEREMY   Stacey tells me I'm going to hell for a lot of things.

BOBBY   [*To* JEREMY.] Where is she tonight?

[*To* TYLER.]

　　　　And, where's your woman?

TYLER   They're both going to bed early because they have to supervise the bus routes tomorrow.

BOBBY   I can't believe my two best friends are engaged.

JEREMY   I'll tell you what—I can't wait to get married.

BOBBY   [*Surprised.*] Really?

[JEREMY *smiles. Their speech and mannerisms are now speeding up with each passing beer.*]

TYLER   We're a little frustrated right now.

BOBBY   [*Realization.*] Youth retreat.

[*Both* TYLER *and* JEREMY *nod.*]

BOBBY   That sucks. Was it a good one?

JEREMY   [*Sorrowful.*] They were speaking in tongues.

BOBBY   Shoot, that's at least two months without hand jobs. Maybe three—that is if rededication was involved. Tell me they didn't rededicate their lives to Christ?

[*Both* TYLER *and* JEREMY *nod, sadly.*]

BOBBY   Guys, I'm sorry.

JEREMY   We're thinking about bumping our weddings up a month.

TYLER   I mean, the retreat could be a good thing, though, you know? It can help us refocus ourselves too.

BOBBY   On hand jobs?

TYLER   [*Pointing.*] Watch yourself.

BOBBY   There's a lot of watching in this town.

JEREMY   [*Easing the tension.*] We've been memorizing verses during the quarter breaks of Madden football.

TYLER   We're almost through Acts.

BOBBY   That's a lot of Madden.

TYLER   I beat your record.

JEREMY   He's won fifteen straight Super Bowls.

BOBBY   [*To* JEREMY.] You can't stop him?

JEREMY   He's too good.

TYLER   [*To* BOBBY.] How many seasons have you played since you left?

BOBBY   I don't really have time for video games anymore.

JEREMY   So, what do you do for fun up there?

BOBBY   I don't know—read.

[*They all laugh. This makes them drink some more beer. And the beer makes them want to smoke some more pot.*]

BOBBY   Seriously, though—read.

[*They all laugh again.*]

BOBBY Six seasons. All-Madden. No Trades. Four Super Bowls.

TYLER We know you.

BOBBY [*Smiling/clinging beers.*] Thanks.

[*To* JEREMY/*casual.*]

How did you get that black eye?

[TYLER *and* JEREMY *exchange a private glance.*]

JEREMY I, uh . . .

TYLER He took a liner to the face in softball.

[JEREMY *says nothing.*]

BOBBY [*To* JEREMY.] Playing right field?

TYLER [*Taking a swig of the beast/changing the subject.*] I saved fifteen souls tonight.

BOBBY [*To* JEREMY.] And you?

JEREMY Twelve.

[*They chug. Their actions and words are very fast the rest of the scene.*]

BOBBY Don't worry, you'll do better next time.

TYLER Thirty-one to twenty this season. I'm winning this season, yep.

JEREMY I'm gonna win 'cause Brother Eric is gonna give whoever saves the most souls a new truck mat for their truck bed and I'm gonna win a new truck mat for my truck bed.

TYLER Winning is cool.

BOBBY When you go soul saving, you're just getting people to agree with stuff they don't understand because you want to score a point, because winning is cool.

TYLER Why do you say that? Don't say that. Be normal.

JEREMY Yeah, be normal for heaven—

BOBBY Normal is relative—more beer?

TYLER Beer is relative. I got some fireworks in my room.

BOBBY Awesome—do you have some more beer in your room?

JEREMY The beer's on the table and you're an alcoholic.

[BOBBY *sees the beer on the table. This makes him happy. He passes it out—two for him and one for everyone else.*]

JEREMY Are you courting anyone up north?

BOBBY It's different there. You don't date girls. You just kind of, like, hook up with girls, you know what I mean? Where are the fireworks?

TYLER Hand job, you mean hand job, right? All the fireworks are in my room. I'll get them, in my room.

BOBBY [*Uneasy.*]
Yeah, sure, I guess . . . sure, hand jobs are kind of sweet and so are buffalo wings.

JEREMY [*Shocked, almost beyond belief.*]
OH . . . MY . . . GOSH.

TYLER You've sullied your soul! You've sullied your soul!

BOBBY uh . . . well . . . um . . . uh . . .

JEREMY [*Excited.*]
What's sex like?!

[TYLER *hits* JEREMY *on the arm, hard.*]

JEREMY Oh, sorry. I mean-sorry. I mean, repent, sinner!

BOBBY It was just one girl, and I really like her, you know. I couldn't do that with someone I didn't really like, you know, and it was just one girl and I really, you know . . . isn't there a *Dukes of Hazzard* marathon on?

TYLER   Are you at least engaged?

BOBBY   We're not together anymore. I'll go get the fireworks.

[BOBBY *gets up to leave.*]

TYLER   Whore.

BOBBY   No, she was cool.

TYLER   I was talking about you.

[*Forgetting what he wanted,* BOBBY *sits back down. They continue drinking.*]

JEREMY   How did this happen? How did you fall so fast? You're just falling and falling and falling and—

BOBBY   One night we just got together. She was in my Shakespeare class and she was beautiful and funny and smart, and I didn't have confidence to talk to her, but she just, well, she just . . . picked me. She walked up picked me and I felt special and we—

TYLER   You live your entire life in Arkadelphia waiting for one person to marry, and you move north—and you move north, and you throw everything away so easy. Too crazy. It's disgusting! You're disgusting! I'm—I'm disgusted—

JEREMY   Falling and falling and falling and—

TYLER   Dumped—you were dumped!

BOBBY   I don't even know if we were dating. Different things, that's what she said we were looking for—different things. I guess I was looking for her and she was looking for someone else—different things.

JEREMY   Someone else?

BOBBY   She was with someone else within a week.

TYLER   Scared—you're so scared. That's why you're home. You're scared. You're coming back to your womb, your geographical womb.

[*Mimes womb.*[2]]

YOUR WOMB.

JEREMY   Your womb.

BOBBY   Okay, okay, okay, enough about my womb. Wombs aren't cool, guys.

JEREMY   Please, Bobby—please, please, please, ask for forgiveness for your immortality, please.

BOBBY   Am I the Highlander?

JEREMY   Immorality. I mean immorality, please, please.

BOBBY   No more—new subject.

TYLER   If you don't ask God for forgiveness, then I'm going to tell your mother that you had sex, and I'm going to tell her that you cuss, and I'm going to tell you that you—that you had sex.

BOBBY   We're twenty years old. We don't have to tell our FUCKING mothers anything.

[*There is a long, awkward pause where both* TYLER *and* JEREMY *take in the horrific obscenity that* BOBBY *has just released into their world.*]

I can't breathe in Arkadelphia. It chokes—it suffocates. You can't breathe—you're dying.

TYLER   Didn't come home for us—came home because you're scared. Scared of Sodom and Gomorrah. Scared of who you are now—probably become a faggot.

BOBBY   That's funny, very funny, coming from you.

---

[2] Yeah, I'm not quite certain what this means either, but I think it would be pretty funny.

TYLER I'm not gay! Are you saying I'm gay? You're gay, that's what you are—gay, gay.

BOBBY Don't care, be gay.

JEREMY Sodom and Gomorrah—and behold I looked out over the mountains and saw—Sodom and Gomorrah—

TYLER Ruined your life—

BOBBY By leaving Arkadelphia—by having sex—by breathing?

TYLER By turning your back on God—classic Bopper back-out.

BOBBY [*Serious/intense.*]
      Stop saying hat—that—

JEREMY Will pray for you really, really hard—

BOBBY Only in public—

TYLER Scared for your soul—

BOBBY [*To* TYLER.]
      You just want a fucking truck mat.

TYLER [*To* BOBBY.]
      You have—you have soul-saving record—

JEREMY [*Praying.*]
      Dear God, help Bobby not to—not to—not—

BOBBY [*To* TYLER.]
      Racist—just like dad.

TYLER Not racist—I don't hate niggers.

JEREMY [*Praying.*]
      Not to be a whore and not to—

BOBBY Can't breathe . . . killing yourselves . . .

TYLER   Kill you—

BOBBY   Kill me? Fuck you!

JEREMY   [*Praying.*]
          Not to—not to cuss and be a whore and—

TYLER   F me?

[*Beat.*]
          No.

BOBBY   Yes.

TYLER   Go F yourself, you mother F-ing F-faced F—

BOBBY   [*Beat.*]
          FUCK YOU!

[TYLER, *indignant, moves toward* BOBBY.]

JEREMY   Okay, okay, okay, okay—I'll get the fireworks.

[JEREMY *gets up to leave.*]

BOBBY   Last night I was here before I moved, I saw.

[JEREMY *stops. Looks at* BOBBY, *scared.*]

TYLER   Huh?

BOBBY   I looked in your room—you two together going at it like—like—

TYLER   ME A FAGGOT?! We not gay—

JEREMY   [*Ashamed.*]
          He saw—

BOBBY   [*Sincere.*]
          Two people in love.

TYLER   [*To* JEREMY.]
          SHUT UP!

[*To* BOBBY]

SHUT UP! SHUT UP!

BOBBY   You drink and smoke—to breathe.

[TYLER *charges* BOBBY *and hits him in the face, viciously.* BOBBY *falls down, hard.*]

TYLER   I hate you! I hate faggots! I hate you! I hate—

[TYLER *keeps hitting* BOBBY. BOBBY *tries to protect himself.* JEREMY *goes to help* BOBBY. TYLER *pushes* JEREMY *down.*]

TYLER   [*To* JEREMY.]

What the F you doing? You—you faggot!

[JEREMY *does not respond.* TYLER *stands over* JEREMY.]

TYLER   Get up.

[BOBBY *moans.* JEREMY *rises, shaking. Blackout.*]

··· scene two ···

[*Lights rise on* JEREMY, *shirtless, sitting on the couch, staring at the framed picture.* BOBBY *is still on the floor. Slowly, he comes around, and picks himself up off the ground.*]

BOBBY   Ohhhhh.

[*Rubbing his face.*]

What the fuck?

[*Beat.*]

I can't feel my legs.

[*Beat.*]

Wait a second. Yeah. Yeah, I can.

[*Looks at* JEREMY.]

What time is it?

JEREMY   Five-thirty.

[BOBBY *gets up. There is an awkward silence.*]

BOBBY   Maybe we could go to McDonald's before church.

[BOBBY *sits down on the couch.*]

JEREMY   You're not going to tell anyone, are you? He's so scared someone will find out.

BOBBY   Have you ever had a McGrittle sandwich? It's a piece of sausage in the middle of two—

[JEREMY *breaks down crying.* BOBBY *is shocked and touched. He moves closer to his friend on the couch. Not knowing what to say,* BOBBY *remains silent. He merely puts his hand on* JEREMY's *shoulder.*]

BOBBY   I won't tell anyone.

JEREMY   [*Regaining composure/pointing to the photograph on the table.*]
How old were we in that picture?

BOBBY   Nine.

JEREMY   [*Smiling.*]
That was the first time we ever went camping by ourselves.

[*Beat.*]

You're mom kept bringing us cookies all night.

BOBBY   That's one of the perks of setting up camp in the backyard.

JEREMY   Bobby?

BOBBY   Yeah?

JEREMY   What's it like to have sex?

BOBBY   [*Laughing, caught off guard.*]
Uh, well . . . it was the . . . worst experience of my life. I remember I was trying to take the girl's panties off and my hands were

shaking so bad it was . . . it was embarrassing. I mean, I had no idea what to do. And, I just . . . I just felt so sorry for the girl because . . . because I knew I wasn't going to be any good.

JEREMY Were you?

BOBBY I used a condom, but I was still scared she might be pregnant. She told me not to worry, however, because it happened so quickly it didn't really count as sex.

JEREMY [*Defensive.*]
Tyler and I don't have sex.

BOBBY [*Uncomfortable.*] Okay.

JEREMY I mean, we mess around, but we don't come—that way we don't commit, you know, sins against God.

BOBBY Do you come with Stacey?

JEREMY Yeah, but I can't stick it in her vagina—only her butt-hole. That way she's still a virgin.

BOBBY [*Grossed out.*] Oh, shit.

JEREMY Why do you cuss? Don't you feel bad?

BOBBY That's one thing I don't miss about Arkadelphia—the guilt.

JEREMY There's no guilt in the North?

BOBBY Not as much.

JEREMY Is that good?

BOBBY [*Reflective.*] I don't know.

[*Beat.*]

Do you feel guilty about Stacey?

JEREMY No. I love Stacey. She's going to be my wife, and I'm going to take care of her.

BOBBY   But, Jeremy . . . you're gay, aren't you?

[JEREMY *moves away from* BOBBY.]

BOBBY   [*Beat.*] I remember the first time I had a wet dream. I woke up covered in sperm, and I was so scared that I just started crying. I rolled out of bed, and got on my hands and knees. I just cried and prayed and cried and prayed and cried and prayed. I knew that God was disappointed with me. I've never been more ashamed of anything in my life. I just felt so . . . dirty.

JEREMY   Every good Christian feels that way whenever he has a wet dream or jacks off or gets a blow job or . . . even worse . . .

BOBBY   It shouldn't be that way, man. I'm telling you—you've got fucking Arkadelphia blinders on. I had the same problem when I first moved to Manhattan. I was in the biggest city in the world, but I had the one-street mindset. I was over a thousand miles away, but still living in Arkadelphia.

JEREMY   I'm tired of Arkansas.

BOBBY   You need to get out. That doesn't mean you shouldn't come back at some point, but you do need to see other places. You fly three hours north, and it's a different world.

JEREMY   If I leave, I don't want to ever come back.

BOBBY   You'll miss the times you went camping, the times you had nothing to do but lay in the backyard and watch the stars, the times you slept in your truck between games at weekend softball tournaments, and the times you just went outside, found a creek, and followed it through the woods soaking up the look and smell and taste and . . . well . . . peace.

JEREMY   I thought you hated the South.

BOBBY   It's part of me. I'm always going to want to come back.

[*Beat.*]

Jeremy, do you really want to get out of here? If so, then . . . well, when I leave . . . come with me. I'll pay for your ticket.

JEREMY   I can't.

BOBBY   Why?

JEREMY   I can't leave Tyler.

BOBBY   Are you shitting me?

JEREMY   I care about him. And, even though I can't tell him, and we can't do anything about it, we both know it. I can't leave him, because, in his own way, I know he cares about me too.

BOBBY   Don't you see how fucked up this is?

JEREMY   I have to stay here. If I go with you, then I'll backslide, and I'll go to hell.

BOBBY   Tyler gave you that black eye, didn't he?

JEREMY   He just loves God so much that sometimes he gets mad at me if he thinks I'm sinning.

BOBBY   Who's he to say that you're sinning?

JEREMY   He's a good person.

BOBBY   That's bullshit.

JEREMY   Remember the time he jumped into the creek in his church clothes to get that stray cat away from a copperhead?

BOBBY   That was a long time ago.

JEREMY   He had to take it to the pound. And his dad beat the S out of him for muddying his church clothes.

BOBBY   Tyler was always getting in trouble.

JEREMY   Maybe his dad was just always hitting him.

[*Beat.*]

I wish . . . I wish Tyler and I both could get away and be as happy as you are.

BOBBY [*Putting his head down, smiling so he doesn't cry.*]
I'm not happy, Jeremy.

JEREMY But you said—

BOBBY Once at a party—

[JEREMY *listens eagerly, expecting something scintillating.*]

—some guys fed me grease.

JEREMY What?

BOBBY It was one of the first parties I went to. I was with the Shakespeare girl. Anyway, they were eating beef noodles mixed with Corona, and all that was left in the bowl was, well, the grease. Some dude told me to eat it because he said it was really good, and no one forced me or anything, but . . . I . . .

[*Embarrassed.*]

. . . just did it.

JEREMY Why?

BOBBY I don't know what's going on up there, or even down here for that matter. I thought he was showing me something new. I thought I was being included. So, I drank it up with everyone watching.

JEREMY That's why Shakespeare dumped you?

BOBBY Her name wasn't—never mind. After the party, Shakespeare never looked at me the same way again.

JEREMY I think I've been drinking grease too. Just to fit in.

BOBBY You're a good person, Jeremy. You're better than me. You slept by my bed when I had pneumonia in the sixth grade, you and Tyler carried me off the court when I broke my ankle in ninth grade, and you-both of you, I think—you're . . . trying to be . . . better people. I really think you are. It's just the racism—and the "not coming so we're not gay" shit—and, well, all of that . . . stuff.

JEREMY   You've lost your faith.

BOBBY   [*Ashamed.*]

I don't like the taste of grease.

JEREMY   The Badgers made it to state.

BOBBY   [*Confused.*]

Yeah, I, uh, know. Congrats.

JEREMY   This town has heart. You know that. What if we're not products of our environment—what if—what if our environment is a product of us?

BOBBY   Where is this coming from?

JEREMY   Something has to change. I can't live like this.

BOBBY   Do you think Arkadelphia is going to change?

JEREMY   Maybe we can progress. Move from the Old Testament to the New.

BOBBY   Do you think Tyler is going to progress?

TYLER   [*Offstage.*]

Jeremy! What the F are you doing in there? Come back in here. And bring the weed.

[JEREMY *picks up the weed, and sighs.* BOBBY *places his hand on* JEREMY's *shoulder.*]

BOBBY   [*Desperate/trying to convince* JEREMY.]

You feel trapped, don't you? It's like the mountains are closing in, and the one street gets shorter and shorter every day. You're being suffocated by this town. It's killing your individuality. Your soul. You.

[TYLER, *wearing nothing save boxers, enters the room.*]

TYLER [*Awkward.*]
  Hey.

BOBBY Hey.

TYLER Burger King? Before church.

BOBBY We were thinking Mickey D's.

TYLER What do you think, Jeremy?

JEREMY I'm going with Bobby.

TYLER Okay, Bobby, where are you going?

JEREMY To Manhattan.

BOBBY Uh, Jeremy, this might not be the best time.

TYLER What?

JEREMY I'm going up north to breathe—and I'm going to come back and create an environment.

TYLER What the heck is he talking about? I really don't care if we go to McDonald's. I don't like their biscuits as much, but—

JEREMY Tyler, I'm sorry.

TYLER Why would you leave Arkadelphia?

JEREMY We're eating grease, Tyler.

TYLER We can go on a diet.

BOBBY No, he means—

TYLER [*To BOBBY.*]
  Shut up.

JEREMY I need to figure some things out.

TYLER Why are you talking like a bad *Lifetime* movie?

JEREMY I want to change.

TYLER Like Bobby? He's gone three months and he comes back talking like a sailor and blaspheming and, well, he's probably got AIDS as well.

JEREMY Tyler, I want to be with you, but—

TYLER Don't say that. Not in front of—

BOBBY You can trust—

TYLER [*To* BOBBY.]
Just like in Mrs. Clean's class? I know you, man. You're going to rat us out and run away—you're always running. Running and falling. Classic Bopper back-out.

BOBBY [*Angry.*]
I swear to God—

TYLER How can you swear to someone you don't believe in?

BOBBY I . . . I . . . believe.

TYLER [*To* BOBBY.]
Liar. Go drink a beer and leave us alone.
[*To* JEREMY.]
Is that who you're leaving Arkadelphia for—a liar?

JEREMY What if someone did find out?

TYLER Our lives would be over. I mean, if Brother Eric or my father—

JEREMY We could—

TYLER No. We couldn't.

BOBBY Tyler, look—

TYLER SHUT UP! Both of you. No one is going anywhere.

[TYLER *grabs the hunting knife and exits.*]

JEREMY   I think we better leave.

BOBBY   Why? Are you scared of him?

JEREMY   Are you?

[TYLER *reenters with the knife and a suitcase. He throws the suitcase on the ground, and stares at both* BOBBY *and* JEREMY.]

JEREMY   Hey, that's my suitcase!

[*While glaring at* BOBBY *and* JEREMY, TYLER *begins to tear the suitcase apart with the knife.*]

BOBBY   [*Holding him back.*]
   Jeremy, stay back.

[TYLER *continues to destroy the suitcase.*]

JEREMY   [*Finally.*]
   Fuck you, Tyler!

[TYLER *stops. All three people are shocked. Blackout.*]

··· scene three ···

[*Lights rise on the living room—empty. The curtains are open and the front door is unlocked.* BOBBY *and* JEREMY *enter, wearing church clothes.*]

BOBBY   [*Tearing off his tie.*]
   Alright, how long do we have?

JEREMY   [*Distant.*]
   What?

BOBBY   Come on, get packed.

[*Unbuttoning his shirt.*]
   Tyler will be back from Little Rock in a few hours.

JEREMY Pack? Now?

BOBBY Yeah, you can stay at my house for a few days.

JEREMY The sermon was beautiful, wasn't it?

BOBBY Brother Eric knows what to say. Do you have any trash bags?

JEREMY The whole congregation was so happy to see you. Your church in Manhattan couldn't be better than this one.

BOBBY I don't have a church in Manhattan. Do you want to take anything from this room?

JEREMY Are you serious?

BOBBY Is the CD player yours?

JEREMY I love sermons that deal with Paul's letters.

BOBBY [*Serious/almost* TYLER-*like.*]
You're not backing out on me, Jeremy.

JEREMY Galatians 5:7. "You were running a good race. Who cut in on you and kept you from obeying the truth?"

[TYLER *enters with a picket sign.*]

TYLER Guys, what's wrong? Why didn't you want to go to Little Rock with everyone else?

BOBBY We don't feel like tailgating at an abortion clinic right now.

JEREMY You didn't go?

TYLER Nope. And, believe me, it was hard not to—Brother Eric's wife was making ribs. And, I just got this new aborted fetus poster. Look.

[*Holding the poster up.*]
I call him Jimmy.

BOBBY You disgust me.

[TYLER *goes to hand the poster to* JEREMY, *but* JEREMY *will not take it.*]

TYLER [*Angry.*]

Do you need a ride to the airport, Bobby?

BOBBY I'm here two more days, Tyler. I wouldn't miss your *Passion* party for anything.

TYLER Go to heck.

BOBBY You can't say "hell," but you can smoke pot and drink?

TYLER I asked God for forgiveness today, did you?

BOBBY You're psychotic.

TYLER Bobby, I think it's time for you to leave.

BOBBY I think it's time for you to stop lying to yourself.

TYLER You think I'm such a hypocrite, don't you? You think I judge people without seeing my own sin?

BOBBY Pretty much.

TYLER Well, what the F do you think you're doing right now, Bobby?

BOBBY [*Beat.*]

Let's go, Jeremy.

TYLER He's not leaving.

BOBBY What if he does? What would you do then?

TYLER [*Afraid, then angry*]

I would . . .

[JEREMY, *curious, looks at* TYLER.]

. . . pray for both of your souls. Violently. Without ceasing. Until I was sweating blood. Until I died.

BOBBY   Well, get to praying then, because we're out.

[BOBBY *goes to leave.* JEREMY *stays.* TYLER *thinks he has won.*]

TYLER   [*To* BOBBY.]
> Don't let the door hit you in the butt, Bobby.

[*Exhales, relaxes/to* JEREMY.]
> Lebron is playing Kobe today. Turn on the television.

[JEREMY *does not move.*]

BOBBY   Turn it on yourself.

TYLER   [*To* JEREMY *the whole time.*]
> Whatever happened to Derek Fisher? He left the Lakers and he just disappeared off the face of the earth. He was so popular in Los Angeles. I bet he wishes he could go back and have everything the way it used to be.

[*Turning to* BOBBY.]
> Don't you think he would if he could, Bobby?

BOBBY   Look, Tyler—

JEREMY   [*Finally, after much thought.*]
> I'm not going with you, Bobby.

BOBBY   Are you fucking kidding me?

TYLER   I knew you would come around.

JEREMY   And, I'm not staying with you either, Tyler.

TYLER   Huh?

JEREMY   You gutted my suitcase like a deer. That's not normal.

TYLER   Hey—I apologized. Seventy times seven, remember? Don't worry—I'll get you a whole new set of luggage at Wal-Mart.

JEREMY   It's not just the luggage.

BOBBY   Jeremy, if you're not going with me, then where the hell are you going?

JEREMY   With my sister. In Chicago.

BOBBY   Well, that's about the stupidest thing I've ever heard.

TYLER   Bobby's right.

BOBBY   What are you going to do—load up your truck and drive there? Do you know what part of Chicago she lives in? How are you going to find her? The phone book? It's not Arkadelphia, Jeremy—it's not thirty pages long—it's thousands. What was her husband's last name? Smith? Yeah, he should be easy to find.

TYLER   Jeremy, you know this is where you belong. If you leave Arkadelphia, then you'll go to hell.

BOBBY   If you stay here—this town will smother you to death. It will kill your soul.

JEREMY   [*Suffocating.*]
I just, I just, I just need . . . room.

TYLER   What about your fiancée, or your job, or your family?

JEREMY   No, no, no more lies.

TYLER   [*Sincere.*]
We can make this work.

BOBBY   Jeremy, don't listen to him. He's scared—scared of being left alone in this town—scared of becoming his father.

JEREMY   [*To* BOBBY.]
Well, maybe I'm scared of becoming you.

[*This shocks and upsets* BOBBY.]

TYLER   Come here, Jeremy.

[TYLER *pulls* JEREMY *to him,* JEREMY *pulls away.*]

JEREMY [*Hyperventilating.*]

> Just, just, back off, alright? You guys need to give me some room.

BOBBY Jeremy, I really care about you.

[JEREMY *heads for the door.*]

TYLER [*Going for broke/to* JEREMY.]

> I love you.

[JEREMY *takes this in, and walks over to* TYLER, *slowly. He embraces him, and then goes into kiss, but* TYLER *looks out the window, and pulls away, horrified.* BOBBY *smirks, thinking he has won.* TYLER *understands this. He closes the curtains and locks the door.*]

BOBBY Jeremy, there's always going to be a place for you in Manhattan.

[JEREMY *looks at* TYLER, *as if searching for an answer.* TYLER *pulls* JEREMY *around and kisses him.* BOBBY—*shocked, defeated, confused*—*grabs his jacket, and begins to exit. He opens the front door, and stares down the one street. He remains in the doorway, unable to move.*]

TYLER Let's play some Madden. Jeremy, get it started.

[TYLER *sits down on the couch with the confidence of a prizefighter.* JEREMY *turns on the video game system, and hands* TYLER *a controller.*]

TYLER Vikings.

JEREMY Cowboys.

[TYLER *and* JEREMY *both look at* BOBBY, *who is terrified—terrified of the North and the South. We can feel his loneliness.* TYLER *picks up an extra video game controller, and holds it out to* BOBBY. BOBBY *turns back to his friends, and stares at the controller, thinking. A few seconds pass. Eventually,* BOBBY *exits, closing the door behind him.* TYLER *and* JEREMY *begin playing video games, and* BOBBY *watches them one last time through the window. He touches the glass. Lights fade to black.*]

• • •

Charlie Blake's Boat

Graeme Gillis

Graeme Gillis

Graeme Gillis is from Cape Breton, Nova Scotia. His plays have been produced in New York at Ensemble Studio Theatre through the Youngblood program for emerging playwrights and in the Marathon of One-Act Plays. He has worked as a playwright at theatres throughout the U.S. and Canada, including Rattlestick Theatre, Cherry Lane Theatre, and the Williamstown Theatre Festival. He has received fellowships from the Banff Centre for the Arts, the Canada Council for the Arts, the Nova Scotia Arts Council, and the Sewanee Writers Conference. He is a member of the Actors Studio and of EST. *Charlie Blake's Boat* was originally produced by Youngblood Ensemble Studio Theatre (Curt Dempster, Artistic Director).

characters

CHARLIE
HELEN

• • •

[*Lights up on the wharf. It is made of logs and iron twine, and stretches the length of the stage. This is Mahone Bay, a small maritime town, present day in late August. CHARLIE BLAKE sits alone, his legs dangling. He is whittling something out of a big block of wood with a Swiss Army knife. A line of unopened champagne bottles sits beside him. Behind him sits his boat. You can hear it bumping up against the wharf and the water lapping in the early morning quiet. In the distance are happy voices, stragglers at the nearby party. It is not yet dawn. A homemade banner stretches over part of the wharf. It reads "Bonne Voyagee Charlie Blake."*]

[*There is also a church banner, purple, like for Easter or Advent, that reads "God Bless Charlie Blake's Boat."*]

[CHARLIE *kills the last of his bottle. He pops another open, and the cork sails into the air.*]

[*From offstage we hear* HELEN *singing "Farewell to Nova Scotia."*]

HELEN   *Farewell to Nova Scotia, the sea-bound coast/Let your mountains dark and dreary be/But when I am far away on the briny ocean toss'd/Will you ever heave a sigh or a wish for me?*

[*Enter* HELEN. *She sees the church banner. When she speaks,* CHARLIE *knows her right away.*]

God bless Charlie Blake's boat.

CHARLIE   Ahh, Jesus.

HELEN   God bless him and keep him from the dangers of the sea. And, God, do not forsake this godforsaken tub of a boat, or this godforsaken tub of a man, amen.

CHARLIE Helen Lucille McNeil. Welcome home.

HELEN Thanks.

CHARLIE Been a long time.

HELEN It has.

[*They begin to shake hands, then laugh and begin to hug, then think better of it and shake hands.*]

CHARLIE You look like about a million bucks.

HELEN And you look like about 75 cents. It's good to see you.

CHARLIE It is?

HELEN Yeah, I'm a little surprised myself.

[*They do the handshake-or-hug thing again, but this time it ends in a hug. This leads to more discomfort. They let go.*]

They're praying for you up at the party, you know. Father Bernie's doing his best but Alec's got his pants on his head and Sheilagh's hanging off the roof. By her ankles. Till Alec pays attention to her, she says. It's that time of night. Anyway you should see it. You might not see it for a while.

CHARLIE So what brings you back this way?

HELEN Heard about the party, you know? Hate to miss a party. [*Reads.*] Bonne voyagee, Charlie Blake.

[*She laughs and shakes her head.*]

Well. Bonne voyagee.

[*She kills the last of her bottle.*]

Farewell to Nova Scotia.

CHARLIE And you came all this way for that?

HELEN   Ah, it was just a plane and a bus.

CHARLIE   Ah yes, the bus from Bullshit City.

HELEN   Come on, Charlie.

CHARLIE   Sorry, I'm sorry. How are things? How are things in Bullshit City?

HELEN   Good.

CHARLIE   Great.

HELEN   Good. Yeah. Onward and upward. All the time.

CHARLIE   Well, that's great.

HELEN   So. What're you whittling there?

CHARLIE   It's a figurehead. For the stem. For the boat.

HELEN   What's it supposed to be?

CHARLIE   Speck.

HELEN   Speck?

CHARLIE   My uncle Speck.

HELEN   Oh. Oh right.

CHARLIE   It's a work in progress.

HELEN   I can see that.

CHARLIE   Yeah, well, I'm a bit behind, so you'll have to excuse me. Got to be done by morning. Last thing before I'm off.

HELEN   To Scotland.

CHARLIE   That's right. Make my mother happy.

HELEN   I've seen your mother up at the party, she's beside herself.

CHARLIE   She's pleased to have the house to herself, I think.

HELEN   So what's in Scotland?

CHARLIE   Ah, I don't know. Bagpipes, I guess. Kilts. Heroin.

HELEN   Right.

CHARLIE   My mother was there once, we've got family over there. Mum says it's more beautiful than Ireland, and they're not as smug as the Irish are either. No "luck of the Scottish" bullshit or anything, you know. I just want to see it. I want to see where I come from.

HELEN   You come from here.

CHARLIE   Well, that's not . . . quite enough. For me.

HELEN   You'd like a little more glam, eh? Little more flash.

CHARLIE   No, man, glam and flash, that's your thing.

HELEN   Is it.

CHARLIE   That's what I hear.

HELEN   Well, you can say you're from wherever you want. You can make it all up. But you belong here.

CHARLIE   Well, I think I'd like to decide. Where I belong. I'd like a say. Instead of someone telling me.

HELEN   So Scotland then.

CHARLIE   For a start.

[*Pops new cork, it sails overhead.*]

So how're you fitting in up there?

HELEN   Just fine, thanks.

CHARLIE   Just asking is all. Old Mahone Bay, you know, the old gang— gone three years and all, it can be a bit awkward.

HELEN   No, I'm fine. They're fine. It's great to see everybody.

CHARLIE   Well, good.

HELEN   Can't wait, can you?

CHARLIE   Well, you know how that feels, right? You couldn't wait, right? To be off? I remember that much.

HELEN   [*Holds her tongue, takes a swig.*]
So let me ask you something, Charlie, how do you figure on making it to Maine, let alone Scotland, in this—

CHARLIE   Careful.

HELEN   What?

CHARLIE   Well—just don't talk bad about her.

HELEN   I wasn't going to say anything bad. In this . . . contraption.

CHARLIE   There's just, a lot of my life in that contraption is all.

HELEN   Right.

CHARLIE   A long time.

HELEN   Yeah.

CHARLIE   And anyway I'm going to Australia first. Then Scotland.

HELEN   But how will you get there?

CHARLIE   Same way you get anywhere from Australia. You go up.

HELEN   But how—

CHARLIE   Port to port, all right, Helen? Port to port. From here to Maine, and from Maine right on down the seaboard. Till I hit the Bahamas. Then get a tow across to Australia and from there just head up to Scotland. Port to port. Down one side and up the other side. It's a circumnavigation, you get it? An old-fashioned, Magellan-style, swabby, scurvy circumnavigation. And if you ever read your own mail, you'd know all this. Goddammit!

HELEN What?

CHARLIE I got a splinter.

HELEN Well, here, come here.

CHARLIE [*Tries to suck his own splinter.*] No, I'm fine.

HELEN Gimme.

CHARLIE Look, will you get out of it and let me handle this, please?

HELEN How long?

CHARLIE What—ow! Fuck!—What?

HELEN How LONG. The whole trip, how long?

CHARLIE Arrgh, three goddam years.

HELEN You're gonna spend three years in that—

CHARLIE Will you quit calling her names? It's not a contraption and it's not a tub either, see? It's a boat. All right? It's a BOAT. It's a ship.

HELEN Well, what kinda ship is that?

CHARLIE It's a schooner.

HELEN That's not a schooner.

CHARLIE It is.

HELEN It's too small to be a schooner.

CHARLIE [*Angrily whittles.*] It's a pinky schooner. And if you knew anything about anything, you'd know that.

HELEN What're you calling it then? Pinky?

CHARLIE No. It's really more of a sloop than a schooner anyway. It's based off the old sloops from the 1800s—

HELEN So then Sloopy.

CHARLIE   No. No. Not Pinky. Not Sloopy. Jesus—fuck!—Ow.

HELEN   Here.

[*Takes his hand.*]

> Now don't look. So what're you going to call it then. If not Pinky or Sloopy.

[HELEN *moves to suck splinter out. It's pretty sexy.* CHARLIE *looks in spite of himself.*]

CHARLIE   I . . . don't know.

HELEN   I told you not to look.

[*Spits splinter out.*]

> There.

CHARLIE   You didn't have to do that.

HELEN   No. So?

CHARLIE   You didn't have to come back here either.

HELEN   Well. God bless ya.

[*Chucks him on the shoulder or chin.*]

> Captain Blake. And God bless your boat.

[*He says nothing, so she finishes bottle.*]

> Aren't you supposed to break one of these over the side?

[*Grabs bottle, brings it to ship's bow.*]

> I christen this contraption, Pinky.

CHARLIE   Her name's not Pinky.

HELEN   Pinky Contraption, the Brave Little Schooner.

CHARLIE   Don't do it on the wood.

HELEN   You said it was all wood.

CHARLIE See. The bow plate's iron, hit the bow plate.

HELEN Your letter said all wood.

CHARLIE My letter. [*Pause.*] Well, that must've been an old letter. I guess you didn't stop reading right away.

HELEN No.

CHARLIE Just stopped answering.

HELEN Yeah.

CHARLIE Yeah, well, the wooden boat idea, that was a Speck thing. Speck's idea, romantic and all but not exactly practical. So now she's some iron and some wood.

[*Brandishes bottle.*]

Anyway here's to the boat then, here's to Pinky, the Brave Little Schooner, the Little Schooner that—

[HELEN *kisses him. For a long time. Champagne goes everywhere. She doesn't leave his arms, just his mouth.*]

HELEN [*In first breath.*] Well.

CHARLIE Well, that . . . beats whittling.

HELEN [*Laughs and takes bottle, still close to him.*] Nice work, Captain.

CHARLIE You keep calling me that.

HELEN I'm just proud of you is all.

CHARLIE Proud. [*Withdraws.*] What're you so proud of?

HELEN Don't be so suspicious.

CHARLIE You think this had something to do with you? It had nothing to do with you.

HELEN   Hey, I know, all right? Get off your high horse.

CHARLIE   You get off your high horse.

HELEN   What?

CHARLIE   Just quit being so PROUD of me. There's nothing for you to be proud of.

HELEN   Fine. Forget it.

CHARLIE   I'm not like I was before, Helen.

HELEN   Look. Just—high horses aside, you don't have anything left to prove. You built the boat.

CHARLIE   So?

HELEN   So you don't have to go sailing off to the bottom of the ocean or wherever the hell—

CHARLIE   I told you, SCOTLAND—

HELEN   Circum-goddam-navigation.

CHARLIE   Down this side, then up the other side. Of the world. Not hard to work out, Helen.

HELEN   What if you need food? Or repairs? You can't pay for that. Or God forbid if you get another SPLINTER? Ya wuss? Ya pansy?

CHARLIE   You'd be surprised at the demand for a fellow can plank and caulk a ship's keel from scratch.

HELEN   Listen to you, caulk and plank a keel. What're you, the Ancient Friggin Mariner?

CHARLIE   Or at how many girls can suck out a splinter.

HELEN   Okay. So you make it to Scotland. What'll you do then? You'll be 35 when you get there.

CHARLIE   I'll decide when I get there.

HELEN   You'll be a bum.

CHARLIE   Well, what am I now, Helen?

HELEN   You're not a bum, Charlie.

CHARLIE   Oh yeah?

HELEN   Not yet.

CHARLIE   Well, that's not what you said before.

HELEN   You were living in your mother's basement before [*Overlap.*] WE were living—

CHARLIE   And I'll be back in that basement tomorrow if I don't get on this boat.

HELEN   It's not the basement or the boat.

CHARLIE   It is for me.

HELEN   There are other things you can be.

CHARLIE   Like you? I could be like you?

HELEN   I wouldn't recommend it.

CHARLIE   I hear, you're a headhunter. I heard that's your job: headhunter.

HELEN   Is that what you heard?

CHARLIE   Well, that sounds great. That sounds like a place where I'd love to work.

HELEN   Well, where WOULD you work?

CHARLIE   Onward and upward, right?

HELEN   Where would you EVER work?

CHARLIE   Where I'm *gonna* work. Out there. On the water.

HELEN Right, unless you're *in* the water, or *under* water.

CHARLIE You know, everybody is happy for me except you.

HELEN Is that right?

CHARLIE Everybody has faith in me, except you.

HELEN That's because nobody gives enough of a *shit* to set you *straight*, except me.

CHARLIE And how're you setting me straight, coming back here—

HELEN Because if you DIE in that thing, man, if you sink, if you get lost, if you get smashed like a bucket of eggs—

CHARLIE I'm not gonna GET LOST.

HELEN Like a bucket of eggs on the fuckin rocks, then what the hell reason will I have to ever come here again?

CHARLIE Same as now, so you can feel better than everybody else.

HELEN Is that what you think?

CHARLIE You're a snob here now. You're a tourist.

HELEN Fine. Go off on your boat.

CHARLIE I have to finish Speck first.

HELEN Fuckin' Speck.

[HELEN *grabs Speck.*]

CHARLIE Hey!

HELEN Speck'll join you in the Bahamas.

[*She grabs the whittling knife.*]

      You can go.

CHARLIE Speck!

HELEN But you won't. Because you're scared.

[*On "scared," she jams the Swiss Army knife into the wood.*]

CHARLIE Speck!

[HELEN *removes the knife,* CHARLIE *watches in horror.*]

That's where his eye was gonna be!

[HELEN *pulls out the Swiss Army corkscrew, winds it into Speck.*]

Holy God, woman, what's wrong with you?

[*She lobs Speck back to him.*]

He's fuckin' blind in both eyes!

HELEN Hey, Charlie.

[*She dangles upside down off the dock.*]

Aren't you gone yet? Why aren't you gone yet?

CHARLIE What're you doing?

HELEN Sheilagh hangs off the roof so Alec'll listen, right? So can I make my point now?

CHARLIE What point? You're being nuts!

[HELEN *gets him in a scissor hold with her legs and hauls him down.*]

HELEN WHOORAGH!

CHARLIE Holy shit!

[*She jumps up, and is now dangling him off the dock.*]

Holy fuck!

HELEN Now you listen to me, Charlie Blake. And excuse my Irish bullshit, but I'm a McNeil and the McNeils are *hardy Irish stock,* you smug Scot bastard. Now maybe I am a headhunter, but that's a talent I've got. And I like it. I'm proud of it. And you built this boat, Charlie. You got a gift. Now I saw how excited everybody got about the boat and the trip.

CHARLIE   They're just glad to get rid of me is all.

HELEN   [*Shakes him angrily.*]
Knock it off! Knock it off or I swear to Jesus you're going into the drink.

CHARLIE   Sorry. Sorry. Holy fuck.

HELEN   I saw the whole town get behind the boat and the trip and you, too, Charlie. Charlie?

[CHARLIE *snuffles.*]

Are you crying?

CHARLIE   No. The blood's all rushing to my head.

HELEN   You don't have to do this, Charlie.

CHARLIE   Hey, listen, Helen, I want to do this.

HELEN   Do you? Because you don't seem that way to me. You seem scared.

CHARLIE   I might be scared. So what?

HELEN   Charlie, I came back to tell you not to waste three more years.

CHARLIE   What'll I do then, Helen? Hang around here? With Alec?

HELEN   If you spend three years in that boat, you're gonna end up like Alec.

CHARLIE   I *am* like Alec. All right, Helen. I'm *just* like Alec. Alec is a bum, right? He's a waste. He is. And this boat is my chance to not be that way. Anymore. And not end up like you. Ever.

HELEN   So why don't you go then?

CHARLIE   Well, why should I stay? For you?

HELEN   Well . . . why not?

[*Pause.*]

CHARLIE   I hadn't thought of that. Not for a while anyway.

HELEN   Right.

CHARLIE   Not till tonight anyway.

HELEN   Right.

CHARLIE   You know, Helen, when I met you I was living in my mother's basement. And when you took off I was still in that basement. You didn't do a thing to me.

HELEN   Thanks.

CHARLIE   So you're off the hook.

HELEN   Thanks. Thanks a bunch.

CHARLIE   You believe me?

HELEN   Sure.

[*Chucks her bottle into the water behind them, looks to the party.*]

You hear those voices? I know every voice up there tonight. Sheilagh. Alec. Your mother. I used to have a voice like that. I used to talk like that. It comes out of me, when I'm drunk. And one night, I got so drunk, I forgot where I was. I thought I was back on your street. I was all hammered, what did I know? I thought I could see your mother's house at the end of the road. And I even yelled out, "Hey, Charlie!" Stupid, right? But I heard it. That voice. And when I left here I couldn't wait to this way of talking out of me. But all drunk to hell that night, I thought I sounded pretty good. And a taxi went by and I thought, "Ah hell, there's no taxis in Mahone Bay." And I took the taxi back to my apartment, and my apartment was empty. And now I'm back. And I still feel gone. I'm sick of feeling like that. And I don't want it to happen to you. It happens when you leave.

CHARLIE   You gotta build a boat.

HELEN   Shut up.

CHARLIE   You're sick of it, right? You said you're sick. Sick of food yet?

HELEN   No.

CHARLIE   You got a while yet then. You'll get sicker yet then.

HELEN   Shut up.

CHARLIE   I mean sick of eating, sick of all of it. That's the way I was in that basement. Sick of the sight of myself, sick of my job, sick of the couch I slept on. Down in the dark, all the time, and it was worse when you were gone, I'll give you that.

HELEN   Thanks.

CHARLIE   But, Helen, about a year after you left, something happened, and it was, it was kind of a miracle. See my uncle Speck came back. Now that wouldn't be much of a miracle if he was just coming back to Canada or even Mahone Bay, but old Uncle Speck came back a lot further. See, my uncle Speck came back to life. You remember the Whitecap Ranger?

HELEN   No.

CHARLIE   See, the Whitecap Ranger was an oil rig. It went down off the coast of Newfoundland in 1978. Old Speck was a rigger on the Whitecap Ranger. When I was a kid I wanted to be just like, well, I wanted to BE Speck, pretty much. And when that ship went down, when Speck went down . . . it's funny, most people forget it. But it was the worst day I could remember.

HELEN   But he came back.

CHARLIE   He came back Christmas morning. Dead for nearly 20 years and we found him sitting under the tree. My mother knew him straight away. "Speck," she says, "you went down and died, how on earth did you end up here, and where've you been for the last 20 years?" Speck just rolls out from under the tree and tells her, "Flossie, it's a long swim." A long swim. Now I thought here's a man who swam back from the dead. Maybe he can help me climb out of the basement. So I said to him, I said, "Speck, what's the secret?" And he said, "Build me a boat, boy, and I'll tell you." I guess Speck always wanted his own boat.

HELEN   So this is Speck's boat.

CHARLIE   Well, it would've been but Speck died, for real, about two weeks after he showed up that Christmas.

HELEN   What?

CHARLIE   Yeah, anchor through the belly.

HELEN   An anchor.

CHARLIE   He was on a new job, showing off, tried to hoist this giant anchor himself, and it slipped.

HELEN   Slipped.

CHARLIE   Yeah. Anyway—

HELEN   Wait a minute, wait a minute, he just slipped? Twenty years back from the dead and then he slipped?

CHARLIE   Can I tell about the boat or are we going to dwell on the death of my boyhood hero?

HELEN   Go ahead.

CHARLIE   Well, see it was the secret. Speck gave me the secret, and he knew it, too. He had to know it. It wasn't his secret FOR a boat, his secret WAS the boat. So come springtime I started Speck's boat. Five o'clock every morning I was in my mother's driveway, drilling and soldering. For five years. I woke up everybody within earshot, building Speck's boat. Mahone Bay got up at dawn every day. For five years I had a reason, not just to get up. I had a reason to get up early. See, Helen, I really was different before I built this boat. I was old before. When you knew me, I was an old man. I'm young now. I'm finally a young man.

HELEN But how—

CHARLIE Getting up early. That's all I can tell you. A reason to get up early. It's still Speck's secret. "Build me a boat." That's all he said. And it was like the secret of the world.

[HELEN *looks at him, then looks back up the hill.*]

Do you believe me? . . . It would be good if you believed me. Helen?

[HELEN *pulls her to him and kisses him. It's quite a kiss.* CHARLIE *doesn't know what to say.*]

CHARLIE Uh . . . was that a yes kiss or a no kiss?

HELEN [*Lets him go.*] Good-bye kiss.

CHARLIE Oh. Well . . . that's not quite fair. I mean, if I'd've known that was my good-bye kiss, I'd've put a little more into it, you know?

HELEN That's all you get.

CHARLIE Damn.

HELEN It's close to dawn.

CHARLIE It's close.

HELEN Sorry about wrecking your whittling.

CHARLIE Yeah.

[*Considers, then exits and speaks from offstage.*]

Well, you know, Alec gave me this for going away.

[*Emerges with a jolly-looking garden gnome statue.*]

Maybe it'll have to do. It actually looks a lot like Speck.

[*Affixes gnome to the bow of the boat.*]

There. Speck had a pretty good sense of humor. And I got to get going.

HELEN   You leaving now?

CHARLIE   Yeah. Good-byes are . . . well it's better just to leave quiet, I think. They'll be here when I get back.

[*Pause, eyes* HELEN.]

You didn't . . . want to come along. Did you?

HELEN   Nah. I'm a landlubber. Pretty devout landlubber. But you belong on your boat.

CHARLIE   You really think that?

HELEN   I know it.

CHARLIE   Thanks.

[*Pause.*]

Well.

[CHARLIE *looks to his boat.*]

Scotland's waiting.

HELEN   Scotland waits.

[*Gathers up her blanket round her.*]

Well. I guess I'll watch you from up the hill.

CHARLIE So long, Helen.

HELEN Bonne voyagee. Captain Blake.

[HELEN *exits.* CHARLIE *watches her go, his hand held up in a good-bye wave. He gets the anchor up. He moves over to the mast to hoist the sail. He pulls the rope down till the sail is all the way up. The sun shines on it. End of play.*]

• • •

Reading List

Susan Miller

Susan Miller

Susan Miller is an award-winning playwright and Guggenheim fellow, whose works include the critically acclaimed one-woman play *My Left Breast*, for which she won an OBIE; *A Map of Doubt and Rescue*, which earned the Susan Smith Blackburn Prize; and *Nasty Rumors and Final Remarks*, also an OBIE winner. Her other plays are *For Dear Life*, *Flux*, *Confessions of a Female Disorder*, *It's Our Town, Too*, and *Sweeping the Nation*. She has been produced at the Public Theatre, Second Stage, Actors' Theatre of Louisville, Naked Angels, and the Mark Taper Forum, among others. Miller has also written for *O, The Oprah Magazine* and was a consulting producer on Showtime's hit series *The L Word*. Her short film *The Grand Design*, directed by Eric Stoltz, starring Frances Conroy and Eric Stoltz, is in postproduction.

characters

3 WOMEN
3 MEN
(Ages of the characters are just suggestions)

BERNIE, woman over 40. A librarian. Engaging. Modern. She loves her work. She could be anything, but she's this.

SNOW, man of indeterminate age. An astronomer. Experience and history show on him.

EAGAN, man in his 40s. Filled with contemporary angst.

SONIA, woman in her 30s. A teacher. Urban.

MILO and **JACOB**, played by the same actor, a man in his late 20s. MILO is an FBI agent, earnest but unsure. JACOB is a trucker, with good intentions.

JANEL, young woman, late teens. Original. Optimistic.

time

Present

setting

The suggestion of a public library

··· production note ···

Reading List was produced in New York as part of the Vital Theatre Company's New Work Festival-Vital Signs. It was directed by Cynthia Croot. With the following cast:

Kathryn Grody
Bridgit Evans
Maha Chelaoui
Jay Smith
Michael Rudko
Happy Anderson

• • •

[*Lush music (Sinatra's "One for My Baby") accompanies the* LIBRARIAN, *as she shreds pink sheets of paper. After a few moments, the music fades and she speaks directly to the audience.*]

BERNIE   It used to be at the end of a day, I'd lock up and take myself out for a cocktail. That was my ritual. I love the sound of that word— *cocktail*. Vodka straight up, three olives. I loved the olives. Well, and the word *cocktail*.

[*Beat.*]

My new ritual—I shred.

[*Beat.*]

What it is, see, certain powers of the Patriot Act give the government the right to review the records of people under suspicion of being suspicious. Which has been interpreted to include the borrowing of books at libraries. So, I shred. Lists of things people want us to locate for them. You know? A day's worth of requests. Like the one I got yesterday asking for places a woman might go if she needed shelter. Then someone tracing the origin of a certain inflammatory phrase. Two queries regarding unpopular Supreme Court rulings. And even the sacred hunt for some rapturous, quotidian detail.

[*Referring to a pink sheet.*]

Okay. Like, here's someone courteously asking for a volume on puppetry, which had a footnote containing an excerpt from *The Pink Code. Pink. Code.* Words to alarm any vigilant homophobe. Actually, *Pink Code*, a book by a lovely man living in Maine, I've since learned—we're in correspondence—is a manual for the use of color and hue in animation. Who knew? Puppets are apparently staging a comeback.

[*She shreds it. Then:*]

It keeps me going. What people have on their minds.

[*A hesitant* MAN *walks up to her desk.*]

JACOB   Hello.

BERNIE   [*Taken with his shy formality.*] Hello.

JACOB   I was wondering. there are so many, you know, well, books, in here. I was thinking if you could maybe narrow it down for me, recommend one. Your personal pick.

BERNIE   [*To audience.*] This fellow. He glowed. As if it were his first time in the library. Like he was excited by information but embarrassed by it, too.

JACOB   Something to keep me in place. Something I could—come back to. See, I'm on the road. I'm miles from anything. Whatever you got.

BERNIE   [*To audience.*] It thrilled me. I mean, a long haul truck driver, taking the time, wanting to know. Who punishes curiosity? But then, I project a scenario. They'd go to his house—this is what I imagined—they'd go to his house, the FBI or whoever they send. They'd already know he pays his taxes. I mean, they'd probably know a fair amount about him, right? Then they look into things and his wife has a Middle Eastern name. He drives a truck. He could be carrying materials. See where this goes? He's obviously a threat, this man who glows in the library and drives to the point of collapse to reach his destination. A man who's gotten himself some books so he doesn't get into trouble on route. He stops for the night. Coffee.

JACOB   No hookers.

BERNIE   And he reads. So he can answer his kids' school questions.

JACOB   And stay honest regarding my vows.

[BERNIE *hands him a book.*]

BERNIE   He reads to keep the stark, abstract fatigue from bearing loneliness. He doesn't want another sexually transmitted disease, either. He's taken out three hardcover volumes. He likes the look of them. The heft. The pages against his rough hands. He's working over a passage in Steinbeck. It just sneaks up on him.

JACOB   [*Looking at pages in awe.*] I didn't know. How it could—I just didn't know this. I didn't know a person could think of this.

BERNIE   So, what could it be about a man crying under a moonlit sky in the cab of his Freightliner Classic XL that sends out a warning to the government?

[*A man,* EAGAN, *seated at a table, looks up from his book and speaks, his rapid delivery makes his ruminations almost comic, were it not for real turmoil:*]

EAGAN   The stars. I was looking up anything I could find on the stars. There was this article about dark matter that scared the shit out of me, and I was putting my whole family through hell about it. Just the way my daughter has pushed me to my limits with her inquiries into the absurdity of language and meaning. Meaning there is none. No meaning. Which I take as bleak and troublesome coming like that from a young person. And, I guess, it challenged something deep and confronted me on a personal level. Like my fatherhood, my being a parent was all of a sudden a pointless and sorry thing. I like talking at the dinner table. It's time well spent if you put aside other concerns. But, I was depressing everyone, and I thought maybe there's another way, you know, with more information, to look at things. To look at this dark matter and my daughter's questions and turn it all into a metaphor of well being instead of what it clearly represented to me now as a crushing void with the power to cancel the present, past and future. Life, albeit the sad and confusing thing though it is, still, it is what we know. And what we want our children to know. Well, apparently in my investigations of the universe there were more than a couple of references to a certain gay astronomer. He kept turning up in the materials I happened to look through. And they wanted to know—*they* being the messengers of secrecy and harbingers of silence—what I had to do with him. What interest did I have in a gay astronomer who was fired from his post in the fifties, and what business did I have with footnotes that referred to the incident in the park, and did I know him.

[*Beat.*]

Well, no, but I want to know him now.

[*The astronomer, SNOW, comes out from the stacks.*]

SNOW   So, what do you want to know?

EAGAN   What happened?

SNOW   What happened was what happens.

[*Beat.*]

I was reading maps with the U.S. Army Map Service. I loved it, really. Ever since I was a boy. The whole idea of—I don't know, pinpointing a place you can find again and again. Well, this one night—it was late. I was on my way home, and I stopped for a while to see the moonlight in Lafayette Park across from the White House. The light fell on two men. Kissing. And I was thinking how beautiful they were. How just—well, that. When the cops descended.

EAGAN   And what? They arrested you for just being there?

SNOW   You're in the vicinity, you must be gay. You're gay—you're implicated. I was taken in for investigation of a morals charge. It was dropped, but I was fired from my job. And—I don't know how to say this without coming off as some kind of fallen protagonist in postwar B movie America—I was banned from all future employment with the federal government.

EAGAN   But you have a Ph.D. from goddam Harvard. You were a World War Two combat veteran, for Chrissakes.

SNOW   Yeah. And I was a Jewish queer in a blue state.

EAGAN   Well, there are plenty of other things to be afraid of. Like, for fucking example, the void in the universe.

SNOW   Not as terrifying as gays having their kiss or marrying, though.

EAGAN   Your name in a footnote that puts people in my business is what scares me. Well, and our finite time on the planet.

SNOW   I have a bad feeling everyone's going to know more than they want to about what it's like to get comfortable with hiding. Living in code. It makes for an anxious world.

EAGAN   Just—How do people with no virtue other than they're straight or white or claim to have God's blessing get the power to ruin lives?

SNOW   The crazy thing is, if our ideas, our acts, our humanness could come from the dark into the light, we'd be seen. And we'd see ourselves. And wouldn't it be better to be judged in full view?

[*Beat.*]

Because we all bear scrutiny.

EAGAN   Jesus. The dark matter. It's *us*. It's *here*.

[*Beat.*]

I think my daughter is gay. I want to tell her something. About you. About the earth from a distance.

SNOW   We're grand and possible from a distance. But, we live here.

[*Lights on another area. MILO, an FBI agent, approaches SONIA's door.*]

MILO   Sonia Federman?

SONIA Yes?

MILO Are you in possession of library books, the titles of which are—

SONIA [*Overlapping.*] They send people now? They send actual people to come to your house and collect fines? God, I know they're overdue. I was meaning to bring them back ages ago. Well, anyhow, what do I owe?

MILO [*Showing his badge.*] Can you tell me where were your parents were born?

SONIA What?

MILO What country are your parents from?

SONIA Do *they* have books overdue?

MILO [*Thrown by her.*] I really don't know. Federman—it sounds foreign.

SONIA We're pretty much all foreign, aren't we?

MILO Meaning?

SONIA We all come from somewhere else. If you trace it back. You know, give me your tired and your poor, your huddled masses yearning to breathe free.

MILO Huddled masses.

[*Beat.*]

Lenin?

SONIA Emma Lazarus. Statue of Liberty.

MILO [*Embarrassed not to have known.*] Right. Right. So, just to verify. You're a teacher in the public school system?

SONIA Senior English and drama. I taught ninth grade for a while but they were all about turning into the next thing not the thing they were, and it was pretty much totally bogus totally all of the time.

MILO   Drama. That's putting on plays. You put on plays?

SONIA   We read plays.

MILO   You don't put them on? I thought you had to put plays on.

SONIA   Well, you can put them on. Some people put them on. But this is a literature class. We read them.

MILO   And these plays, you took them out of the public library.

SONIA   They didn't have them in the school library.

MILO   So, the school didn't authorize them.

SONIA   They didn't *not* authorize them. I do this all the time. We all do. Supplementary materials. Oil for education, not so much left for books. We all do this.

MILO   [*Reading titles on his notepad.*] *There's a Dead Mule in the Street. Silverstein & Company. It's Our Town, Too. My Burka, Your Bris.* Do these play titles sound familiar to you?

SONIA   You want them back. I'll get them. Jesus.

MILO   I tried out for one in school. A play. I mainly wanted to get next to a girl named Cheryl. I wanted to touch her sweater. She was in all the plays. She was in the halls. She was everywhere. I wanted to get her pregnant.

SONIA   You wanted to get her pregnant?

MILO   In the play. The guy in the play.

SONIA   Your character.

MILO   My character. *He* wanted to. I would've—I mean, me myself, who *I* am, I would've pulled out.

SONIA   Do you remember what play this was?

MILO   I kissed her. And I said something. I don't know if it was even in the play, the words I used. And then I got an erection and I didn't get the part, and Cheryl, she sees it. She sees I'm hard and says to the drama coach I think he'd be good in the part.

SONIA Maybe he didn't want her to get pregnant. You know? It was the dramatic event. It was messy. It complicated things. That's why it was in the play, probably. I mean, *you* would have been careful. But then your life isn't literature.

MILO I have to do this, you know. I'm in the world of undercover. I'm looking for inconsistencies and subtexts. Subtexts of peril. I don't just wait for it to unravel. I'm supposed to recognize a warning.

SONIA We're the same then. Always looking for something. Except, I don't report people for their thoughts. Or their questions. Or their boners.

MILO I'm sorry I let that slip. I didn't mean anything towards you. I'm not—

SONIA I know the moment of taking someone else's words, of thinking them, of being in a play and saying someone else's idea of things. Because we *can*. We can kiss and not actually get pregnant. We can subvert ideas and reconstruct history and express ourselves with our cocks and our breasts and our intellect and our hands all over each other. We can say what we mean and don't mean and might do and would never do and get hard and wet and thankful. That's why I took those plays out of the library. That's what you can do in a play.

MILO I have to make a report. I have to write something down. I have to say something.

SONIA "It is difficult to get the news from poems but men die miserably every day for lack of what is found there." Say that.

[*Lights up on* BERNIE.]

BERNIE [*To audience.*] When I was a girl, I wanted to be a choreographer. I didn't know what a choreographer was. It just sounded good. So, my father sent me to the dictionary. Go look it up, he said. Go to the library and look it up. And I looked up as many words as I could so I could stay there all afternoon. I went to the shelves and opened books to passages that were exciting even though I didn't understand most of what I read. There was always something I found wherever the books fell open that kept me coming back. And keeps me. To this day.

[JANEL *approaches the desk and hands* BERNIE *a piece of paper.*]

JANEL   I know I shouldn't be asking, Miss Bernie, but I was sleepless over that novel you got me started on, and I have a paper due on something not anywhere near as compelling, so if you could just find this one fact I need, or tell me where *I* could, you'd be my hero.

BERNIE   Did you try the Internet?

JANEL   That's just a thing that leads me astray. And it doesn't have the same good smell as in here. Whiff of pencils and eraser. The dusty stirring paper thing.

BERNIE   [*Pleased, enjoying her.*] So, did you get to that passage where I put the Post-it?

JANEL   It was wicked original. And sad, a little bit.

BERNIE   I've got something else I want to show you—but not until after you turn in your paper. Deal?

JANEL   I can't totally make that promise.

[BERNIE *takes the paper from* JANEL *and walks to stacks.*]

[*To audience.*]

My librarian. She's always got a list of things for me to read. I do that thing with people. Make them mine. Anyhow, sometimes she just sends me to the stacks and says, just take any book. Read the first sentence. Tells me, Janel, one thing leads to another. You go to a place you didn't think was where you needed to go, and it maybe takes you to the place you were meant to find.

[EAGAN, *sitting nearby, responds to her.*]

EAGAN   But what if on our way to the thing we were meant to find, we come across a—paragraph, a footnote, something irreverent, something ardent and unpopular. Does that make you part of a conspiracy? Or are you just part of the fabric of things, part of the mystery, searching for some place to land.

JANEL   Yeah. Looking for home.

[BERNIE *re-enters.*]

BERNIE   [*To audience.*] An older person came up to me very distressed one day. She said, "There is a giant—well-organ," she said. "On the screen and I can't get it off." New way to flash someone, I guess. Well, no, we don't want to encourage people in the library to surf pornography on the Internet. We don't want that. But what becomes of us when a place that gives permission to get lost in a book is turned into a place where you can be found. What do you call that?

[*Then echoing her father.*]

Go. Look it up!

[MILO *walks in.*]

MILO   Excuse me, I need a poem.

BERNIE   You need a poem.

MILO   I'm looking for a poem. Can you get me a poem?

BERNIE   Which one?

MILO   I don't know.

BERNIE Well, can you give me a line or something to go on? The name of the poet.

MILO A poem about a poem.

BERNIE You'd think that would narrow the field.

MILO How about a play, then?

BERNIE We've got plays. Again, though—

MILO A truly great play.

BERNIE About love or heroes or social injustice or ordinary struggles or a family saga or one person's place in the sweep of history? Betrayal, redemption, loss?

[*He refers to his notebook.*]

MILO The one about a *Streetcar*. Or a *Salesman*. Or a *Town*. Or, *Angels*. Or—a *Raisin*? Do you have any of those?

BERNIE [*Surprisingly moved by him.*] We have them all. Every one.

[*She walks toward stacks, speaking to audience.*]

You know, librarians go to jail for this. For giving someone a play. A poem. Losing sleep and teeth and years in prison. This is hard for us here to know. We don't see what goes on in other places. This is how we're imprisoned in this country. By not seeing.

[BERNIE *offers some books to* MILO.]

JANEL [*To the entire place.*] Listen up! I want to make a bitch beautiful poem to my librarians in other places.

[*A moment. Then, in spoken word, def poetry jam style:*]

Someone gives you a book
Don't close it
She chose it

Turn a page to possess it
Finesse it
Stress on the words that repeat you
Any life can complete you
Arranged on a shelf is a wealth is your stealth
Is the health of your mind and my mind is my own and I own
what I know, what I don't, what I will when I chill with the pages
I read when I need to know
So, my eyes are wide to go inside and find what's behind the
world unfurled when I open a book
Yo, open a book. Don't hurl it.

[*After a moment, one by one,* EVERYONE *in the library begins* reading out loud *from his/her books. This builds, until their lush cacophony fills the air.*]

[BERNIE *takes in the music of words. Then, as if issuing a sweeping challenge to anyone who would silence this joyful noise:*]

BERNIE   Shred that!

• • •

The News

Billy Aronson

Billy Aronson

Billy Aronson's plays have been produced by Playwrights Horizons, Ensemble Studio Theatre, Woolly Mammoth Theatre, and Wellfleet Harbor Actors Theatre; they have been awarded a grant from the New York Foundation for the Arts and a commission from the Magic Theatre, and published in three previous volumes of The Best American Short Plays. His TV writing includes scripts for Cartoon Network's *Courage the Cowardly Dog*, MTV's *Beavis & Butt-Head*, Nickelodeon's *Wonder Pets* (head writer first season), and PBS's *Postcards from Buster* (Emmy Nomination). His writing for the musical theatre includes the original concept and additional lyrics for the Broadway musical *Rent*. He lives in Brooklyn with his wife, Lisa Vogel, and their children, Jake and Anna. For more, visit billyaronson.com.

··· **production note** ···

The News was originally produced by Ensemble Studio Theatre—The LA Project, Michael C. Mahon and Laura Jane Salvato, Artistic Directors. The cast featured Jacqueline Wright, Liz Ross, Ray Xifo, and Hiram Kasten, under the direction of Lisa James.

The New York premiere was produced by Ensemble Studio Theatre, William Carden, Producing Artistic Director. The cast featured Diana Ruppe, Geneva Carr, Thomas Lyons, and Grant Shaud, under the direction of Jamie Richards.

• • •

[*A hospital bed and two chairs.* KAREN *sits in the bed wearing a smock.* HILLARY *sits in a chair wearing a suit and holding a wrapped bouquet. Both have cell phones within reach.*]

HILLARY   So the thing is still there.

KAREN   They decided not to take it out at the last minute. I had symptoms that didn't add up, so they did a test and they found something else.

HILLARY   So when will they take out this other thing?

KAREN   Well, they can't because of where it is and how far it is along.

HILLARY   But I don't see why they don't get the first thing. They said they could just go in and get it, the sooner the better.

KAREN   There's no point in going in there because this new thing's a lot further along.

[HILLARY *starts to cry.*]

KAREN   I'm not crying because tears don't help.

[HILLARY *struggles not to cry.*]

KAREN   There are things they can give me and methods that might slow things down.

[HILLARY's *cell phone rings. She ignores it.*]

> I'm going to make every choice with my eyes open, just like I've been doing from day one. I've been getting the name of every doctor and every hallway, otherwise you run the risk of waking up in the dark with no idea why parts of you are numb and all these smells are coming out of you.

[KAREN's *cell phone rings. It has a different tone than* HILLARY's. *She checks it, touches a button to stop the ringing.*]

KAREN I'm only taking it if it's George, which it's not because he thinks I'm in the operating room 'til four, he doesn't know they did the test. You thought I was supposed to be out of the operating room at two because that was the original plan, but they pushed it back to four and I forgot to tell people, but it's good you came early after all. Talk to me about work.

HILLARY It's okay.

KAREN I can't wait to get back, you have no idea about these new drugs, or maybe I could work from home, there are side effects but it's a trade-off, like the ones I'm on now.

[HILLARY's *phone rings. She reaches to turn it off.*]

HILLARY I'm sorry, I'll turn it off—

KAREN Leave it on. Sound is good. Maybe I should call George but he's at work, he really has to get caught up and he'll be here soon anyway. The only other call I'd take would be Abigail, who's on a trip with her choir, I said she should go.

HILLARY How is she?

KAREN She's fine. She's a fine child. She's her own person. She's become her own person and I love the person she's become. She expresses herself. She makes her own decisions. She's so aware of the world and her position in it. How did it happen so fast, she's only ten years old, do you realize that? But you can already see the person she's become, and I'm so proud of that little girl, I adore her so much.

[HILLARY*'s cell phone rings. She ignores it.*]

KAREN We had some hard times, she and I. She didn't like me for a while. But it turns out the reason she didn't like me is because she thought I didn't like her. Imagine that. But now she knows I really like her and she likes me again.

HILLARY [*Nods.*] Mmm.

KAREN The thing is to do what you can, that's the challenge, if you want to jog, you jog or there are machines, or if you want to go to the movies, then you just do it and people understand and if you can't sit there or there's trouble controlling the muscles in your face at a restaurant or if there are sounds that you're making, people accept that, or if you're embarrassed, you can pace yourself or go home if you have to and there are tricks you can learn, like if your balance tilts, you can compensate, or if things spin or there's a shaking in your chin, you can compensate, or if it stings when you press down your foot.

[KAREN*'s phone rings. She checks, doesn't answer.*]

But the thing is to keep going because everybody's working within a clock, nobody knows it but we all have a different clock and you can't possibly know what it says so the thing is to get in as many meaningful moments with people who mean something to you, a meaningful moment just happens in a time and a place, planning doesn't help, you can organize all you want but then nothing happens but then something just presents itself and you try to enjoy it.

HILLARY You mean so much to me, Karen.

KAREN Well, sure we mean a lot to each other, all of us, we've done so much and we appreciate each other and what we've done.

[HILLARY's *phone rings. She ignores it.*]

And of course we've been angry, we've had these tensions, but that comes from trying to accomplish what's best for us all, which we each try to do in our individual ways, so of course there's frustration, but of course we forgive without even explaining because there just isn't time for it all.

HILLARY Sure.

KAREN It's so important, to just, to stop with the, I really need to just do what I, you know, to get out, and go to the beach. Sunshine. The sound of water. To look out at all that water. To feel the wind and the sunshine on your arms and hear the water and people talking, and laughing. There's laughing. And you can join right in with the laughing. As long as you can breathe you can laugh.

[*Pause.* DAVID *enters wearing a suit, carrying a wrapped bouquet and cell phone.*]

DAVID Karen, it must be so great to have it over.

[*To* HILLARY.]

Hi.

HILLARY Hi.

[DAVID's *cell phone rings, in yet a different tone. He ignores it.*]

KAREN They didn't take it out after all, they did another test and they found something else because I had these symptoms.

DAVID Shit.

KAREN There are treatments that can slow things down and I'll make my choices with my eyes open.

DAVID Shit. Karen.

KAREN I'm not cursing and I'm not crying. I'm going to do what I can do.

DAVID You need another opinion.

KAREN What do you mean?

DAVID People make mistakes. It happens all the time.

KAREN I know they're right.

DAVID Who told you? A specialist?

KAREN My body told me.

DAVID That's not a . . . what does George say?

KAREN He's at work, he doesn't know about the test yet.

DAVID I'll talk to him. You're getting a second opinion, and you're joining a group. There are all kinds of groups. I'll help you find just the right group.

KAREN A group of what?

DAVID You know, people who know all about your situation.

KAREN I should get into, a situation?

DAVID I mean a group of people who understand what you're going through. You can just open up, believe me, it's an opportunity. We're all so covered up. We have to be, to get by. But they have ways to help you let everything go. And these bonds develop, these wonderful bonds, and there's a whole new quality. What exactly did they tell you? Was the person a specialist? What exactly did they say?

KAREN When they prick your arm to knock you out there's a flash where you're fifteen and you're standing at the sink and there's a twitch in a part of you that you didn't know you had but when you touch it it's crawling away.

[*Pause.*]

KAREN What's it like out?

HILLARY It's nice.

KAREN   They said it was going to rain.

HILLARY   It cleared up.

DAVID   They don't give you anything to put flowers in. I'll round something up.

[DAVID *stands.*]

KAREN   Sit. Bodies in the room is good.

[DAVID *sits. Pause.* GEORGE *enters, wearing a suit, carrying as many balloons as he can hold.*]

GEORGE   You're supposed to be in the operating room.

KAREN   I thought you were working.

GEORGE   I got halfway there and it hit me I should have balloons in your room when you got out.

[HILLARY *and* DAVID *stand.*]

KAREN   Sit.

DAVID   We can walk around while you guys talk.

KAREN   Sit down.

[HILLARY *and* DAVID *sit.* DAVID*'s cell phone rings. He reaches to turn it off.*]

KAREN   Leave it on.

GEORGE   These balloons are wet. How did they get wet? Something happened to these balloons to make them wet. Okay. Specks on the sidewalk. It rained for a few seconds. That's right. It rained. But that was before I bought the balloons. So that's not it. Oh wait. My hip is sore. I was lying on the back of a car. A car backed into me as I crossed the street. I was in the middle of the intersection on the back of a car. People were shouting are you all right. So the balloons got wet from the back windshield. Except they were still in the bag, and the bag wasn't opened, so that's not it. Wait, wait. When I came out of the elevator I ran right into a guy who had a cup of soda that he probably spilled all over. But it was cola, and the droplets on the balloons are clear. So maybe I went back out and it rained again. Or maybe the ceiling leaks. Or maybe the balloons are sweating.

[GEORGE's *cell phone rings, in yet a different tone. He ignores it, drops the balloons.*]

KAREN Don't leave them on the floor if they're wet.

GEORGE Hi.

DAVID Hi.

HILLARY Hi.

KAREN My friends are here because I didn't tell them the operation got pushed back.

GEORGE They're always changing things here and I'm sick of it.

KAREN They decided not to operate after all because they ran another test.

GEORGE I could have gotten you the best doctor in the world if you could have just been ready one day sooner.

KAREN This hospital has the best reputation in the world.

GEORGE What does a reputation do? Nothing. I could have gotten you the number one guy.

KAREN The doctors here are the best anywhere.

GEORGE They're not number one. The number one guy is in Europe by now.

KAREN Could you pick up the balloons?

GEORGE I'll blow up the last one so you can see the whole effect.

KAREN Pick up the balloons and sit down 'cause we have to talk.

[GEORGE *tries to blow up the last balloon. He's out of breath, so it's difficult, noisy and messy.*]

GEORGE Fuck.

[*He stretches the balloon again and again, tries to blow it up again, finally fills it up. Then he tries to tie it, but his fingers are weak and shaky so it's a struggle. Unable to tie the balloon, he finally lets it go; it shoots away in all directions.*]

KAREN Pick up the balloons.

GEORGE You can't talk to me like that.

KAREN I've said it every other way.

GEORGE You can't use that tone on me.

KAREN I'll say what I have to say in the way I need to say it to be heard.

GEORGE If you want me to hear you, you can't use that tone.

KAREN I don't want the floor to be slippery and the balloons bother me down there.

GEORGE Please explain how balloons on the floor is more disturbing than phones ringing.

KAREN I just wasn't expecting balloons.

GEORGE At your surprise party you said they made all the difference.

KAREN That was for Abigail's party and she was six.

GEORGE It was for your birthday and you said they made all the difference.

KAREN It was for Abigail.

GEORGE It was for you, it was your surprise party.

KAREN If you keep saying it does, that make it true?

GEORGE I don't even hear you when you use that tone.

KAREN Do you realize that you're yelling?

GEORGE I don't even hear you when you use that tone.

KAREN Do you realize you're yelling?

GEORGE I don't hear what you're saying.

KAREN You're yelling. Do you hear yourself?

GEORGE You're the one who's yelling at me in front of your friends.

[DAVID *and* HILLARY *stand.*]

KAREN and **GEORGE** Sit down.

[DAVID *and* HILLARY *sit. Their cell phones ring.*]

GEORGE I'm sorry I didn't bring flowers like your friends but you used to love balloons.

KAREN Please just get them off the—

GEORGE [*Shouts.*] I'm getting the balloons off the floor! Are you happy I'm getting them up even though there are no strings to hang them on and not one desk to put them on just like there are no vases here? If this is the best hospital in the world oh I'd hate to see the worst hospital in the world, I really would hate to see that. Get up. Get up up up.

[*In a frenzy* GEORGE *bats the balloons up into the air. As they scatter* GEORGE *runs around the room to keep them up.* GEORGE *and* KAREN *break into laughter. They're laughing so hard they can hardly get the words out:*]

GEORGE The time with your uncle and the—

KAREN Yeah—, yeah—

[*Overwhelmed by laughter, Karen flops back and George sinks to his knees. The laughter subsides.*]

KAREN I'm gonna miss you.

[GEORGE *hides his head between his legs.* KAREN *covers her eyes with one hand.* DAVID *and* HILLARY *look away in different directions.*]

[GEORGE *rises, moves slowly towards* KAREN.]

[GEORGE*'s phone rings.* KAREN*'s phone rings.* HILLARY*'s phone rings.* DAVID*'s phone rings. All four phones ring, forming a strange chord that repeats in a certain rhythm, to provide a musical background.*]

GEORGE   You're coming home tonight?

KAREN   Do we still have the chicken?

GEORGE   I'll send out for chicken.

[DAVID *and* HILLARY *hold their bouquets in one hand, phones in the other, move closer to* GEORGE *and* KAREN, *sing softly into their phones as they observe.* GEORGE *and* KAREN *rub one another.*]

DAVID and **HILLARY**   They're having dinner at home.

KAREN   At our table? On our plates?

GEORGE   With our forks and our knives.

DAVID and **HILLARY**   They're having dinner at home.

KAREN   What's on TV?

GEORGE   Your show's on at nine.

KAREN   Is it a rerun?

GEORGE   It's a good one.

DAVID and **HILLARY**   They're watching TV.

KAREN   And then can we go for a walk?

GEORGE   Let's go for a walk.

DAVID and **HILLARY**   They're going for a walk.

[GEORGE *and* KAREN *put their hands together, rub one another's hands.*]

DAVID and **HILLARY**   They're holding hands.

• • •

Heights

Amy Fox

Amy Fox

Amy Fox is a playwright and screenwriter. Her plays include: *By Proxy*, *Summer Cyclone*, *One Thing I Like to Say Is*, *Heights*, *Honeymoon Hotel*, and *Farm Boys* (co-writer). *By Proxy* was commissioned by the Alfred P. Sloan Foundation in 2006. *One Thing I Like to Say Is* was named a finalist for the 2006 Susan Smith Blackburn Prize, and was produced by Clubbed Thumb in its Summerworks Festival in 2007. Amy's other plays have been produced or developed by the Ensemble Studio Theatre, Primary Stages, the Lark, Soho Rep, New River Dramatists, and the Blue Heron Arts Center. Her work has also been produced in London, San Francisco, Austin, St. Paul, Albuquerque. and Orlando. *Summer Cyclone* and *Heights* are published by Dramatists Play Service. She was a member of Youngblood for five years and is currently a member of the Ensemble Studio Theatre.

Fox adapted her one-act play, *Heights*, for the screen, and the resulting Merchant Ivory film was released in theatres nationwide in 2005. *Heights* premiered at the Ensemble Studio Theatre. She has an MFA in fiction writing from Brooklyn College and teaches screenwriting at NYU's graduate film program. She lives in Brooklyn, New York.

characters

ALEC, a man in his early 20s
ISABEL, a woman in her early 20s
JONATHAN, a man in his early 20s

• • •

[*The rooftop of a city apartment. Night. The surrounding apartment buildings can be seen, many of their windows lit. There is a door leading to stairs inside the apartment building. ISABEL is lying on a deck chair half asleep. She has headphones on and a large sweatshirt draped over her. ALEC enters, speaking on his cell phone. He is also carrying a bottle of wine, two glasses and several candles. ISABEL's chair is off to the side and turned away from ALEC, and he does not notice her. As he speaks, ALEC sets a bottle of wine and two glasses on a small iron table, and places the candles carefully. ISABEL notices him and watches, removing her headphones.*]

ALEC   Right, sesame chicken, imperial chicken, right, and steamed dumplings. Well, I'm on the roof. The roof. The top, right. Well, you've come up here before. We've done this before. A few weeks ago, you sent the guy up here, right. Okay. Okay fine. We'll come down. Okay, in the lobby, okay. No, don't call. Don't call me up here. We'll come down, let's say three o'clock, we'll come down. Right.

[ALEC *hangs up the phone and puts it in his coat pocket. He attempts to light the candles, but without much success.*]

[*Continuing.*] Come on now. Come on. There you go. Theeere you go.

ISABEL   Excuse me.

[ALEC, *startled, lets the match go out.*]

ALEC   [*Muttering.*] Fuck.

ISABEL   Sorry. The thing is . . . the thing is—

ALEC Hi.

ISABEL It's—is this some kind of occasion?

ALEC Pardon me, I didn't see you there. I didn't realize anyone was . . .

ISABEL You reserved the roof for this occasion.

ALEC No. I didn't. Pardon me but at two o'clock in the morning, I honestly didn't think anyone would be . . .

ISABEL Everyone's asleep, you thought.

ALEC Possibly. Possibly they're asleep, possibly they're not asleep, I don't care honestly. What I care is, they're not on the roof. They're asleep, they're at work, they're drinking chicken soup . . . what I care is—

ISABEL I'm on the roof.

ALEC Right. Which is why you and I have . . . we have a little situation.

ISABEL I haven't slept in three nights.

ALEC Right. And my situation is this. I was planning to come up here and eat some Chinese food.

ISABEL Chinese food.

ALEC Right. And you were planning, well, God knows what you were planning, but since you haven't slept in three nights, allow me to suggest—

ISABEL What? What's your suggestion? I should go back to bed. I should go back downstairs and climb into bed.

ALEC Well, I don't know. Maybe you were planning to sleep on the roof. But I should tell you I don't think it's a particularly wise idea.

ISABEL And why is that?

ALEC Well, for one thing, sleepwalking. There's always sleepwalking to think about. And there's another thing. You could get all kinds of weirdos coming up here with all kinds of weirdo ideas. Chinese food, well, that could be the least of it, if you know what I mean.

ISABEL I haven't slept in three nights. I came up here for peace and quiet.

ALEC There must be other places. Other peaceful, quiet places.

ISABEL Are you expecting someone?

ALEC What?

ISABEL You're expecting someone.

ALEC Yes. I am, in fact, expecting someone.

ISABEL Of course.

ALEC And the truth is, if you must know, the person I'm expecting does not expect to see the two of us. Only one of us is expected.

ISABEL Who is she?

ALEC Nobody you know, I'm sure.

ISABEL Your girlfriend?

ALEC Right. My girlfriend.

ISABEL Does she have a name?

ALEC Yes. Rhonda.

ISABEL You're right, I don't know any Rhondas.

ALEC Well, that's fine. No reason you should know any Rhondas. No reason you should be standing here when Rhonda comes up those steps.

ISABEL You could introduce us.

ALEC Yes, but this, this was supposed to be a private rendezvous. So I would appreciate it, I really would appreciate it, if you could go and do your not sleeping someplace else.

ISABEL I was here. I was here first.

ALEC Yes but—

ISABEL I made this decision. I unplugged the clock and got out of bed and decided to come to the roof. I don't have the energy to make a different decision.

ALEC That's ridiculous. That's the most ridiculous thing I've ever heard.

ISABEL I am not going to sit here, at two o'clock in the morning, and brainstorm other alternatives. I was . . . comfortable.

ALEC Fine. Nobody's asking you to brainstorm. I am simply asking that you consider my situation.

ISABEL Your situation.

ALEC Yes. My situation. Maybe tonight's the big night. Maybe I was going to propose.

ISABEL Were you?

ALEC Yes. I was going to propose to my girlfriend.

ISABEL At two o'clock in the morning.

ALEC Rhonda works nights. She gets off at one.

ISABEL So where is she?

ALEC I don't know. She'll be here any minute.

ISABEL Because if she isn't coming—

ALEC She's coming. And I'll tell you another thing. If you can't respect that, if you can't respect the fact that my girlfriend is coming up here and I was going to propose, I'll tell you something else. Rhonda has suspicions. She's got all these suspicions. So here I am, ready to propose, and Rhonda's going to come up those steps and see us here, talking like this, wine and candles all around, and she's going to make assumptions. Is that what you want? You want Rhonda to make assumptions.

ISABEL Listen Mr. . . .

ALEC Alec.

ISABEL Okay, Alec. Listen for a sec, can you? That doesn't make sense. Rhonda knows you're up here, right? So why would she, why would she come up those stairs, and think that you would plan this thing and get her up here, and then accidently be here with some woman you're seeing? It doesn't make sense.

ALEC That was an explanation. You want to psychoanalyze, take it apart, fine. You don't like that explanation, I'll give you a different one. Your own explanations haven't exactly been satisfactory. You decided to come to the roof. So what?

ISABEL I can't explain it.

ALEC Why not?

ISABEL I don't know. Because I can't.

ALEC Try.

ISABEL Why?

ALEC I don't know.

ISABEL Ever had insomnia?

ALEC Not really.

ISABEL You do things, when it's two in the morning and you can't sleep, you do things you wouldn't do at any other time. Because you can't stay in bed. It's not an option. Maybe there's this person breathing next to you, not snoring even, just breathing, but it's loud, and you tell yourself, it's not loud, it's like the ocean roaring,

and you can sleep next to that. But then all you want to do is
swim into the ocean, and there isn't one. There's just this man
next to you, and maybe you had a fight before bed, and maybe
you didn't, but there wasn't a wild passionate anything. And he
turned off the light, and fell asleep right away, but you have to get
out of there. So you take taxis. That's what I do, usually, get in a
taxi and ride around and get back before my cash runs out.

ALEC Taxis.

ISABEL You asked for an explanation.

ALEC I asked—

ISABEL I know, the roof. I'm getting there. The taxi thing gets
expensive. And the funny thing is, it was my fiancé who suggested
the alternative.

ALEC Your fiancé?

ISABEL Yeah. You'd think he'd hate it, waking up alone all the time.
And he does, I guess, but maybe he's used to it. I was complaining
about the taxi thing, and he said what do you want, and I said
privacy, my own space, where do you find that, and he said I don't
know, sometimes I go up to the roof. It was a couple of months
ago that he said it. And he's right, you know. It's . . . very . . .

ALEC Private?

ISABEL Yes, private. The other night, it was private. Tonight, well,
we're dealing with tonight.

ALEC Are we?

ISABEL You were going to give me a different explanation.

ALEC A what?

ISABEL A different explanation. You said, a few minutes ago, that if I
didn't like your explanation, you had a different one.

ALEC   I never said that.

ISABEL   You did. You said those words exactly.

ALEC   I'm wondering something. Do you think, do you think there are many . . . couples, in this building? Engaged couples?

ISABEL   Excuse me?

ALEC   Such as yourself. I'm only wondering, if it's a common thing, if there are an infinite variety of . . . combinations, such as yourself and . . .

ISABEL   Jonathan.

ALEC   Jonathan. And your name, I seem to have forgotten to . . . your name is . . .

ISABEL   Isabel.

ALEC   Right. Isabel.

ISABEL   You were going to give me an explanation.

ALEC   Right.

ISABEL   I'm beginning to think Rhonda's not coming. I'm beginning to think . . .

ALEC   What are you beginning to think?

ISABEL   I have no idea.

ALEC   Here. Take this, take thirty bucks, and grab yourself a cab.

ISABEL   You're giving me thirty dollars?

ALEC   Yes.

ISABEL   What, to leave the roof?

ALEC   Yes. Now.

ISABEL   Now?

ALEC   Preferably now.

ISABEL   I'm not taking your money.

ALEC   I don't want it.

ISABEL   You don't want thirty bucks.

ALEC   Not this thirty bucks. I mean it. Go downstairs and take a cab. Have fun.

ISABEL   You're crazy.

ALEC   Just go. Please.

ISABEL   Okay.

ALEC   Okay?

ISABEL   Okay.

[ISABEL *crosses to the door, opens it, and steps into the stairwell. She reemerges a moment later.*]

ISABEL   [*Continuing.*] Somebody's coming.

ALEC   What?

ISABEL   I can hear her coming up the stairs.

ALEC   Shit. Just a sec. Just give me a sec.

[ALEC *crosses to the door and begins fiddling with the lock.*]

ISABEL   What are you doing?

ALEC   I'm trying . . . I am trying to . . .

ISABEL   You can't lock her out.

ALEC   I am trying to . . .

[ALEC *begins opening and closing the door to see if his efforts are successful.*]

ISABEL   You're crazy.

[ALEC *turns to shut the door, but finds himself face to face with* JONATHAN.]

JONATHAN Isabel. What are you doing up here?

ISABEL Well, that's a funny question. What am I always doing at two o'clock in the morning?

JONATHAN Riding taxis. I thought you rode taxis.

ISABEL Sometimes you want a change, something different. You want to go up to the roof and find a total stranger, and argue over contested territory.

JONATHAN Contested territory.

ALEC That's right. Contested territory and total strangers. That just about sums it up. I'm Alec Yoshka.

JONATHAN [*Pause.*] Jonathan Dodd.

ISABEL And then there were three.

JONATHAN Excuse me?

ISABEL It's a nursery rhyme, isn't it? And then there were two, and then there were three. Four, if you count Rhonda.

JONATHAN Who's Rhonda?

ISABEL His girlfriend. He's going to propose.

JONATHAN Are you?

ALEC Yes.

JONATHAN Big step.

ALEC Very big. But when the time is the time . . .

JONATHAN I guess.

ISABEL You guess. You only guess?

JONATHAN I wasn't . . . I really wasn't . . .

ISABEL What?

JONATHAN   I wasn't talking about us.

ISABEL   Jonathan and I have been engaged nine months. He wasn't, however, talking about us.

JONATHAN   I was talking in the general. People do talk in the general.

ISABEL   Of course they do.

JONATHAN   So, where is she?

ALEC   Who?

JONATHAN   Rhonda?

ALEC   Late. Very late. Which is probably a good thing, seeing as Isabel came up here, and you came up here . . .

ISABEL   Why did you?

JONATHAN   What?

ISABEL   Come up here.

JONATHAN   I was . . . looking for you. Why did you come up here?

ISABEL   Fresh air, space, I don't know.

[*Pause.*]

You never come looking for me.

JONATHAN   Well, tonight I did. Maybe I was concerned.

ISABEL   You're all dressed up.

JONATHAN   Well, some of us don't like to go about in our pajamas.

ISABEL   Some of us? What is that supposed to mean?

JONATHAN   I felt like getting dressed. That's all I meant.

ISABEL   And all I meant was that it's odd. You don't usually get up and get dressed in your nicest clothes and come looking for me. And how did you know I'd be up here?

ALEC   Excuse me, I'm sorry to interrupt, but seeing as Rhonda is so late, and the two of you have some business to sort out, I'm thinking I'll wait downstairs after all. If Rhonda does show up, if you wouldn't mind explaining the situation . . .

JONATHAN   Of course.

ALEC   If you wouldn't mind explaining, if she's looking for me later, that I'll be in my apartment for the rest of the night. I should be awake.

JONATHAN   Okay.

ALEC   So then the two of you can have some privacy.

JONATHAN   Okay.

ALEC   To sort out your business.

JONATHAN   [*Pause.*] We don't have any business.

ALEC   Well, maybe you do, and maybe you don't.

JONATHAN   We don't.

ALEC   So what you're saying is that there isn't any business. You came up here to find Isabel, and you found her, and you're going to go back downstairs and go to bed, and I'll go downstairs, and if Rhonda never shows up, well, that's fine. She and I will have dinner another time, and that will be it. No business of any kind.

JONATHAN   That's what I'm saying.

ALEC   Well, I don't know.

JONATHAN   You don't know.

ISABEL   What's happening?

JONATHAN   Nothing.

[ALEC *crosses to the door to go downstairs and finds it to be locked.* JONATHAN *and* ISABEL *do not see this.*]

ISABEL   Because there's this conversation happening, and I can't really understand it, but it's happening . . .

JONATHAN   Nothing's happening.

ALEC   There's just this business . . .

JONATHAN   Would you stop saying that, would you stop saying business. What are you saying?

ALEC   Maybe this was supposed to happen. That's what I'm saying. Maybe things are supposed to happen. What is it they say about truth, truth will, what is it, out?

JONATHAN   No.

ALEC   Isabel—

JONATHAN   No.

ALEC   There's somebody I want you to meet.

[*Pause.*]

This is Rhonda.

ISABEL   Excuse me?

JONATHAN   There's nobody by that name here.

ALEC   Nobody? Are you sure?

JONATHAN   Yes.

ALEC   I beg to differ, Rhonda.

JONATHAN   Don't call me that.

ALEC   Why not?

JONATHAN   Because it's a game, and I don't like games.

ALEC   Oh, it's not a game. This is serious business, Rhonda.

ISABEL   Stop it.

JONATHAN   Don't call me that.

ALEC   Isabel asks me if I'm expecting someone, I say yes, she says what's her name, I say Rhonda. Why don't you tell Isabel who I was expecting.

ISABEL   Oh my God.

ALEC   Exactly.

[*To* JONATHAN.]

Which makes you Rhonda.

JONATHAN   Nothing makes me Rhonda. My name is Jonathan Dodd.

ALEC   Mr. Jonathan Dodd, were you or were you not, on the night of April 26—

JONATHAN   No.

ALEC   Were you or were you not planning to join one Alec Yoshka—

ISABEL   Oh my God.

JONATHAN   Why are you doing this?

ALEC   Were you or were you not—

JONATHAN   Why are you doing this?

ALEC   Because it's time. When the time is the time—

JONATHAN   This is crazy. Isabel, you can't listen to him.

ALEC   You think I'm crazy, Isabel? Is that what you think? He got dressed up to look for you, and my girlfriend Rhonda is two hours late, and I'm crazy?

JONATHAN   This is like . . . an ambush.

ALEC   What do you think, Isabel?

ISABEL   I'm going to be sick.

JONATHAN You can't do this to me. Isabel—it's an ambush, you can't do this to me.

ISABEL Do what? I'm not doing anything.

ALEC It's not an ambush. It's a coincidence. She can't sleep.

ISABEL Maybe because I'll have nightmares like this.

ALEC She can't sleep so she came up here. At your suggestion, I might add. Why the fuck, pardon me, but why the fuck would you tell your wife—

ISABEL Fiancée.

ALEC Yes, exactly. Why you would tell her to come up to the roof is beyond me.

JONATHAN I never—

ISABEL You told me, a few months ago you told me, you said it was . . .

ALEC Private.

ISABEL So I came up here. And you, the two of you came up here because . . .

ALEC Because it's what we do. Where we meet.

ISABEL Jonathan. [*Pause.*] Jonathan.

JONATHAN . . . Yes.

ISABEL Yes?

JONATHAN Yes.

ISABEL For how long?

ALEC Jonathan. I think it's time . . .

JONATHAN No.

ALEC I think it's time—

JONATHAN   No. You keep saying that, but you're wrong. This is not the time. This is some random, ridiculous encounter, on a fucking rooftop. You don't do these things on a rooftop. Most people do not, at two o'clock in the morning, do these things on a rooftop.

ISABEL   Most people.

JONATHAN   Isabel, listen to me. I didn't want it to happen like this.

ISABEL   Right. And most people, they would do this how? Nine o'clock in the morning—coffee and croissants—could you pass the marmalade—and by the way there's this man downstairs—

ALEC   Upstairs.

ISABEL   What?

JONATHAN   He lives upstairs.

ISABEL   Does he? Does he, in fact, live upstairs? And do you, in fact, are you . . .

ALEC   Yes.

JONATHAN   Yes what. Am I what?

ISABEL   . . . I don't know.

JONATHAN   What's your question?

ISABEL   I don't know.

ALEC   Good, because he doesn't know the answer.

ISABEL   Just tell me one thing. How long has this been going on?

JONATHAN   About five months.

ISABEL   What were you thinking, this whole time, what were you fucking thinking?

JONATHAN   I don't know.

ALEC I think she deserves an answer.

JONATHAN You think you deserve an answer. Would you stop, would you please stop pretending you're worried about Isabel. You don't, I'm sorry, but you don't give a fuck about Isabel.

ISABEL I feel sick.

ALEC For your information, for your information Isabel and I were on this roof for a good long time before you graced us with your presence.

JONATHAN And what . . . you bonded? The two of you bonded?

ISABEL Really sick.

JONATHAN Well, that is rich, you know, that's really nice, if you bonded, because, because, you're my two favorite people in the world.

ISABEL You make me sick.

[ISABEL *crosses to the edge of the roof, leans over the side and tries to vomit.*]

JONATHAN [*Crossing to* ISABEL.] Isabel, baby—

ISABEL Don't touch me. Don't even think about touching me.

JONATHAN Okay . . . okay.

ALEC [*To* ISABEL.] Are you okay?

ISABEL Don't talk to me. You knew? You knew the whole time? About me.

ALEC Yes.

ISABEL He said he was engaged. And what did you say?

ALEC I don't . . . remember.

JONATHAN He laughed.

ISABEL You laughed?

ALEC It was . . . unbelievable.

ISABEL You laughed at me.

ALEC No—

ISABEL I'm not stupid.

ALEC No—

ISABEL You think I'm stupid.

ALEC I never—

ISABEL Well, I'm not. Ever have insomnia?

ALEC No. We talked about that already.

ISABEL No. We didn't. We didn't talk about it. Ever go to bed with someone and some nights they won't touch you? Other nights there's something, maybe not passion. A touch. Enough to make excuses, explanations. Not everyone can take your breath away. People have inhibitions, you have to understand that. But then there were those nights I couldn't begin to understand. He wouldn't even meet my eye. Can you imagine that?

ALEC You wanted to marry this person.

ISABEL I don't know.

ALEC It was okay to marry this person.

ISABEL I don't know. I don't know who it's okay to marry. The guys before, where it was all about the sex. Like they somehow slept through everything else and woke up when we went to bed. The thing is he was there in the morning. Not the morning, that's circumstance, that's nearly everybody. The afternoon. That's the one you marry, the one that gets you through the fucking afternoon.

JONATHAN Yes, I think that's right.

ISABEL I'm not talking to you.

JONATHAN It's the afternoon.

ISABEL I don't want your opinion, okay? I don't want that. I want—

JONATHAN What, what do you want?

ALEC We want the truth.

ISABEL We. We want?

ALEC The truth. Something definite.

ISABEL You want definite? How about marriage? That's supposed to be definite.

ALEC I wouldn't know.

ISABEL No, neither would I. I've got to get out of here.

[ISABEL *rushes to the door and struggles to open it, but it is locked.*]

[*Continuing.*]

Fuck. Alec, what did you do, what the fuck did you do to the door?

ALEC I was trying to—

ISABEL Yeah, well it's locked. You fucking locked it.

JONATHAN So we're stuck. What you're saying is we're stuck.

ALEC I'm sorry. I didn't realize . . .

JONATHAN We'll get down. There are ways . . . we'll get down.

[JONATHAN *crosses to the door and struggles with the lock.*]

ALEC Now this I'd like to see. Jonathan finding a way out. Sorry, down, not out. A way down.

JONATHAN Thank you. We're stuck on the fucking roof, and you're playing word games. Thanks so much, very helpful.

ALEC Couldn't resist.

JONATHAN We will get off this roof.

ALEC Ever consider jumping?

ISABEL Yes.

ALEC Please don't. You gonna be okay?

ISABEL What do you think?

JONATHAN Do you need some water?

ISABEL No.

ALEC What kind of question is that? Do we have any water? Do you see any water to be had?

JONATHAN I was trying to help.

ALEC Yeah, keep trying.

JONATHAN Where's your cell phone?

ALEC My what?

JONATHAN Your cell phone that you bring everywhere, like you're some Wall Street kid. For once it could serve a purpose.

ALEC . . . I left it downstairs.

ISABEL You what?

ALEC Left it downstairs. My cell phone.

[ISABEL *gets up and crosses to the chair over which* ALEC'*s jacket is draped.*]

JONATHAN Of course.

ALEC Isabel. What are you doing?

ISABEL [*Taking the jacket.*] Maybe I'm cold. Maybe I'm going to throw up all over your jacket.

[ISABEL *pulls the cell phone out of the jacket pocket.*]

[*Continuing.*]

Maybe I'm looking for this. You ordered the fucking Chinese food, remember?

JONATHAN You said it was downstairs.

ALEC I forgot.

JONATHAN You forgot?

ALEC I was confused. This whole night has been so crazy…

JONATHAN You had, in your jacket pocket, the one thing that could get us off this roof, and you forgot.

ALEC Isabel was kind enough to remind me. Who are you going to call?

ISABEL That's the thing. I don't know.

ALEC Two thirty in the morning.

ISABEL I have a friend … she's in Brooklyn, but she could call somebody.

[ISABEL *dials and waits.*]

Hi, Doris, it's Isabel. Either you're asleep, or you're out dancing or something. But if you're there, would you please WAKE UP. It's a bit of a crisis. So please WAKE UP and PICK UP THE PHONE. WAKE UP, DORIS.

[*Pause.*]

Okay? I guess you're not there. Okay. Bye.

[ISABEL *hangs up the phone.*]

ALEC I know somebody. He's perfect. Lives just down the block.

[ALEC *holds out his hand.*]

> Here.

[ISABEL *hands* ALEC *the phone.* ALEC *takes it and begins to dial. He stops dialing and slides open the battery compartment.* ALEC *takes the batteries out of the phone and pockets them. He holds out the phone to* ISABEL.]

[*Continuing.*]

> Here.

ISABEL   What are you doing?

ALEC   He's not home.

JONATHAN   You didn't even dial.

ALEC   He's not home. Here.

ISABEL   [*Taking the phone.*] You have the battery pack.

ALEC   True.

ISABEL   What are you doing?

ALEC   Things happen for a reason. People get stuck for a reason.

JONATHAN   We're not stuck.

ALEC   Everyone's always running away. Until one day they get stuck. They have to face things.

JONATHAN   We're not stuck. Just give us the batteries.

ALEC   Of course. Just give us some answers.

JONATHAN   Give me the fucking batteries.

ALEC   No.

[JONATHAN *lunges for the batteries, the two men struggle violently, nearing the edge of the roof.* JONATHAN *has lost control;* ALEC *attempts to defend himself.* ISABEL *watches, attempting to stop them.*]

ISABEL   Stop it—please—what are you doing??...STOP IT!
I said—JONATHAN!

[ISABEL *comes between them.*]

[*Continuing.*]

Stop it. Both of you. We're twelve stories up.

JONATHAN   [*To* ALEC.] What is it you want? What do you fucking want?

ALEC   I want you to figure it out. You're in the same goddamn fog you were the night we met. You do remember that night?

JONATHAN   Yes. Of course.

ALEC   Where we were.

JONATHAN   Oscar's. Across the street.

ALEC   Why did you go in there?

JONATHAN   I had an argument with Isabel. I wanted to sit somewhere and think things through.

ALEC   It's a gay bar. Oscar's for God's sake.

JONATHAN   I wanted a beer.

ALEC   Yes, but—

JONATHAN   It's across the street.

ALEC   Fine. Whatever.

JONATHAN   I was minding my own business.

ALEC   Yes. You were. And I checked you out, but I saw it right away.

JONATHAN   Saw what?

ALEC   That you were so far beyond confused that you came out the other side with some ridiculous kind of clarity. Sitting there in your suit, telling me about your life, about law school, interviewing at all these firms. About your girlfriend. All these words, and all I could think was, this man needs something, he needs help.

JONATHAN Help?

ALEC Yes.

JONATHAN Fuck that. No, no thank you. What was it, some kind of power trip for you, I needed your help?

ALEC No, it wasn't that. I felt for you. Because I've been there too, knowing things you can't let yourself know—

JONATHAN Alec—

ALEC Constructing this whole other life, I know that, how hard it is. But then, the first time you meet somebody—

JONATHAN Alec—

ALEC You meet somebody, and this thing that's so hard in the abstract is suddenly so right. I know that too. How you meet somebody, and for the first time—

JONATHAN Alec—

ALEC It's . . . it's . . .

JONATHAN You weren't the first time.

ALEC What?

JONATHAN There was—

ALEC What are you talking about?

JONATHAN This guy. Before.

ISABEL When?

ALEC Why didn't you tell me?

ISABEL Jonathan? . . . When?

JONATHAN   Four years ago. His name was Pete. We met in London, on Goodge Street. He used to say that word over and over, to make me laugh. He would whisper it sometimes, first thing in the morning. Before I even opened my eyes. Goodge.

ISABEL   What happened.

JONATHAN   He left me. For somebody else, this other guy. And nobody knew, it was this big secret and I couldn't talk to anybody back here, and I came home and thought maybe I imagined the whole thing. Maybe it never happened.

ALEC   You never told me.

JONATHAN   Maybe it never happened.

ALEC   Bullshit.

JONATHAN   After he left, I used to wake up to that word, like somebody had whispered it. But nobody was there. And one morning, I thought I can't do this, if it's going to feel like this ever again, I can't do it.

ISABEL   And then what, you went back to women.

JONATHAN   When I met you, it was something, it was, you were—

ALEC   Safe?

JONATHAN   A friend. That's what I needed. Like you said, if it gets you through the afternoon.

ALEC   What are you talking about? Both of you, going on about the afternoon. Wake up, it's called fear, no matter what time it is.

JONATHAN   I said I needed a friend.

ALEC   Fine. Get yourself a friend. Marry her. Plan an afternoon wedding. How about three o'clock? Let's finalize this thing right now. I think you should propose, just to clarify things. Just in case there's been any confusion.

JONATHAN What are you talking about?

ALEC I think you should propose to Isabel.

JONATHAN No.

ALEC [*Demonstrating.*] Isabel, will you marry me.

ISABEL Stop it.

ALEC Come on, just so we know where we stand.

[*To* JONATHAN.]

>Go ahead, get on one knee.

[ALEC *pushes* JONATHAN *onto his knees.*]

ISABEL Stop it. We're not—nobody's getting married.

ALEC I just want to make sure.

JONATHAN I told you already—

ALEC I just want to know what you want. Who you want. Isabel, will you . . . will you—

JONATHAN [*Breaking away.*] I won't do this.

ALEC You can't do it. You can't fucking say it. Marry me. Marry me, Isabel. On your knees. That's how it's done, isn't it?

[ALEC *pushes* JONATHAN *onto his knees again, harder this time.*]

ISABEL Please. Don't.

ALEC On your fucking knees.

[JONATHAN *breaks away and crosses to the edge of the roof to get away from* ALEC, *trying to catch his breath.* ALEC *moves back, watching.* ALEC *turns to look at* ISABEL *and then slowly crosses to* JONATHAN. JONATHAN *stares at* ALEC, *then suddenly goes to embrace him.*]

>[*Continuing; holding* JONATHAN.] You never told me, about that guy. This whole time, you were lying to both of us.

ISABEL   [*To* ALEC.] Welcome to the roof. It's a scary place.

[ISABEL *crosses to a different corner of the roof, too close to the edge.*]

JONATHAN   [*Noticing* ISABEL.] Isabel, what are you doing?

ISABEL   Were you ever, scared of heights. None of us.

JONATHAN   Please, come away from the edge.

ISABEL   Most people are terrified. They call it vertigo.

JONATHAN   Alec, the batteries. Now, before something happens.

ALEC   She'll be all right.

JONATHAN   How do you know?

ALEC   Because she's leaving you.

ISABEL   Vertigo. I'm looking. At all the windows. I just want . . . I just want to look.

JONATHAN   What about you?

ALEC   Me.

JONATHAN   Are you leaving me?

[ALEC *stares at* JONATHAN, *but does not answer. He crosses to* ISABEL *and holds out the batteries.*]

ALEC   Here. Call somebody.

[ISABEL *replaces the batteries and dials.*]

ISABEL   Yes, I'm on the roof, of my building. Three of us. And we can't, right now, get down. Yes. Please. Thanks. Yes.

[ISABEL *waits.* ALEC *and* JONATHAN *watch her. The lights fade slowly to black. Curtain.*]

• • •

He Came Home One Day While I Was Washing Dishes

K. Biadaszkiewicz

K. Biadaszkiewicz

K. Biadaszkiewicz (Christine Rusch) is a member of the Dramatists Guild and the Authors League. She has a MS.Ed. from Temple University and is the co-founder of Human Values in New Plays program at the NC Humanities Committee. Her professional affiliations include: Best Lunch Theatre Ever, Greenville Museum's New Works Theatre, Southeastern Playwrights' Conference, Playwrights' Fund of NC, and I People's Theatre, Darlington, SC. She is a fellow in Drama, SC Academy of Authors, and instructor of Fiction/Playwriting (UCLA, 1998-2001).

Her drama honors include: *Past Angry* (play), first place, Judith Siegel Pearson Award (Wayne State University); *Potato Girl* (play), Best Play (Institute for Southern Studies); *Selected One-Acts*, Special Collections, Green Library, Stanford University; *The Man Who Buried...*, Producer's Choice Award, Turnip Theatre Festival; *He Came Home One Day...*, Letter of Recognition, O'Neill Theater Center.

She has had numerous fellowships and publications in books and magazines of poetry, prose, and drama. She was the founding–artistic director of Playwrights Fund of NC & Southeastern Playwrights' Festival, and has served on ScriptWriters board of directors, Columbia, South Carolina.

characters

ACLIMA, a woman of middle age

CADI, her son, late teens

setting

Aclima's kitchen, a refugee camp in Gaza. Today.

synopsis

A young man hurries home to tell his mother the good news. It is the news she has dreaded. She does not hurry at all.

• • •

[*A tabla plays softly, perhaps the rhythms of the huda, the ancient song of the desert.*]

[*At rise* ACLIMA, *a woman of middle age, is washing dishes.*]

[*She hears the sound of her son's voice.*]

CADI'S VOICE Mama! Mama!

[ACLIMA *addresses audience.*]

ACLIMA He came home one day while I was washing dishes.

[*The door opens and* CADI *enters, excited.*]

CADI Mama!

ACLIMA Whew, you startled me, Cadi.

CADI I'm sorry.

ACLIMA Is everything all right?

CADI Yes. Oh, yes!

ACLIMA Well, what is it? Your smile is bigger than your face!

CADI I have some good news.

[ACLIMA *pauses, addresses the audience.*]

ACLIMA [*To audience.*]
> I was a little worried when I heard those words. There is no good news in the camps.

CADI I have been accepted!

ACLIMA Where?

[*To audience.*]
> Of course I knew where. And my heart beat like a tabla, alone in an endless desert on a dark and moonless night.

CADI To the ranks of the brigades.

ACLIMA [*To audience.*] That's the Izz-a Din Al-Qassam Brigades.

CADI From now on, I'm going to be counted among the warriors!

ACLIMA That's . . . wonderful, my son.

CADI Are you proud of me?

ACLIMA . . . Yes. Of course I am, dear Cadi. Of course I am.

CADI The commander needs your approval for me to become a Istishahadi [suicide bomber].

ACLIMA Oh.

[*The wind blows the door open, and* ACLIMA *shivers.*]

CADI . . . What's wrong?

ACLIMA Nothing. Just a little chill.

[CADI *latches the door.*]

CADI If he has a letter from you, that means our operation will be very successful.

ACLIMA . . . Successful?

CADI Yes!

ACLIMA [*To audience.*] I am known in the camp for my handwriting.

CADI And there's a film, too. Today!

ACLIMA A film? I don't have time to watch a film.

CADI No, Mama. Not to watch it. To appear in it, with me.

ACLIMA [*To audience.*] His farewell video. A powerful encouragement for other mothers and sons, to strengthen the hearts of our people.

CADI Will you, please?

ACLIMA [*To audience.*]
There is so little else to strengthen their hearts. . . . Actually, there is nothing else.

CADI Please?

ACLIMA . . . I can't appear in a film looking like this.

CADI Thank you, Mama!

[*He starts to run out, excitedly. She hesitates, hurries after him.*]

ACLIMA Cadi?

CADI I'll be outside while you get ready.

ACLIMA Are you . . .

CADI What, Mama?

ACLIMA Are you sure that this is what you want?

CADI Oh, yes! They're going to show the film to the whole camp! All my friends will see it!

ACLIMA But are you sure it's what you want to do?

CADI   I want to show that we are a people, Mama.

ACLIMA   Of course you do.

CADI   I want to honor the memory of Papa and little Taqir.

ACLIMA   You are a good son.

CADI   I want them to know what happened to Grandpa's orchard.

ACLIMA   I know you do, but . . .

CADI   They don't hear you weeping, Mama.

ACLIMA   You imagine things. It is only the wind, my son.

CADI   It is a very strong wind that reddens my mother's eyes.

ACLIMA   You are a brave son, but surely . . .

CADI   At last everyone will see!

ACLIMA   [*To audience.*] I am . . . so proud of him.

CADI   They will understand!

ACLIMA   [*To audience.*] My son, I am so . . . very proud of him . . .

CADI   You will cry no more, Mama.

ACLIMA   I will cry no more.

CADI   At last people will understand, and everything will be the way it should be.

ACLIMA   You are the finest son in the whole world.

CADI   Don't you see? At last there will be peace!

ACLIMA   [*To audience.*] He is the finest son in the whole world.

CADI   Hurry, Mama. Hurry!

[*The tabla continues to play, softly.*]

• • •

Letty on a Bench

Jolene Goldenthal

Jolene Goldenthal

Jolene Goldenthal is an award-winning playwright and a former columnist and art critic for the *Hartford Courant*. *Describing Life: Monologs for Women*, a collection of fifty of her original monologues, was published in 2007 by Bleich Books. Her other plays have been seen at Hartford Stage, Ensemble Studio, Victory Gardens, Bailiwick Rep, Mill Mountain, Florida Studio Theater, Mercyhurst College, and the 92nd St. Y, among other venues.

Jolene Goldenthal is the founding artistic director of Hartford Playwrights Inc. and a member of the Dramatists Guild.

characters

LETTY

YOUNG LETTY

MA

CAP

PA

YOUNG CAP

• • •

[*The waiting room of a deserted urban train station.*]

[*A darkened stage. Low music heard off. A beat. A woman enters slowly, warily. She is enveloped in layers of mismatched clothing, topped by a large tattered shawl. Her hair is disordered. She wears stockings but no shoes and carries an oversized handbag. She moves to a long bench, with intense care places her bag on the floor. Reaching into it, she pulls out several small wooden figures, one by one, and places these carefully on the surface of the wide bench next to her.*]

[*The music fades. She begins to speak.*]

LETTY   In the beginning there are four.

[*She places a small figure gently on the bench.*]

        Ma . . .

[*She hesitates briefly, then pulls out another, slightly larger piece and places this firmly next to the first.*]

        Pa . . .

[*She now pulls two similar but much smaller pieces out and places these, side by side, near the MOTHER figure.*]

        Cap . . . and Letty.

[*She reaches down once more, brings out a miniature wooden house and places this to one side.*]

They live in a nice little house . . . in a nice little town.

[*She steps back to view her handiwork, moves one of the small houses slightly, moves the* MOTHER *figure nearer to the house and the figures representing the* TWO CHILDREN *closer to each other. The* PA *figure she leaves where it is.*]

Ma stays home. The kids go . . . to school.

[*She has now rearranged the figures so that* MA *is near the small house and the* TWO CHILDREN *figures are together, side by side.*]

Pa . . . goes to work.

[*She picks up the larger figure and shifts it to face away from the others.*]

It's a nice life for Ma and the kids.

[*Pause.*]

But when Pa comes home . . . things change.

[*Hastily she shifts the* CHILDREN *figures nearer to* MA.]

The kids are scared. Ma gets sick. There's a *terrible fight*!

[*With a quick sweep of her arm she crashes the figures, houses and all to the floor. She then wraps her shawl tightly around herself, climbs onto the bench, ignoring the figures scattered on the floor, and curls herself into a sleeping position.*]

[*A voice is heard off, calling. She tries to ignore it, covering her ears with her hands.*]

CAP   [*Calling off.*] Letty . . . ? Letty . . . ?

[*Entering, anxious.*]

[*The woman, silent, sits up abruptly, points a finger at him, and then curls herself up as before.*]

Letty. It's me. Cap . . .

[*A silence. The woman hugs her torn shawl tightly about her body.*]

I want to help you.

[*She sits up slowly and stares intently at him.*]

LETTY   Say that again.

CAP   I want to help you.

LETTY   Right.

[*She pulls the shawl over her head this time, stretches out once again.*]

[CAP *waits for a moment, then touches her shoulder tentatively.*]

CAP   Letty . . . Please.

LETTY   Go away, Cap. Scrambo ambo.

CAP   Forget it. That scrambo ambo stuff won't work with me.

[*She sits up with a loud sigh.*]

LETTY   Too bad.

CAP   It never worked. You ought to know.

LETTY   Guess I forgot.

CAP   [*Sitting down near her on the bench.*] I'm the only one knows you don't mean it.

LETTY   *Hell I don't!*

CAP   Come on. I'm not just anybody.

LETTY   [*After a moment.*] Yeah.

[*A small silence.*]

They . . . want to . . . take me away . . . Cap.

CAP   [*Painful.*] I know. That's how I found you.

LETTY   [*Indignant.*] *You knew I was here!*

CAP   How in the name of God's green apples . . . ? How do you figure that?

LETTY [*Sweetly.*] I sent you lots of messages.

CAP How come I never got any?

LETTY You probably weren't concentrating.

CAP Guess that's it.

LETTY I told you once I told you a zillion times. Clear your mind and concentrate and you're sure to hear from me. [*A pause.*] But you have to be thinking about me, Cap.

CAP Think about you? That's all I've been doing. I thought you were dead. I thought . . . Ah . . . Forget it.

[LETTY *reaches out, grabs his hat in one swift teasing movement, and shoves it on her head, laughing. Then, watching him eagerly, she pulls off the hat, examines it carefully, hands it back to him.*]

LETTY Nice.

CAP [*Absently shoving the hat on his head.*] Yeah.

LETTY Don't you worry yourself about me. I'm fine.

CAP [*Worried.*] Where're your shoes? Haven't you got any shoes?

[LETTY, *disinterested, gestures toward a basket nearby on the floor.*]

LETTY In there. Safe.

[CAP *promptly rummages in the basket, filled with assorted junk, and pulls out a pair of worm shoes, laces tied firmly together.*]

CAP Call this safe? [*He waves the knotted shoes at her.*] How in hell you going to get them on your feet?

LETTY When I want them I untie them. Okay?

CAP [*Struggling with the knots.*] Seems as if you haven't wanted them much lately.

[LETTY *is silent for a moment.*]

LETTY [*After a moment.*] I don't know. Sometimes I wake up . . . and it's like . . . Like I'm dreaming. I'm free, see? For the only time in my whole life . . . I'm free.

CAP Yeah.

LETTY [*A gesture, she pulls out her pocket.*] Nothing. Zilch. You got nothing. Nobody bothers you. It's great, Cap. Maybe you ought to give it a shot.

CAP Free, huh? That why you keep your shoes tied up?

LETTY [*Uncomfortable.*] Oh . . . That.

CAP Seems to me if I was doggoned free, I'd wear my shoes, if I felt like it.

LETTY Maybe I don't feel like it.

CAP Seems to me if I felt so great about everything, I'd give my brother a call. "Hey. I'm okay, Cap. Don't you worry about me now."

LETTY [*Studying her foot intently.*] Yeah.

CAP Seems to me I'd do that.

LETTY Quarter. Maybe more . . . even . . .

CAP How's that?

LETTY Phone call's a goddam quarter. What's the point of wasting a quarter . . . when you don't know if maybe anybody wants to talk to you . . . at the other end . . .

[*Her voice trails off.*]

CAP They'd want to. Take my word.

LETTY I don't know . . .

CAP When we were kids. You'd come to me anytime. With any old thing.

LETTY   You. Yeah.

CAP   Meaning?

LETTY   [*Reluctant.*] You're all right . . . But those others . . .

CAP   Ma and Pa?

[*She nods, silent.*]

They're gone, Letty. You know that.

[*She is silent.*]

Ma died. Then Pa died. You remember that.

[*She is silent for a moment.*]

LETTY   Far as I'm concerned, they're still there.

[*A long pause.*]

I don't want to talk about . . . them.

CAP   Okay. What do you want to talk about?

[*She is silent.*]

CAP   You pick, we'll talk.

[LETTY *glances at him briefly, then stretches out on the bench, her head buried in the shawl.* CAP *studies her thoughtfully, then walks to a neighboring bench, sits, watches her for a moment. He then walks over to her and shakes her gently.*]

Letty?

LETTY   [*Muffled.*] Yeah?

CAP   Look . . . I . . . I'm going. Okay?

[*She sits up quickly.*]

LETTY   What for?

CAP   Not much point hanging around here.

LETTY   We could talk . . .

CAP   If you want to.

LETTY   You pick.

CAP   I was going to let you.

LETTY   [*Pointing at him.*] You.

CAP   [*Apologetic.*] I guess I want to talk about Ma and Pa.

[LETTY *claps her hands over her ears in a single swift movement.*]

    Letty . . . Come on . . .

LETTY   No.

[CAP *takes her hands gently.*]

CAP   My pick.

LETTY   [*Looking everywhere but at him.*] Okay . . .

CAP   Honest. I don't know where to start.

LETTY   Beginning.

CAP   [*Holding her hands.*] In the beginning there was Ma . . . and Pa . . . and you . . . and me . . .

[LETTY *nods, silent.*]

    And it was okay. Pa worked. Ma stayed home. We went to school.

LETTY   After school we'd watch tee vee . . .

CAP   Have supper.

LETTY   Do some homework.

CAP   Go to bed.

LETTY   Saturday was different. I used to go shopping with Ma.

CAP   Pa took me fishing once.

LETTY [*A sudden laugh.*] You came home with that sailor hat. Wouldn't take it off your head!

CAP So you started calling me "Cap." You're the one that named me.

LETTY [*After a moment.*] Yeah.

CAP That makes you kind of special . . .

[*She is silent.*]

I used to wish . . . This is sort of crazy. [*Pause.*] I used to wish every day was Saturday. Mostly so's I could grab a hot dog someplace and skip that lousy eating business.

LETTY [*Quite suddenly younger, timid.*] Ma says to pass the salt, Pa.

CAP [*Deep voiced, strong, harsh.*] You can tell her it's over there.

LETTY She says where, Pa?

CAP If it had teeth, it'd bite her.

LETTY [*Frightened.*] Ma says . . . she says . . . "Shut up, Pa."

CAP I'll give her *shut up!* I'll give her . . . I'll give her . . . *a push in the face!* . . . I'll ! . . . I'll ! . . .

LETTY [*After a moment, in her own voice.*] You all right?

CAP [*Heavily.*] Sure.

[*A silence.*]

LETTY You're the only one I think about. Ever.

CAP I wish You'd come home with me, Letty.

LETTY I'm fine.

CAP Yeah. I know. But I figure . . . [*Attempting a laugh.*] I can make you finer . . . Maybe.

[LETTY *is silent. She stretches out, flat, gazing at the ceiling.*]

What're you looking at?

LETTY I don't know. Lights and . . . stuff . . . Makes me kind of dizzy

[CAP *grasps her arms firmly, sits her up.*]

CAP Come on now. I've got to get you out of here.

LETTY What for?

CAP I want you to come home with me. Now.

LETTY I won't stay.

CAP Stay as long as you want. That's okay. Just come home where you belong.

LETTY I don't belong! That's what I've been trying to tell you! *I don't belong there!*

CAP You can try it . . . for a while. Long as you'd like to stay . . .

LETTY How long do you think you'd want me? *How long could you stand it?*

[*A small silence.*]

I don't know. [*Pause.*] I'm all mixed up, Cap. I'm mixed up in my head . . .

CAP [*Gently.*] That's all right.

LETTY I'm so . . . I don't know . . . Like—It's me . . . And it's not me . . . And a whole bunch of people are sitting inside my head . . . Talking . . . talking . . . talking . . . Till I yell "shut up" at them and they stop for a little while and then they start again . . .

[*She rolls over, tugging the old shawl tightly around her as a protective covering. There is silence for a moment. CAP moves to her, sits on the edge of the bench, waiting, hopefully, for a response from her.*]

CAP Letty . . . ?

[*Silence.*]

Letty...?

LETTY [*Muffled.*] Go away, Cap. Go away.

[CAP *rises, walks to her, then carefully removes the shawl from her face.*]

CAP I can't leave you here like this.

LETTY I'm fine.

[*She tries to roll over, to hide herself from him. But* CAP *gently stops her.*]

CAP I've got one sister.

LETTY Big deal.

CAP Maybe it's winter, okay. I'm home, nice and warm. Food on the table. My sister's out here someplace. Cold. Maybe hungry.

LETTY You're breaking my heart.

[*She sits up.*]

So I'm hungry. So what? I'm hungry a lot.

[CAP *reaches into his pocket, finds half of a candy bar, hands it to her.*]

CAP Here.

LETTY [*Suspicious.*] What's this?

CAP You're hungry.

LETTY Don't be stupid.

CAP Eat it. Then we'll get some real food. Where do you want to go?

[*She is silent.*]

Place across the street looks okay. [*Pause.*] How about it?

LETTY I don't want to go there.

CAP Why not?

LETTY   They don't like me there.

CAP   Okay. We'll go someplace else.

LETTY   Forget it. I bet they won't let me in.

CAP   [*Pulling out a wallet.*] Money talks.

LETTY   Forget it. I'm not hungry. What gave you the idea I was hungry?

CAP   [*A shrug.*] I don't know. I just sort of figured . . . Besides you said you were hungry.

LETTY   Grow up, Cap. You can't go on believing everything any fool tells you.

CAP   You're not a fool.

LETTY   Pretty near.

CAP   Letty . . . *Please.*

LETTY   Give me my shoes.

[CAP *promptly searches in her basket, finds the shoes, unties them, hands them to her—first one, then the other.*]

CAP   Here you go.

[LETTY *places the shoe on one foot, takes the other shoe in her hand, prepares to slip it on, then stops with no warning. She stares at the shoe as though it is a strange, unknown object, then at her foot, and again at the shoe.*]

LETTY   [*Confused, she glances up at* CAP.] What am I doing this for?

CAP   Don't play games with me, Letty.

LETTY   [*Vaguely.*] I don't wear shoes. Unless I'm going someplace . . .

CAP   Well, that's okay, then. You're going with me.

LETTY   Where?

CAP   First off, we'll get something to eat.

[LETTY *obediently puts on the second shoe, stands up tentatively for a moment, then sits, defeated.*]

LETTY   Bet you no place'll let us in.

CAP   I told you. Money talks.

[*She is silent.*]

Come on. I'm starving.

LETTY   You go on ahead. Okay? I'll catch up.

[*She sits, slowly begins to remove her shoes.*]

CAP   Letty... Please. I'm trying to help you.

LETTY   You ought to stay away from me. I'm bad news. I'm like one of those things everybody's afraid of. A plague. That's what I am. Some kind of a plague. All by myself...

CAP   [*Sad.*] Don't talk crazy.

LETTY   Why not? That's what I am, I guess.

CAP   Not to me, you're not.

LETTY   [*Suddenly, in a strong, older voice.*] You can tell him I said he can go right straight to *Hell*!

CAP   [*Younger, fearful*] Pa... Ma says... she says... you can go to...

LETTY   [*As before.*] Tell him! Tell him what I said! You afraid of that... fat... old... fraud? You afraid of that... old... *nothing*!?

CAP   [*As before, after a moment.*] Pa... Ma says to tell you... [*Low.*] I can't do it, Ma. I... I'm sorry... I... I... can't...

LETTY   [*In her own voice.*] Forget it. I'll tell him myself. Someday.

CAP   [*Own voice.*] That's what I figured. The right time and everything. He got older... I got older...

LETTY And there never was a right time.

CAP [*After a moment.*] You got it.

[*A silence.*]

LETTY We were going to be rich. Make stuff and sell it in the front yard . . .

CAP Key chains and wallets.

LETTY And Kool-Aid. [*Pause.*] What's rich, Cap?

CAP Having everything you want. I guess.

LETTY I'm rich then. I've got a place to sleep. Nobody bothers me.

CAP What about food? What've you got to eat?

LETTY [*Blithely.*] People give me stuff. Money. Sometimes I get so much money I pitch it.

CAP You what?

LETTY Money's a headache, Cap. People got it, they can't get rid of it fast enough. Come in here in a big hurry. Throw some money at me. What am I going to do with it? I need maybe five bucks.

CAP You could buy yourself something.

LETTY [*Defiant.*] What?

CAP Some clothes or something.

LETTY [*Laughing.*] You've got to be kidding! If I was to walk into one of those stores, money in my pocket. You think they'd sell me anything? Throw me out, more like it.

[*A silence. She reaches for her shoes, begins to slowly knot the laces together, studying them intently all the while.*]

Besides. What'd I do with the clothes? Probably somebody'd steal them from me anyhow. If I had any, that is . . .

CAP   [*Sits on bench next to her.*] Look. I'm not too good at this . . . I want you home. You don't belong in this place. You ought to be home. With me . . . taking care of you.

LETTY   [*Suddenly.*] Who the hell are you?

CAP   No games. Cut it out.

LETTY   [*Fiercely.*] I asked *who are you*?

CAP   [*Quiet.*] I'm Cap, Letty. Your brother Cap.

LETTY   I don't have a brother. [*Long pause.*] Do I?

CAP   You sure do. I'm it.

LETTY   That's nice.

[*She wraps herself in the shawl and curls up, as though to sleep.*]

CAP   *Wake up! Dammit!* I want to talk to you! You're my only sister dammit! There's nobody else . . .

[*A silence. CAP waits, watching her hopelessly. After a moment LETTY turns, stares at the ceiling as she speaks.*]

LETTY   Your sister's dead. Didn't anybody tell you? Ashes. Rags. Rocks . . . She never was much good anyhow . . . Worthless . . . Pa said . . . See? He was right. Right the first time . . . *Good for you, Pa!*

[*She sobs silently, her body moving back and forth in a continuous rocking motion.*]

CAP   [*Low.*] Shut up, Ma.

MA   You're talking to me now?

CAP   I'm talking.

MA   Your Pa never talked to me . . . After she . . . After she . . . was . . . born . . .

[*Sobbing.*]

Made me feel so . . . bad . . . Made me feel . . . awful.

[*A silence.*]

CAP [*After a moment.*] Letty?

[*He bends down, close to her, whispers.*]

      Letty?

[*A silence.*]

      I'm going, Letty . . .

[LETTY *is silent.*]

[CAP *turns slowly, walks a few steps away from her, waiting.*]

      You take care. Okay . . . ?

[*Silence.*]

      I'll keep coming back until I get you to come home.

[*A beat.*]

LETTY [*Suddenly.*] Do the happy ending.

CAP Oh, no.

LETTY [*Eager.*] Come on. Do it with me.

[*She bends eagerly and begins to gather the small figures from the floor where she had discarded them earlier. She places one on the bench, watching him as she does this.*]

      Ma . . . Come on, Cap.

[CAP *picks up another figure slowly and places it on the bench.*]

CAP Pa . . .

LETTY More.

[CAP *picks up another figure and places it near* MA.]

CAP Me.

LETTY [*She picks up the last figure and places it near the* CAP *miniature.*] And me. [*She looks at him.*] Oh, we were so happy together.

CAP Sometimes.

LETTY Don't spoil it.

CAP [*Sadly.*] We were happy together.

LETTY And we thought it would be for always . . . Come on, Cap . . . You say it.

[*Music comes up now, faintly.*]

CAP We thought . . . We thought . . . it would be . . . for always.

[*Music up. Lights begin to fade.*]

• • •

Erros—Love Is Deaf

Cherie Vogelstein

Cherie Vogelstein

Cherie Vogelstein has been produced over 150 times Off-Broadway, Off-Off-Broadway, and across the country. Her one-act plays are a favorite among college students and have received over sixty campus productions. A recipient of the Hobson's Scholarship for Dramatic Writing, the James Hammerstein Fellowship for Best Emerging Playwright of 1999, and the winner of the Jury Prize at the HBO Arts Festival, Cherie is currently published by Applause Theatre Books, Smith and Kraus, Farrar Straus Giroux, and Dramatists Play Service.

··· **scene one** ···

[*E.L.O.'s "Mr. Blue Sky" segueing into Frank Sinatra's "Fly Me to the Moon." The lights come up on* MITCH's *Upper West Side apartment as* MITCH *is running to the door. A soggy but still gorgeous* ANNETTE *enters as the music dies out.*]

MITCH   [*He speaks with night guard in his mouth; bear-hugs her.*]
You're late! Sweetie!

ANNETTE   I know, I know, I'm sorry.

MITCH   Oh, I don't care—you're here! That's all that matters. [*Hugging her as he removes night guard.*] I just had to put my, ya know, night guard in cuz when I worry, I start to grind—[*Hits his head.*]—unh! I forgot the music . . . [*He runs to stereo system.*]

ANNETTE   I started walking over so I could . . . I could get my head clear . . .

MITCH   [*Still looking for CD.*] In the rain? At night? Pookie!

ANNETTE   [*Mumbling.*] It wasn't raining when I . . .

MITCH   Dvorjak?

ANNETTE   What?

MITCH   Dvorjak. He's a famous composer from the—

ANNETTE   [*Weary.*] I know who Dvorjak is, Mitch.

MITCH   You do?

ANNETTE   Yes, I do!

MITCH   Okay, Pookie! I just—you said "what."

ANNETTE   Because I didn't hear what-can you-can you just come . . . sit with me?

MITCH   [*Music plays, he rushes to her.*] Of course I can, of course we can—
[*Holds her as they sit.*]

Look at you—look at us—sitting here together in our little . . .
warm . . . womb of a room-try saying THAT five times fast.
[*He tries.*] Little warm womb of a room little warm womb of a
room little worm room of a womb—

ANNETTE [*Tilts her head back, mournful.*] Oh God, God—

MITCH [*Suddenly on the alert.*] How was the audition?

ANNETTE I—I don't want to talk work—

MITCH Neither do I—you're tired—

ANNETTE I am tired, I'm so—

MITCH I know, Pookie, lie your head down.

[*He tries to push her head down.*]

ANNETTE No, I don't want to lie my—

MITCH [*Still pushing.*] Listen to Big Daddy—lie your head—

ANNETTE Mitch. Mitch. Please—

MITCH [*Pushing her head down all the way.*] Down on my lap, baby. Come
on. Get down—

ANNETTE Stop it!

[*He stops.*]

I really don't like when you do that, Mitch—

MITCH Do what?

ANNETTE Push my head down—

MITCH Aw, I wasn't pushing it down for that, baby—I just wanted you
to relax, because tonight . . . tonight is going to be . . . so magical.

ANNETTE But wait. I need to—

MITCH [*He smushes her lips with his finger.*] Shh, let's not ruin the magic.
SHHH—

ANNETTE   Mitch, we have to talk!

MITCH   Yes, yes, I want to talk! And laugh and drink with you—you love to drink! [*Jumps up, moves to table.*] Look!

Champagne! Real napkins like in a restaurant and lamb chops— your favorite—

ANNETTE   It is?

MITCH   Oh well, maybe it's mine, but you love it too, don't you—

[*Phone rings.*]

ANNETTE   You . . . you know what it is I want to say, don't you?

MITCH   [*Answers phone.*] Hello? Hello?! They hung up.

ANNETTE   Because I mean . . . we can't say we haven't . . . because we have—I have—

MITCH   Have what?

ANNETTE   Tried to—I really have, Mitch.

MITCH   Have what?

ANNETTE   Tried!

MITCH   Tried to what?

ANNETTE   To make this work! [*Phone rings.*]

MITCH   Hello? HELLO?!.

ANNETTE   I really have. You know I have!

MITCH   [*Hangs up.*] Have what?

ANNETTE   Stop it! God! This is not Abbott and Costello, I don't want to be in a Woody Allen movie with you all the time!

MITCH   Well, Abbott and Costello I can understand but Woo—

ANNETTE   You can't do it, though, can you? You can't be serious for even a—

MITCH   No, I can, I can but—I've spent my whole life being serious—a serious student, a serious practitioner—look—[*Points to baby picture on mantle.*]—I was a serious BABY even—so now I just want to . . . laugh with you and eat and look at you—you're so beautiful, Annette, and my feelings are so intense sometimes, it scares me. So I joke. But this relationship is . . . the most serious thing in my life. I love you.

ANNETTE   And . . . I love you too—

MITCH   [*Taking her hands.*] Thank you.

ANNETTE   Like an uncle, Mitch—I love you like an uncle—

MITCH   Today. Today an uncle. Tomorrow . . . a first cousin. In time—

ANNETTE   No, don't you . . . you could never be more than a . . . brother to me—

MITCH   Ya see? Already I'm a brother! That's what I'm talking about—you've gotta grow into the—it's like shoes!

ANNETTE   Shoes.

MITCH   I know the way it-the woman grows into the . . . love—works her way around till it fits like a—a . . . glove—shoe and—I'm good for you, you know I am—

ANNETTE   I do, I DO know—it's me! I'm the one who can't—that's why I'm—for YOUR good—I'm doing this for you too—

MITCH   Don't do anything for me, PLEASE—

ANNETTE   But I mean, listen to yourself! You—you want to be my shoes!

MITCH   And what's so wrong about that? It means I—I want to walk with you and support you and hold your . . . feet in my . . . soul—that's so . . . nice!

ANNETTE   It IS! It is nice! But . . . nice . . . is not what I'm looking for, Mitch. I'm sorry, I can't . . . I can't do this anymore . . . it's over.

MITCH Wow. [*Pause.*] Wow. You . . . you've never said those words before.

ANNETTE I—but . . . I'm so sorry.

MITCH [*Long sigh.*] Well. [*Pause.*] So. So . . . what you ARE looking for, Annette? Do you even know?

ANNETTE No.

[*Beat.*]

But I don't think it's . . . "nice."

MITCH Why you dirty piece of fucking shit!—

ANNETTE Mitch!

MITCH I—I was just trying to be, ya know . . . mean—

ANNETTE [*Coming over to him.*]

It's not in you, though. You're just the good, solid, decent guy every woman dreams of meeting.

MITCH Yeah. Every woman but you.

ANNETTE No, no, I'm so glad I met you!

MITCH Are you?

ANNETTE Yes! And I really hope . . .

MITCH Yes, Annette?

ANNETTE You'll still be my periodontist—I mean, I understand if—

MITCH Ya know, I wish I were dead—

ANNETTE God forbid!

MITCH Here I thought this was gonna be the most beautiful night of my life—

ANNETTE It does look beautiful—

MITCH   Great, thank you! Now I can kill myself . . .

ANNETTE   Stop it!! [*Pause.*] Can you even be buried in a Jewish cemetery if you commit sui—

MITCH   Damn it, Annette! I don't care where I'm BURIED!—it's how I want to spend my LIFE—and I was hoping it was gonna be with YOU!

ANNETTE   Oh, Mitchy, come on, we always knew there was a good chance this wouldn't work.

MITCH   We did? *I* didn't know.

ANNETTE   I told you—I tried to but you wouldn't hear me—

MITCH   Because you never said those words before, you never said, "It's over!"

ANNETTE   But I told you I wasn't in love with you millions of times!

MITCH   Yes, but you never said," It's over!" And as long as you were willing to let me try—try to make you fall in love, I knew there was a chance you would . . . fall in love. A *chance* you wanted to . . . be made to.

ANNETTE   I DID want to but . . . can I tell you something? [*Almost a whisper.*] I—I don't know if I'm even capable—

MITCH   Don't tell me that, don't whisper it—

ANNETTE   [*Whispering.*] It's the truth. Only a—

MITCH   [*Kicks couch.*] Don't whisper!

ANNETTE   [*Talking loudly.*] A challenge excites me—because of my—my low self-esteem—

MITCH   Oh please don't try and console me, alright? It only makes it worse.

ANNETTE   Alright. I'm sorry.

MITCH [*Checking.*] So you were? You WERE just trying to console me? It's not your self-est—[*Newly upset, kicking couch again.*] Oh, what's the difference? I'm watering a PLASTIC PLANT and thinking it's growing—it's "over." IT'S OVER!

ANNETTE [*Pause.*] I don't know what else to say . . .

MITCH I just, I need to be alone—[*She turns to go.*]—not yet. [*Pause.*] The truth is, I thought . . . I thought I had enough love for both of us, ya know? I mean, I'd rather love than be loved anyway, if I had to make the choice . . . but I don't, right? Have the choice. Do I?

ANNETTE Ya know, it's funny but . . . suddenly, I feel so close to you, ya know? Now that we're saying good-bye?

MITCH Yeah, that IS funny.

ANNETTE And this has always been the hardest part—the fear that you'll stop being my friend.

MITCH I *will* stop being your friend.

ANNETTE So I was right—

MITCH [*Rises suddenly.*] NO! No, you were wrong—you ARE wrong— we're a work in progress, Annette! Every great objective requires work—please! Don't walk out on me—us—tonight! Of all nights!

ANNETTE Mitch, I know it doesn't feel like it now, but this is—this is just your ego talking—

MITCH My ego? Oh no, no, my ego doesn't talk like that—my ego says things *like*, "What are you doing, Mitch? You're a prominent periodontist with dozens of women sitting in your chair every week wishing they could be with you and yet you prostrate yourself like a schmuck before this uneducated little dancer who never even reads the paper"—you see? But that's NOT what I'm saying—

ANNETTE   Well, but maybe that's what you should be saying—maybe in the end, I'd just be too dumb for you and—

MITCH   Is that it? Is this some kind of . . . preemptive strike?

ANNETTE   Does it matter? I mean, would it really help if it was?

MITCH   Is it?

ANNETTE   [*Beat.*] No, Mitch. It's not.

MITCH   Ya know, it WOULD'VE helped.

ANNETTE   [*Rising.*] Well . . . I guess . . . I guess I should . . . go—

MITCH   Wait! Before you leave, I just want you to know that this— [*He leads her to table.*]—all this? The 200 dollar champagne, the fancy doily stupid napkins, everything—this was going to be my proposal. Tonight, I was going to ask you to be my wife! Because when I close my eyes? At night? The only reason I want to open them again in the morning . . . is to see you. I've never felt this way about anyone ever—[*Kneels.*]—so consumed, so delirious, so without pride—I'd do anything for you, Annette, I'd die for you—

ANNETTE   And I so, SO appreciate that, but I have to stay strong—I have to do this. [*At door.*] You'll find someone else, Mitch. She's out there somewhere—

MITCH   [*He goes to window, looks out.*]
You really think there's someone out there for me?

ANNETTE   [*Gently.*] I KNOW there is. [*Beat.*] I promise you.

MITCH   You promise?

ANNETTE   [*A whisper.*] I promise.

MITCH   [*Beat, then, ala Charles Laughton in* Witness for the Prosecution.]
THEN YOU'RE A LIAR! [MITCH *jumps out the window.*]

ANNETTE   [*Screams.*] MIIIIITCH!!! [*Blackout.*]

··· scene two ···

[*"My Sharona" blasts loudly.* PAUL *and* JANET *play Ping-Pong in any empty game room.*]

PAUL   Okay. Volley for serve.

[*He throws ball. They volley, she misses.* PAUL *catches ball.*]

Okay, my serve.

JANET   It didn't go over six times.

PAUL   Yes it did.

JANET   No, five times. I counted.

PAUL   [*Tense.*] Alright then. You serve then, all right?

JANET   Okeydokey.

[*She's about to serve.*]

PAUL   You need the advantage.

JANET   What?

PAUL   You obviously need the advantage.

JANET   That's a mean thing to say.

PAUL   Oh, I'm sorry.

[*Pause.*]

Serve.

[*She serves, they volley, he misses.*]

JANET   Okay. One nothing.

[*She serves again, she misses. Gets ready to serve again.*]

PAUL   Why don't you announce the score?

JANET   What?

PAUL   You announce it when *you* win the point. Why don't you announce it when *I* win the point? Unbelievable.

JANET   What are you talking about?

PAUL   I'm talking about your little psychological tactics.

JANET   Oh you mean—

PAUL   It's very obvious what you're doing, Janet. I mean, it's *very* obvious. And very distracting.

JANET   You mean like when you—

PAUL   I said to myself today, if she pulls that crap again—

JANET   Like when you—

PAUL   I'm going to say something.

JANET   [*Snorts.*] Oh, right.

PAUL   You're damn straight.

JANET   Like you usually don't say things? You STARTED OUT by—

PAUL   No, no—

JANET   Okay, Paul, this is just *your* way of psyching *me* out. Don't you think I know that?

PAUL   Now, now—

JANET   [*Snorts derisively.*] "Now, now"—so patronizing-

PAUL   Alright now.

JANET   SO fucking competitive—

PAUL   Who, moi? *You, YOU* are the most cutthroat woman of all time!

JANET   And you are just the worst sport that ever lived!

PAUL   Really? What else am I?

JANET   You really want to know?

PAUL Absolutement.

JANET Let's just play, all right? We came here to play, didn't we?

PAUL Bon. Very well. Let's play. Serve.

JANET [*Pointedly.*]
> One to *one*.

[*She serves, he misses.*]
> *Two* to one.

[*She serves, he misses.*]
> *Three* to one.

[*Serves again, he misses again.*]
> Four to one.

[*He takes ball, hits it at her as hard as he can.*]
> Hey!

PAUL You've ruined my concentration.

JANET That almost hit my eye.

PAUL Tell me what I am.

JANET You're crazy. You almost blinded me.

PAUL What am I? I want you to say it.

JANET No, I'm not giving you the satisfaction.

PAUL I want you to tell me. Now.

JANET Why should I? It's your serve.

PAUL Keep that ball—

[*He comes around to her side, she half-moves to other side.*]

JANET [*Slightly scared.*] We switch at 11—

PAUL I'll switch whenever I want!—

JANET [*Not fully convincing.*] You're scaring me, Paul—

PAUL Good.

JANET No, I mean it. You're, you're really scaring me.

PAUL Excellent. Tell me what I am.

[*They keep moving around the table.*]

JANET Stay away from me.

PAUL I'm faster than you, Janet.

JANET Just, just go back—

PAUL And stronger!

JANET I don't want to—

PAUL But you will! Now tell me what I am.

[*He grabs at her shirt, rips at it as she just escapes.*]

JANET Ah, my good shirt!

[*He catches her, gets on top of her.*]

JANET No.

PAUL What am I?

JANET [*Whispers.*] It's too soon.

PAUL Shut up.

[*Slaps her.*]

Goddamnit.

JANET [*More annoyed than angry.*]
Paul . . .

PAUL [*He rips her pants button off.*]

You little cunt. Go ahead.

JANET   [*Resigned.*] You're a man.

PAUL   What kind of man?

JANET   A big man.

PAUL   Don't humor me.

[*Pulls her hair.*]

Don't humor me, Janet.

JANET   Ow. A strong man.

PAUL   I'll hurt you. I really feel like—

JANET   [*A trace of nervousness.*]

A big, strong, hard man who has to fuck me in the light because you're not ashamed.

PAUL   I'm not ashamed.

JANET   You're not ashamed.

PAUL   I'm not ashamed.

JANET   You're not ashamed.

PAUL   I'm not ashamed, I'm not ...

[*He gets off her, checks himself.*]

I'm ...

JANET   Well?

[*Waits.*]

Nothing?

PAUL   Nothing to speak of.

JANET   [*Getting up, coming over.*]

Let me see.

PAUL No! There's nothing to see.

[*He bends, picks up the Ping-Pong ball, hands her ball and racket.*]

Come on.

[*She takes racket, goes to other side.*]

PAUL Serve.

JANET Paul.

PAUL What?

JANET Why can't we . . . just . . .

PAUL [*Annoyed*] What?

JANET I don't know.

[*Pause.*]

Try to do it . . . normally.

PAUL [*Jack Nicholson craze.*]
Normally? What's normally?

JANET Well, you know, in an apartment, a bedroom, not at a Ping-Pong club—

PAUL Goddamnit! Goddamnit, Janet. Why are you like this?

JANET [*Genuinely frightened.*] Like what?

PAUL You don't put your heart in it and it shows.

JANET I try—

PAUL You're just like my wife—

JANET No, I love you—

PAUL I don't want to be loved. I want to be . . . feared!

JANET   Why? I don't understand-

PAUL   Maybe—maybe if you feared me, you'd try to please me. You wouldn't laugh.

JANET   Laugh?

PAUL   Oh, I see it. You and Diane. You think I can't read people? I'm a psychiatrist, for God's sake. A mental defective.

JANET   A what?

PAUL   Detective, detective. [*She giggles.*] What's the matter with you? What's happening?

JANET   Nothing.

[*Containing her laughter.*]

     Seriously.

PAUL   You're laughing, aren't you—

[*She is struggling to keep it in.*]

     Aren't you?! Right in my face.

JANET   Paul, I'm not! [*Suppressing it.*] You're trying to make me laugh!

PAUL   I am? I'm trying to be funny? I'm funny to you?

JANET   NO, NO! You're NOT, you're not funny to me at all.— [*Guffawing.*]

PAUL   Then why're you GODDAMN LAUGHING?

JANET   [*Doubled over.*] I can't help it!

PAUL   Goddamnit. No respect!

JANET   I'm sorry, I'm sorry. It's just—

[*She laughs too hard to speak.*]

PAUL   [*Shaking his head in fury and disgust.*]

A mistress, no less.

JANET   When you tell someone not to laugh—

[*Another wave of laughter.*]

They have to laugh.

[*She tries to regain composure, finally.*]

Paul?

[*Picks up racket.*]

Paul, come on, let's play—we'll play Ping-Pong—start over—
zero–zero.

PAUL   [*Calm as can be.*] I don't need your charity, Janet.

JANET   [*Happy.*] Alright then: one–four, your serve.

PAUL   And you GO BURN IN HELL!

[*Blackout.*]

··· scene three ···

[*Therapist's office. MAX and PAUL. Schoenberg atonal music plays under, but quietly. PAUL covers half his face with his hand as MAX looks up and down for a good 15 seconds of silence.*]

MAX   It's just that now that I've built this rapport with her, I don't want to ruin it, ya know? [*Beat.*] I just don't know . . . if I can . . . take the chance.

PAUL   [*Another LONG beat.*]
The chance.

MAX   But I mean. What am I supposed to do with these, you know, all these . . . EMOTIONS I have? Rubbing her shoulders is not enough anymore.

PAUL   What would be enough?

MAX   I don't know but . . . she just has these unearthly qualities, ya know? I mean—and I'm not only talking physical things. She's also this super feeling woman.

PAUL   What kind of unearthly qualities?

MAX   Well, OK. For starters, her skin. It's—it's poreless. Just one smooth sheet of hardened, golden honey. My hands glide over her flesh like a Ouija board. The skin tells me where to go, it controls me and I . . . uh . . . I . . .

PAUL   [*Clears his throat.*]
You—

[*Beat.*]

A Ouija board.

[*Pause.*]

Max. Why don't you tell me about your fantasies.

MAX   Here we go.

PAUL   How do you mean?

MAX   Why do you always want to know about my fantasies, Paul?

PAUL   I don't understand.

MAX   Do you get off on my fantasies or something? Why can't I just tell you my thoughts?

PAUL   Your fantasies *are* your thoughts.

MAX   [*Pause.*] OK. Sometimes, I picture her wrapping her hair around my naked ass.

PAUL   Her hair around your . . .

MAX   That's it.

PAUL   [*Disappointed.*]
        Hmm.

MAX   You know, I'm very self-conscious about my ass.

PAUL   No, I didn't know that. [*Beat.*] Why are you . . .

MAX   Well . . . it's hairy.

PAUL   I see.

MAX   Is yours?

PAUL   What?

MAX   Is your ass hairy?

PAUL   My? Hmm . . . What do you think, Max?

[*Beat.*]

MAX   I don't know. I mean, how would I know?

PAUL   Well. Why would you want to know?

[*Beat.*]

MAX   [*Quickly, defensive.*] Well, I wouldn't I—I was just being polite.

PAUL   By asking me if I had a hairy ass?

MAX   God, yeah, I was making conversation, I don't know. Man!

PAUL   All right. Now, about Lauren . . . her hair around your . . .

MAX   Her, her . . . ass also is . . . just these two, perfect mounds of vanilla scoops I have to . . . stop myself, literally force myself from just bending down and burying my face right into the . . . ice cream of her . . . ass. Ya know?

PAUL   Ice cream.

MAX   But it's more than superficial. Her mind is so in tune with her body. Emotionally in sync—

PAUL   How do you restrain yourself from burying your head up her...
ass, as you say.

MAX   I said "into," not "up." Um...it's hard, it's really not easy, I
mean...

[*Pause.*]

Sometimes I feel you're just this sick pervert.

PAUL   [*Hand on chin.*]
I see.

MAX   Who just sits there hiding behind his hand.

[PAUL*'s hand covers part of his face.*]

PAUL   Uh huh. And what else do you think of yourself?

MAX   What?

PAUL   Did you hear what you said?

MAX   [*Turning in his seat in frustration.*]
Oh man...

PAUL   Who were you describing? Who hides behind his hand? Who
uses his hands?

MAX   You do.

PAUL   I do? Am I a masseur?

MAX   You know, I'm a better therapist than you. I should be the
therapist.

PAUL   Maybe you should.

MAX   When Lauren talks to me, I get her to relax, to feel better.

PAUL   Is that what you want me to do? Try and make you feel better?

MAX   No. I want you to just jack off on my fantasies. Okay?

PAUL [*Lighting up.*]

Hey, now where did that fantasy come from?

MAX [*Very annoyed.*] Oh God! Forget it.

[*Beat.*]

You don't help me.

PAUL How should I help you, Max? Do you think it'd help you if I soothed you? If I just gave you a mental massage in here?

MAX [*Resigned.*]

I don't know, Paul. I'm a massage therapist.

PAUL [*Leaning forward.*] What do you need help to do, Max? What do you want to do to her?

MAX I want—I want to make contact. I can't make any—

[*Covers his eyes.*]

Contact. I want . . .

PAUL Yes, Max?

MAX I want to rip off my pants—

PAUL Good! And?

MAX And get on the table on my knees, straddle her, have her locked between my knees and watch her eyes go wild. Like a little kaleidoscope. I want to see the pupils dilate, the irises spread with the triangles spinning around. I want to see . . . I want to see—

PAUL Fear? Do you want her to fear you, Max?

MAX [*Thinks.*] Uhhh . . . no.

PAUL No? Why not?

MAX What? What do you mean, "Why not?"

PAUL [*Also annoyed.*] What do you think I mean?

MAX   I—I don't know! I'm just telling you my fantasy—I don't know "why I DON'T want her to"—you tell ME why not. I feel like punching you in the fucking head.

PAUL   Do you? [*Pause.*]

MAX   No. It just passed. [*Beat.*]

PAUL   You know, it's all right to feel violent. We all feel violent impulses sometimes . . . in the afternoons—

MAX   [*Over him.*] I'm just a pair of hands to her. A pair of powerless hands.

PAUL   And you want power?

MAX   Respect. I want respect.

[*Points to head.*]

I've got a good head in here. A poetic mind. You know?

PAUL   Listen. About the ice cream—

MAX   I'd rather be respected than loved. I'm a man. You know? I don't want to be ignored.

PAUL   [*Looking at his watch.*]
All right, Max.

[PAUL *rises.*]

MAX   My mother never respected my father. [*With conviction, rising.*] I'm a man, Paul.

PAUL   You certainly are. And now it's—

MAX   Ahh, what's the difference.

PAUL   I'll see you next week, Max.

MAX   [*Sad.*] Okay, Paul. [*Beat.*] Thanks.

[*Blackout.*]

··· scene four ···

[*A masseur's room.* LAUREN *lies facedown on table.* MAX *sensually massages her throughout scene. Vangelis New Age music plays softly. The scene is relaxed, slow-paced.*]

LAUREN Ahh. I've been so . . . so . . .

MAX Mmmm . . . ?

LAUREN Uch, I'm almost embarrassed to . . . say.

MAX Oh come on, you can say anything in here—you know that.

LAUREN Well . . . it's just been so long since . . . you know.

MAX Tell me. All about it.

LAUREN I am just—it's like the Hoover Dam in there! I'm a vault of shit! Three days of constipated agony.

MAX [*Momentarily disgusted.*]
Ooh—okay, well . . . let's just try and relax, now—

LAUREN My body's just got a mind of its own, Max, you know? I mean, when I feel good, my skin glows, my hair shines, my breasts swell—

MAX Mmmmmn.

LAUREN But when I feel . . . like this, my muscles . . . ache, my eyes . . . sting, my gums bleed, my—

MAX [*Alarmed.*] Your gums bleed?

LAUREN Yeah, when I'm upset, or . . . down.

MAX That's bad. That's really bad.

LAUREN Yeah . . . I know.

MAX Do you floss, Lauren? You have to floss.

LAUREN   I'm just such a vessel, Max, such a—

MAX   [*Sweetly.*] Lauren, Lauren, Lauren . . .

LAUREN   What?

MAX   [*Severe.*]
   You have GOT to floss.

LAUREN   Alright! [*Pause.*]

MAX   Now—[*Massaging sensually again.*]—tell me what's really going on.

LAUREN   What's really going on?

MAX   With your body, with your soul . . .

LAUREN   Well, it's all just so . . . senseless.

MAX   Life. Is senseless.

LAUREN   It's not even my problem.

MAX   Oh but it is.

LAUREN   It is?! How can you tell?

MAX   How I can tell? I can *feel*.

LAUREN   Ooh, right there, right there, it's so—

MAX   All of your worries have gathered right in this little area, right
   back here, Lauren. If we can untangle this coil of knots—then . . .

LAUREN   Yes?

MAX   We can solve all your problems.

LAUREN   Ahhhh, Max. Max . . . you know my friend Annette? I've
   mentioned her—

MAX   Sure, sure—the dancer—

LAUREN   The temp actually, but . . . so I fixed her up with my
   periodontist, who I love—

MAX   Mitch, right?

LAUREN   How do you remember—you are so great!

MAX   [*Stops massaging.*] So are you.

LAUREN   So anyway, they really hit it off—

MAX   Wonderful!

LAUREN   Yeah, well . . . you don't know what happened. I mean, this is why I can't sleep, I can't eat—which is good—plus I'm losing hair—gobs of hair.

MAX   Your beautiful hair?

LAUREN   Yesterday, I counted 146.

MAX   You counted?

LAUREN   I just held 'em all in my hand. Looked like a little vagina. [*Beat.*]

MAX   How . . . how long did it take to count all those hairs?

LAUREN   That's not the point, Max. The point is . . . she doesn't even really like him—

MAX   She doesn't even really like . . . Mitch?

LAUREN   No! That's the thing! He's this wonderful person who she doesn't even appreciate! So she goes to break up with him!

MAX   Oh, what a shame—

LAUREN   Yeah! And so he jumps out the window!

MAX   What?!

LAUREN   Can you believe it? I fixed them up!

MAX   Oh my God! No wonder you're so upset!

LAUREN   I mean, she's always had the worst taste in men, so I thought I'd introduce her to a good, stable kind of guy—

MAX   He doesn't sound that stable really—

LAUREN   And she would, ya know, get on the right track—I never thought he would end up falling madly in love with her!

MAX   [*Confused.*] Is he . . . is he dead?

LAUREN   He's in very critical condition.

MAX   Oh, man!

LAUREN   I just wanted for everybody to have fun!

MAX   Of course you did. You meant so well—

LAUREN   But then Annette has to be this little, little, self-involved, anorexic, motherfucking slut—oh, what am I saying? It's not her fault! It's not her fault!

MAX   Lauren, Lauren, listen to you! You are such a friend!

LAUREN   I try to be—

MAX   The way you care—your whole body cares—

LAUREN   But where does it get me, Max, where?

MAX   So full of passion and—

LAUREN   I story of my life—

MAX   Ohhh, Lauren . . .

LAUREN   What am I gonna do?

MAX   You? You're gonna keep on caring—

LAUREN   I don't wanna care—

MAX   And you're gonna breathe—breathe deep. Deep, deep into your soul.

LAUREN   I don't want to breathe deep into my soul.

MAX   We're gonna untie the knot.

LAUREN It hurts to breathe.

MAX Loosen the knot.

LAUREN I feel so guilty—

MAX Smooth out the knot.

LAUREN She never even loved him, Max—

MAX Unwind the knot.

LAUREN She never loved him at all—and I—

MAX Let it go.

LAUREN I did!

MAX [*Alarmed, he stops massaging.*]
        What?

LAUREN For THREE years. And probably the rest of my lonely,
        pathetic life.

[*Beat.*]

        Isn't that so horrible?

[*He continues massage, very upset and angry now.*]

MAX Yes. Yes, it is.

LAUREN I mean, I know it's not her fault that men go crazy for her—

MAX [*School marm.*] Mmhmm—

LAUREN And maybe it was weirdly self-destructive of ME to fix them
        up in the first place but—

MAX [*Chopping her back now.*] Yes, well, it all sounds very, very
        dysfunctional, Lauren—

LAUREN I know! It is! But why couldn't it be me, you know? Why her?

MAX Lie still. [*Chops harder.*]

LAUREN Why couldn't he love me like that? She never even thought he was funny, Max!

MAX [*Really hard chops now.*] And YOU, you think he's hilarious!

LAUREN I guess that's always the way it is, though, isn't it—OW!

MAX Did that hurt? I'm Sorry.

LAUREN The ones who don't know how to love, get the passionate lovers. The ones who don't need the needy, GET the needy. You know what I mean?

MAX I think I can figure it out—

LAUREN People don't think I have needs but—

MAX Oh, who cares?

LAUREN What?

MAX What people think—

LAUREN I DO—I do have needs, Max—I need to be needed! I think I'd even rather be needed than loved, because when they need you, they can't leave you or replace you, even when the love runs dry—ow!—ya know? And nobody will ever need me the way he thinks he needs her because I'm just the Rosalind Russell character who—Max, Jesus! What're you doing?! It really hurts.

MAX [*In a burst.*] Because I need you too, Lauren!—[*Regaining his composure.*]—To relax. Just . . . breathe. Can you breathe for me, Lauren? Just once?

LAUREN I'll try.

MAX That's all I ask.

[*Blackout.*]

... scene five ...

[*In a restaurant. Nora Jones music plays softly in the background.* ANNETTE *and* LAUREN.]

ANNETTE   So that was . . . yeah. Totally awful.

LAUREN   [*Dispassionate.*] Look. He was lucky . . .

ANNETTE   Lucky?! He's mutilated! Broken into so, so many parts. His legs, his ribs, his hip, his feet, his arm, his thumb—

LAUREN   "His thumb." He could've been killed, the fucking maniac—it's a miracle he didn't die.—[*Motions to waitress.*]

ANNETTE   [*Timid.*] I know but . . . the thing is? Have you thought about this, Lauren? The man was willing! He was actually WILLING to die for me!

LAUREN   I think I'm gonna get the nicoise—would you split that with me or are you just gonna not eat as usual?

ANNETTE   [*Nods.*] So listen . . . I wanted to ask you something,

LAUREN   Okay.

ANNETTE   But don't you think it's kind of amazing when you think about it?

LAUREN   What?

ANNETTE   Ya know, that kind of . . . pure, unconditional kind of love—

LAUREN   Is that what you wanted to ask me?

ANNETTE   No, I was just . . . saying the LOVE—

LAUREN   Oh, come on, Annette, gimmee a break. That's not love and you know it!

ANNETTE   What?! It is! It absolutely is—

LAUREN [*Very patiently.*] No, that's what we call: mental illness, insanity, a chemical imbalance, codependence, dysfunction, lazy eye— anything BUT—

ANNETTE Look, I know. I know it was "crazy,"—but it was crazy for ME—

LAUREN They're ALL crazy for you, Annette, don't you get it? He's just another one of the crazy psychos in your life who wants to bring you down—down on the sidewalk right with him—[*Opening menu.*]—and it would've been on MY head!

ANNETTE What?

LAUREN [*Reading menu.*] Who introduced you? I practically threw you at him—

ANNETTE Because you KNEW—

LAUREN What?

ANNETTE Something in you SENSED that—

LAUREN Are you kidding me?! I had NO idea—

ANNETTE God, Lauren! Can you just be on my side? Please?

LAUREN Of course I'm on your—what does that even mean?

ANNETTE Just that . . . Mitch loves me intensely! He loves me like nobody ever EVER will!

LAUREN [*Calmly.*] Oh, I don't know, Annette—I'm sure there're plenty of other suicidals out there who'd be interested in you.

ANNETTE That's exactly what I'm talking about—

LAUREN Anyway, the problem was never *his* idiot love for *you anyway*!

ANNETTE But maybe that *was* the problem—maybe I couldn't handle all that unconditional love because I felt I didn't deserve it! I felt I wasn't worthy—

LAUREN   Oh that fucking Al-Anon fucking bullshit—

ANNETTE   [*Hushed.*]

That kind of devotion, that kind of LOVE!

LAUREN   [*Hissing.*] Would you stop calling it love? [*To a guy walking by, sexily.*] Hi.

ANNETTE   All I'm saying is THAT kind of love can make up for— [*Whispers.*]—I OWE him, Lauren!

LAUREN   [*Also whispers.*]

Oh my God. Do you hear what you're saying?

ANNETTE   For that kind of devotion he deserves . . . he DESERVES—

LAUREN   Oh God! Please tell me you're not considering going back to the jumper!

ANNETTE   [*Looking down, barely a whisper.*] He deserves love.

LAUREN   Then let him find it! Let him meet someone who loves him!

ANNETTE   I love him, Lauren!

LAUREN   Then why were you constantly trying to break up with him then?! [*Whispers.*] Why did you need lubricants during sex?

ANNETTE   [*Also whispering.*] Because of . . . vaginitis, I was insecure—it was preemptive, I—I thought I needed to be challenged but now . . . now I realize . . .

LAUREN   What?

ANNETTE   . . . I'd rather be loved. I'd rather BE loved than love, if I had to make the choice—

LAUREN   But you don't have to—!

ANNETTE   I want to ask you—

LAUREN   [*Takes her hand.*] Annette. Netty. Listen to me: You're a young, beautiful woman with big boobs—you could have it all, love, passion, everything! This is not a William Styron novel, you're not saving—

ANNETTE [*Unfamiliar with Styron.*] What?

LAUREN Anyone by acting out of . . . guilt or some misplaced sense of . . . gratitude—

ANNETTE I hear what you're saying, I do—

LAUREN Do you? Because this is so important—

ANNETTE Of course I do. I know I don't HAVE to be with him—

LAUREN [*Holding her hand.*] Of course you don't!

ANNETTE And I never had the right feelings—

LAUREN That's right, that's right, you didn't at all!

ANNETTE But now I do. [*Beat.*] We're getting married, Lauren. I want you to be my maid of honor—please say yes. [*Beat.*] Please. [*Longer beat.*] No one cares the way you do. PLEASE. I need you by my side. [LAUREN *remains frozen.*] Okay. I'll take that as a yes.

[*Blackout.*]

··· scene six ···

[*"Here comes the bride" music. A wedding.* JANET, *in bride's maid dress, moves to the standing microphone at the head of the dance floor to make a toast.*]

JANET [*Everyone quiets down.*] Hi, everybody. [*Voices say, "Hi! Hi, Janet!,"* *etc.*] I—I just wanted to say a few words about my beautiful sister—who's never looked more beautiful and happy than she does today. [*Voices murmur in agreement.*] Lauren and I were very different growing up—she was blond, I was brunette. She was neat, I was messy. She was thin, I was fat. She was a whore, I had morals—just kidding, just kidding! We were both whores—KIDDING! [*Laughter.*] But the truth is, we WERE both a little boy crazy, that we were. Luckily, we didn't go for the same type—I always went for the ambitious, mentally-ill type while Lauren, Lauren searched for... true love. The first day she met Ivan, she said to me, "I think this is the one I've been waiting for all my life." [*Choking up a little.*] And she was right! The more I get to know Ivan, the more and more I grow to love him with all my heart and soul and wish that—[*Progressively starts to lose it.*]—I could meet someone just exactly like him because the... absolute... pain and... excruciating humiliation of living in the DATING WORLD OF DANTE'S *INFERNO*—[*Regaining her composure.*]—can be difficult—but today... TODAY is really fantastic! So let's just—let's all raise our glasses to my wonderful sister, Lauren, and her true love, Ivan Oblomovitch... nikov: May you help each other... to complete yourselves... and each other... and everyone. [*A brief, confused silence is followed by light applause. JANET quickly walks off dance floor. MITCH, in a wheelchair, rolls over to stop her.*]

MITCH   I—I really loved your speech.

JANET   What?

MITCH   Your toast—I thought it was incredibly... touching.

JANET   Really? [*Covering her face.*] I—I completely humiliated myself—again.

MITCH   No, you didn't! It was so funny and sweet and... personal—

JANET   [*Holding her face in her hands.*] Oh, God—right! [*Looks up, kind of just noticing him now.*]—I'm sorry—thank you, that's very nice of you to say. [*Extends her hand.*] I'm Janet, the bride's—

MITCH   [*Shakes.*] Mitchel. Mitchel Reisner.

JANET   [*Putting it together.*] Mitchel Reisner? Aren't you—aren't you the uh... [*Recovers.*] ... periodontist?

MITCH Who jumped out the window? Yes, that's me. [*They laugh a little awkwardly.*] Your sister is one of my favorite patients. She fixed me up with my fiancée, in fact.

JANET Oh, Annette, that's right, yeah . . . She's in Europe now, isn't she? That's . . . so when're you guys getting married?

MITCH Oh, we're not—I'm not—we broke up.

JANET You did? Uh-oh!—I mean . . . I'm so sorry.

MITCH No, no, it's okay. I've learned a lot about myself these past few months.

JANET Oh? [*Beat.*] Like . . . ?

MITCH Like how much I hate Annette—no, I'm just . . . I hope they're happy, I do.

JANET They?

MITCH She, uh, she ran off with the married, attending psychiatrist I was seeing in the hospital, while I was in traction.

JANET [*With slight alarm.*] A married psychiatrist? Really?

MITCH Yeah, they make you see somebody, ya know, whenever there's . . . an attempt of that . . . nature.

JANET Right, uh-huh. Which hospital were you . . .

MITCH Oh, um, Sinai Hospital?

JANET Oh my God.

MITCH Yeah, well . . . anyway . . . I just wanted to say—

[*He falls out of the wheelchair.*]

JANET Oh God, are you alright?!

MITCH Yeah, I'm—thank you—I'm fine, I'm—[*Struggling up, she helps.*]—I was just going to say . . . how much I could relate to the . . . absolute pain and excruciating humiliation . . .

JANET   [*Helping him still.*] You were really listening—

MITCH   [*Smiles.*] "Excruciating humiliation of Dante's *Inferno*," I think it was. My favorite book, by the way.

JANET   Really?! Mine too!

MITCH   Oh, you like to read?

JANET   Ohh, just give me a good book or a Woody Allen movie and . . . [*Almost shyly.*] . . . that's all I need.

MITCH   Hey, you wouldn't want to roll me around the dance floor a little, would you? You can lead.

JANET   I'd love to. [*They gaze into each other's eyes, falling in love.*] I'd love to . . . [*The lights slowly fade as Sinatra's "Fly me to the Moon" serenades us and our sweethearts roll off into the sunset.*]

• • •

I'll Do It Tomorrow . . .

Michael Roderick

Michael Roderick

Michael Roderick, originally from Rhode Island, moved to NYC to teach at LaSalle Academy, where he currently holds the position of English department chair and drama director. He graduated from Rhode Island College with a BA in secondary education, English, and theatre performance and finished his master's degree at NYU in educational theatre in July 2006. Michael has produced twenty shows in NYC since he began writing and directing while he was an undergraduate. He also runs his own producing organization, Small Pond Entertainment Play Production and Casting. He has written fifteen plays and has had numerous shows produced in Off-Off-Broadway and Off-Broadway venues. His play *Three in the Bed* was a selection of the Samuel French 2007 Off-Off-Broadway One-Act Play Festival and his play *PROPS* was a selection of the 2006 Midtown International Theatre Festival. He also plans on eventually publishing a book about his first year teaching called *Stage Fright*, as well as a young adult novel titled *Norin's Quest: Beyond the Gates of Lavender*.

characters

KENNETH, a procrastinator

LEE, an angel

MISSY, Kenneth's sister

ANNA, Kenneth's mother

BE BE, a waitress

(*Note:* Roles can be double cast)

...

... scene one ...

[*We open in complete darkness. The sound of loud obnoxious snoring is heard for a few beats and then a lava lamp is turned on, creating an eerie glow around the space. We now discover that this is somebody's bedroom. A crowded bedroom with unwashed clothes piled on the bed, Post-it notes over every available furniture item and one is in fact stuck to the foot of the person snoring. It reads "Wash socks." LEE stands above the bed. She is an angel, but her outfit would remind one of a Paula Abdul video. She wears a fedora hat and what seems to be a suit without the suit jacket. She allows the snoring to continue for a little while KENNETH slowly wakes up.*]

KENNETH Mmmmmm. What's that? You want me to drip candle wax there . . . mmmm ohhh, you naughty girl . . . [LEE *is slightly appalled by this and kicks the bed.*] Ow! Oh, I see you like it rough. . . . Well, we can OWWWWWWWWWWww! [LEE *has now grabbed* KENNETH's *ear and succeeded in waking him up.*]

LEE Good morning, Kenneth.

KENNETH What's going on? Where am I?

LEE In your bed, Kenneth. Where you've been for the past 24 hours.

KENNETH What the fuck do you think you're doing in my room? Who the hell are you? You better speak up, you crazy bitch, or I'm gonna call—[KENNETH *can suddenly no longer speak. He* *continues to talk for a few beats, realizes this and begins to scream. When no sound comes out he eventually begins to cry. Once he is done, LEE begins.*]

LEE   You have a potty mouth, you know that? I bet you'd curse me out even worse if I let you speak. Don't you dare get up. I just made you dumb, imagine what else I can do, huh? OK, that's better, now listen. In the past twenty four hours you woke up, walked to your fridge, ate some pop tarts and then turned on the TV. You watched TV for a couple of hours and then proceeded to go into your room, where you did some *other things* until you eventually fell back asleep. Oh, don't look so shocked, we know when you do it. You woke up again a few hours later and did nothing .What do you think is wrong with this picture, in fact what do you think is wrong with this day? [LEE *then causes the room to flood with light and picks up the lava lamp. She switches it off.*]

KENNETH   Ahhhh. You don't get to ask me a damn thing! I mean what—[*She flicks the lamp back on and* KENNETH *goes dumb again.*]

LEE   Not smart, dear. Try again. [*Flicks the lamp off.*]

KENNETH   How in the—

LEE   Kenneth. Are we going to have to spend all night doing this? OK, here's the deal. You answer my question and I'll let you keep talking. You digress and I shut you down. Agreed? [KENNETH *nods.*] Good. [LEE *flicks the lamp on.*]

KENNETH   What's wrong with this day is, it's like any other day, I haven't done anything. I've got papers due, people I should call, laundry to finish, e-mails to send, and I haven't done any of it. . . .

LEE   See? Now was that so hard?

KENNETH   Now can you at least tell me what's going on? Who are you?

LEE   My name's Lee

KENNETH   Like the jeans?

LEE   Do I have to silence you again? OK. As I was saying. My name's Lee. I'm a detective for God. You are under investigation for one of God's highest crimes. Wasting life. So far the evidence is against you. Kenneth. You haven't done a single productive thing in over a year. You haven't left your house in three days. Do you have any idea how much work you have to do?

KENNETH   I'll do it tomorrow.

LEE   That's the problem, Kenneth. Tomorrow comes and goes and still nothing has moved forward. You are wasting life! Life is not to be wasted! I'm sorry but there's too much evidence, you're under arrest.

KENNETH   Wait a sec, what do you mean arrest? I—[*Suddenly* KENNETH's *arms fly behind his back and an unseen force pushes him to stand.*]

LEE   Shhhhhhhhhh. [*Takes a large wax candle out of her pocket and lights it; the lights go out.*] Kenneth Nelson, as a result of your lack of respect for the gift of life, I, in concert with God, your almighty father, have decided to sentence you to one week of advanced aging to commence now. This candle shall be the monitor by which you will observe your life. As its wax dwindles so shall you. You are now at an age of 25 years, by tomorrow, Monday you will be 35—

KENNETH   But that's impossible—

LEE   Kenneth, do not interrupt me. Tuesday you shall be 45, Wednesday 55, and so on and so forth until your death. The hope is that in these last few days of your life you will do that which you have been putting off forever. These are the rulings of the high court of heaven and cannot in any way be revoked with the exception of a pardon by God himself, who I doubt will have pity on your soul.

KENNETH   He does forgive, though, right? There's gotta be a way to solve this. I mean, I'm not a bad person, I just put some things off. I mean, you can help me, right? Please tell me, there must be something—

LEE   OK, OK. Geez. You guys are all the same. Sooooo big and tough, and the second you get sentenced to die in a week you become a little pansy. Anyway. There is one way to save yourself. No one has ever done it, but if you think you can, hey, who am I to stop you?

KENNETH   What is it?

LEE   Well, most people in life never realize the impact they have on everybody else. We live in a world where everyone is so concerned with themselves that they never stop and think about what they do for others. It's said that if you can truly touch a person's soul, then in your pocket you'll find a seashell. You see, in heaven there's an ocean that's filled with seashells and every bad thing that anybody has ever let go within themselves ends up in heaven in that ocean. If a shell appears in your pocket, it means that somehow you caused someone to let go of something that was killing them inside and therein reserved that terrible thing a place in the ocean. God has decided that if someone can deliver him a collection of seashells for every day of that last week of life, he will give that person one more chance. It's nearly impossible.

KENNETH   But not entirely?

LEE   No, not entirely. [LEE *flicks off the lights and all we see is* KENNETH *staring at the candle.*]

[*Blackout.*]

··· scene two ···

[*Monday. 35-year-old* KENNETH *is sitting at a counter talking to* BE BE *the waitress. She is an attractive young girl with very bouncy hair. He wears a hooded sweatshirt.*]

BE BE   Wow. That's a really good story. You should write that down.

KENNETH   It's not really a story, Be be. I mean, I've been coming here for years and have I ever worn a sweatshirt?

BE BE You're acting really weird, Ken. I mean, come on, do you expect anybody to believe this?

KENNETH If I expected anybody to help me with this, it's you, Be be. You always listen to me no matter how crazy the story was. Please, I need your help. I have a day to figure out how to get a seashell.

BE BE I still don't get it. So you have to help someone be happy to get one?

KENNETH Not really. I have to help them to let go of something bad in their life and I don't know the first place to start. I'm going to die at the end of the week, Be be.

BE BE Stop saying that! You're going to be fine. It's just really hard to believe. Ok, let's see . . . Well, you got in trouble for procrastinating, right? So maybe you didn't finish something and it left somebody with bad feelings towards you. Now if that person lets go of those feelings, maybe you'd get a shell.

KENNETH That's genius! Thanks, Be be. I know what I have to do! [*Exits.*]

[BE BE *wipes down the bar looking out at* KENNETH, *who is running across the street. lights fade.*]

··· scene three ···

[*Tuesday, 45 years old.* KENNETH *comes into the restaurant much slower than he left, his voice has changed. He still wears the same hooded sweatshirt.*]

KENNETH Be be! It worked. I did what you said and went to see a business partner of mine. We were working on a big project and on the day we were supposed to present it, I slept in and told him I'd send my half that afternoon. I never sent the other half and we never got the company to sign on. I went to him and told him I was sorry. I never thought that it would be that big of a deal. I always thought he'd get back on his feet, but it hit him really hard. I didn't realize how much he was counting on me and I let him down. I told him all of this and he didn't want to hear it. Finally, I took the plans for the project out of my briefcase and handed them to him signed. I told him I didn't care about the money. He could have everything. I just wanted to know that we were square after I let him down. I realized at that moment that the project didn't matter! It was the fact that I almost ruined someone else's life that mattered. It was like a revelation or something. You should have seen it, Be be! Then, just as I'm leaving, I feel something in my pocket and [*Takes out the shell.*] I did it! I got him to give up something bad, probably his hatred for me. The important thing is I did it!! [*He looks at* BE BE *and she looks at him with shock. She can now see his face.*]

BE BE   Oh my god. Ken your face, it's—

KENNETH   I know, I'm 45 today. Happy birthday to me, huh? [*Manages a weak chuckle.*]

BE BE   You only got one shell?

KENNETH   So far. I know what I have to do, though. I've avoided so many people throughout my life and so many things. I have to use this week to confront them. No matter how old I get, I have to set things right. That's the only way I'll get the seashells.

BE BE   Well, it sounds like you know what you're doing at least.

KENNETH   Will you help me?

BE BE   Um. How can I help you with this?

KENNETH   I need somebody to be there, to keep me on track, and help me if I start to get too old to move. You're the only friend I have left. The rest can't stand me.

BE BE   I can't do that. I'm not a nurse, I'm a waitress. How could I possibly help you?

KENNETH   You can be with me while I try to do this. This may be the last you'll ever see of me.

BE BE   Stop saying that! Maybe we can find you a doctor or—

KENNETH   NO! No doctors. They can't help me. I have to do this and I NEED YOU to help me. Will you?

BE BE   OK. But I'm still not sure what all of this means.

KENNETH   Don't worry about it, let's go. I don't have much time

BE BE   My shift's over in ten minutes. I'll meet you outside, OK?

KENNETH   OK. [*He stumbles out, obviously still rapidly aging as the lights fade again.*]

··· scene four ···

[*Wednesday, 55 years old. KENNETH walks across the stage with BE BE and takes out a shell; they hug. KENNETH begins to laugh and then cough uncontrollably. BE BE hugs him closer and smoothes his gray hair.*]

··· scene five ···

[*Thursday, 65 years old. BE BE is sitting in a chair in KENNETH's apartment with the candle burning. It appears as if a large portion of the wax has now burned down. She looks at her watch impatiently. KENNETH enters now even slower and slowly reaches into his pocket; he shakes violently and pulls out a seashell. He manages a weak smile before coughing uncontrollably again. This time he falls to his knees from the force of the cough. She goes to him and holds up the shell smiling and mouths the words "only two more"; it looks as if she may cry.*]

··· scene six ···

[*Friday, 75 years old. We see MISSY, KENNETH's sister, sitting alone on the whiteness of an institution. She is disheveled and her nails appear to have been bitten to the point where they bleed. Her clothes are tattered and destroyed and she appears to have a black eye. KENNETH enters, now much older with a cane.*]

KENNETH Missy?

MISSY How-how do you know my name, old man?

KENNETH I know your brother.

MISSY What does that fucking asshole want? He left us! Left me and Mom to fend for ourselves while he went off to have himself a life somewhere else. Selfish prick. What does he want, old man? What does he want? Is he upset 'cause sis has lost it and is giving him bad publicity amongst his friends? Does he want to send me the six Christmas cards or birthday cards I've never gotten while I've been rotting in this place? What is it? WHAT? YOU KNOW WHAT, GET THE FUCK AWAY FROM ME. I hate my brother! OK? You tell him that, you fucking prune-eating asshole! I HATE HIM!!!!!!!!!!

KENNETH Calm down, Missy. He loves you. He does. He just . . . he wanted me to tell you that.

MISSY He loves me? He loves me? Where is he? Huh? Do you see him here? No, he has to send you. My own brother can't even look me in the face he's so embarrassed by me. It wasn't my fault, OK? I was on the drugs when I did that stuff! I didn't mean to hurt anybody! I didn't mean to hurt his—

KENNETH It's OK. It's OK! He knows. He knows. He knows you didn't mean to—

MISSY Then why did he never come back? Why has he never come to see me? He thinks it's all my fault. He hates me. He—

KENNETH Listen to me! [*Goes to her and looks her right in the face.*] He . . . He . . . I do not hate you. [*She backs away staring in disbelief.*] I just couldn't face you after all of that happened. I loved . . . You don't need me to say it again. I . . . I forgive you. You're my sister, I forgive you . . . I . . . [*Goes to her and hugs her. He cries.*] I should have come back. I was wrong. It wasn't your fault. It wasn't—

MISSY   Kenneth. What happened to you? Why . . . Why are you so old?
I don't understand. I—

KENNETH   [*Hugs her again and kisses her on the forehead.*] Merry
Christmas, Missy. Happy Birthday . . . Good-bye . . .

MISSY   Wait, Kenneth, why—

KENNETH   I should have come sooner. Now there's no time. I have
to go.

MISSY   Wait! [*She reaches into her pocket and takes out a seashell.*] I found this
today when they took me for a walk on the grounds. I—I want you
to have it. I miss you, Kenneth. Please don't hate me. I . . . I . . .

KENNETH   Shhhhhh. I know. It's OK. Good night, Missy.

[*He takes the seashell and looks up to the sky as he exits.* MISSY *watches him go as the
lights fade.*]

· · · scene seven · · ·

[BE BE *is sitting again waiting by the candle as* KENNETH *enters. Hobbling with
the cane. He shows her the seashell and smiles again weakly; he then sits down and she
comes over to him. He coughs again very violently and the coughing only ends when he
starts to cry. Lights fade.*]

· · · scene eight · · ·

[*Saturday, 85 years old.* ANNA, KENNETH'*s mother, is sitting in a rocking chair
rocking back and forth as he enters from behind. It is startling how much younger his
mother looks compared to him. He is a broken old man, wrinkled and with white hair.*]

KENNETH   Mom?

ANNA   Kenneth? Is that you? You sound like you've got quite a cold. It's
been a long time

KENNETH   I know, six years. I just couldn't bring myself to come back
after—

ANNA   I know. I know. To be honest, it was hard to stay here after all of that. I wanted to come with you, but I had to take care of Missy and then, well, we know how out of hand that got, but I loved her. I still love her and I still love you. Come here so I can get a look at you.

KENNETH   I . . . I don't look so good, Mom. I'm not doing too—

ANNA   Stop being so sill—[*She turns around and sees* KENNETH *now, 85 years old, a shaking and sickeningly thin old man.*] What oh what . . . Oh, my poor baby. What's happened to you? Why do you look so—

KENNETH   I'm about to die, Mom. I wanted to come and see you because I'll die tonight. I didn't want to leave you without saying good-bye first.

ANNA   I don't understand. How? Why? My baby. My—

KENNETH   Shhhhh. It's OK, Mom. [*Hugs her.*] It's all going to be alright. I just wanted to say [*The coughing starts again.*] I love you, Mom. Don't ever forget that. I know I haven't been around, but I don't want you to ever forget that I love you. I wasted so much time doing things that didn't matter when I should have been there for you and Missy. I'm so sorry. I'm—[*He kneels down and cries. ANNA holds him and cradles him in her arms.*]

ANNA   It's OK. I forgive you . . . shhh, it's OK. Let it out. There, there.

[*Blackout.*]

··· scene nine ···

[*12:01, Sunday, 95 years old.* BE BE *and* KENNETH *sit on the couch while the candle dwindles. He holds the seashells in his shaking hands.*]

BE BE   So how will you know if He's forgiven you?

KENNETH   I don't know. It may be over, Be be. I want you to listen to me. I used to think that life was full of minutes, but I was wrong. Life is full of moments and too often we are so concerned with ourselves that we never stop and give respect for the moments. I spent my entire life ignoring opportunities and saying I'll do it tomorrow or I'll do that later and what did it get me? Life is so precious that if we waste even a second of it, we are cheating ourselves of the greatest gift ever. This week I finally saw moments in my life. Before this week there were minutes, hours, days, dates and none of that matters. It's the moments that matter. The times when you can do something in life that you can be proud of, that someone else can be happy about. You're so young, Be be. You have so much to live for. Don't be like me. [*Starts to cough again.*] I can only hope God'll have mercy on my soul.

BE BE   God has.

KENNETH   What?

BE BE   I can take many forms, Kenneth. Even female forms. I have been with you the entire time. Watching and guiding you and you have done well. Sleep now, Kenneth, and all will be restored in the morning, but never forget what you have learned from this.

[KENNETH *drifts off to sleep while* BE BE *watches. She then takes the small candle and replaces it with a brand-new fresh one.*]

Live life for the moments . . .

[BE BE *then shuts off the lights and lights the new candle. The lava lamp is turned on again and we see the figure of* KENNETH *at peace as the lights fade down.*]

• • •

acknowledgments

I would like to thank my publisher, Michael Messina of Applause Books—The Hal Leonard Group, and my agent, June Clark, for their support of this edition and my position with Applause Books.

Furthermore, I'd like to thank Rick Pulos, administrative/production coordinator of the theatre program at Long Island University, my graduate assistants, and the administration of LIU—Dean David Cohen, Associate Dean Kevin Lauth, and Assistant Dean Maria Vogelstein.

I would also like to express my gratitude to all the theatres around the country and their literary managers, as well as all the playwrights whose work I read, enabling me to compile my first edition.

I follow in the footsteps of more than sixty editions of The Best American Short Plays/The Best Short Plays series, and I would like to thank all the previous editors of this series: the late Stanley Richards, Ramon Delgado, Howard Stein, Mark Glubke, Glenn Young, and anyone I may have left out who came before these fine editors who helped make this series a success for over eighty years.

I would like to quote from the 1989 edition of The Best Short Plays, edited by Ramon Delgado:

> From the beginning of this series the past and present editors have sought to include a balance among three categories of playwrights: (1) established playwrights who continue to practice the art and craft of the short play, (2) emerging playwrights whose record of productions indicate both initial achievements and continuous productivity, and (3) talented new playwrights whose work may not have had much exposure but evidences promise for the future. An effort has also been made to select plays not anthologized elsewhere and, when possible, plays that are making their debut in print. . . . The value of these considerations is to honor the artistry of the established playwrights, encourage the emerging, acknowledge the promising, and offer a varied selection of new plays in one volume.

As the new editor of this series, I plan to keep the tradition moving into the future.